why we watch

why we watch

The Attractions of Violent Entertainment

edited by Jeffrey Goldstein

New York □ Oxford
Oxford University Press
1998

Oxford University Press

Oxford   New York
Athens   Auckland   Bangkok   Bogota   Bombay
Buenos Aries   Calcutta   Cape Town   Dar es Salaam
Delhi   Florence   Hong Kong   Istanbul   Karachi
Kuala Lumpur   Madras   Madrid   Melbourne
Mexico City   Nairobi   Paris   Singapore
Taipei   Tokyo   Toronto   Warsaw

and associated companies in
Berlin   Ibadan

Library of Congress Cataloging-in-Publication Data
Why we watch :
the attractions of violent entertainment
/ edited by
Jeffrey H. Goldstein.
p. cm.
Includes bibliographical references and index.
ISBN 0-19-511820-0 (cloth);
ISBN 0-19-511821-9 (pbk.)
1. Violence in mass media—United States.
2. Popular culture—United States.
I. Goldstein, Jeffrey H.
P96.V52U68   1998
303.6'0973—dc21   97-33066

1   3   5   7   9   8   6   4   2

Printed in the United States of America
on acid-free paper

Acknowledgments

The generous support of the Harry Frank Guggenheim Foundation (HFG) made it possible to explore the attractions of violence by hosting three meetings of scholars who themselves are attracted to the topic. The resulting book is a collaborative effort involving not only its distinguished contributors but also the many colleagues who met with us to discuss the subject of violent entertainment. We are especially grateful to David Altheide, Ehor Boyanowsky, Manohla Dargis, J. William Gibson, Jo Groebel, Wendy Lesser, Errol Morris, and James Twitchell for steering us in the right direction and contributing their considerable experience and wisdom.

The officers of the HFG not only encouraged this project but also contributed substantially to it on every level. But for his modesty, Joel Wallman, Program Officer at HFG, would be listed as coeditor of this book. His meticulous reading of chapter drafts and his insightful comments during meetings have done much to broaden the scope and quality of this project. If the book is not up to Joel's usual standards, it is only because we did not always heed his advice. The editor and contributors benefited enormously from the thoughtful comments of Karen Colvard and James Hester, Program Officer and President, respectively, of the Harry Frank Guggenheim Foundation, who supported this project from the beginning.

David Hawtin, Akko Kalma, Pawel Mlicki, Erica Simon, and Peter Waterman offered thoughtful observations on violent entertainment, which appear throughout this book. The assistance of Lara Cajko and Ineke Wagenaar is inestimable.

Contents

Contributors

MAURICE BLOCH is Professor of Social Anthropology at the London School of Economics and Political Science. His empirical research has been carried out mostly in Madagascar. He is the author of many articles and several books, the latest of which is *How We Think They Think: Anthropological Approaches to Cognition, Memory, and Literacy* (1997).

JOANNE CANTOR is Professor of Communication Arts at the University of Wisconsin at Madison. Her research interests include the psychological effects of mass media, with emphasis on the effects on children. Her most recent contributions include the prosocial effects of television and factors influencing children's interest in viewing violence, as well as children's fright reactions. She is the author of *Mommy, I'm Scared!*, which gives advice to parents about children's fright reactions to mass media.

VICKI GOLDBERG is a photo historian and journalist. Her work appears regularly in the *New York Times*.

JEFFREY GOLDSTEIN has taught at Temple University and the University of London and is now with the Department of Mass Communication at the University of Utrecht, the Netherlands. His books include *The Psychology of Humor* (1972), *Aggression and Crimes of Violence* (1986), *Sports Violence* (1983), and *Toys, Play, and Child Development* (1994).

ALLEN GUTTMANN has written a number of books in the field of sports studies. The best-known of them is *From Ritual to Record: The Nature of Modern Sports* (1978), which has been translated into several European and Asian languages. The most recent of his publications are

Games and Empires: Modern Sports and Cultural Imperialism (1994) and *The Erotic in Sports* (1996). Most relevant to his contribution to this volume is *Sports Spectators* (1986). Guttmann teaches at Amherst College and has been a guest professor at Yale and at several German and Japanese universities. His *Women's Sports: A History* won the NASSH Prize for best book of 1991.

J. HOBERMAN is the senior film critic for *The Village Voice*. He teaches cinema studies at New York University and The Cooper Union. His film and cultural criticism has been collected in *Vulgar Modernism: Writings on Movies and Other Media* (1992) and *The Red Atlantis: Communist Culture in the Absence of Communism* (1998).

CLARK McCAULEY is Professor of Psychology at Bryn Mawr College and Adjunct Professor of Psychology at the University of Pennsylvania. His current research interests include group dynamics (stereotypes, groupthink, group conflict, terrorist groups) and individual differences (sensitivity to disgust, relations to work, patriotism, and nationalism). His interest in horror movies arose in trying to understand why people sometimes want to expose themselves to disgusting stimuli.

MARIA TATAR teaches folklore and cultural studies at Harvard University. She is the author of *The Hard Facts of the Grimms' Fairy Tales* (1987), *Off with Their Heads! Fairy Tales and the Culture of Childhood* (1992), and *Lustmord: Sexual Murder in Weimar Germany* (1995). She is also the editor of *Classic Fairy Tales* in the Norton series of critical editions.

DOLF ZILLMANN received his Ph.D. in 1969 from the University of Pennsylvania. Much of his teaching has been at that institution and at Indiana University, where he created and directed the Institute for Communications Research. After excursions to European universities such as Oxford, England, and Klagenfurt, Austria, he came to the University of Alabama, where he is Professor of Communications and Psychology and Senior Associate Dean for Graduate Studies and Research. Zillmann has conducted and published hundreds of investigations into a great many aspects of human behavior. His theories and his primarily experimental work can be found in the journals of the psychology and psychophysiology of emotions, aggression, sexuality, and media effects, as well as in journals that embrace the psychology of entertainment and the exploration of comedy, erotica, suspense, mystery, horror, tragedy, sports, and music. Among his single-authored and coedited books are *Hostility and Aggression* (1979), *Connections between Sex and Aggression* (1984), *Selective Exposure to Communications* (1985), *Perspectives on Media Effects* (1986), *Responding to the Screen* (1991), and *Media, Children, and the Family* (1995).

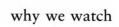
why we watch

Introduction

JEFFREY GOLDSTEIN

Violent entertainment is never absent for long from the public agenda. Today violent entertainment is much in the news on both sides of the Atlantic and around the world. Much publicity has been given to studies of violence in children's television, and to the fear that violent films and video games have given rise to recent murders by young boys in England, the Netherlands, Norway, and the United States. According to *Market Focus: Toys* (Feb. 1995), "if there is one issue confronting toymakers and entertainment producers right now, it is the level of violence that children are exposed to in the course of their daily lives and what role they play in promoting that." As this is written, politicians in Washington are considering legislation to limit violent entertainment in television, film, video games, and pop music. The United States and Canada have decided to require a V-chip on all new television sets to enable violent offerings to be filtered out. The device is also under consideration by the European Parliament.

While parents, teachers, politicians, and social scientists often bemoan the violence in entertainment, they neglect to ask why a significant market for violent literature, films, cartoons, video games, toys, and sports exists in the first place. Politicians and others who debate violent entertainment focus only on its *production* while ignoring its public *reception*. Psychologists, too, have ignored the *appeal* of violent entertainment, focusing untiringly on its *effects* (Cole, 1995). *Why We Watch* addresses squarely the neglected question of the appeals of violent imagery. What is the attraction of violent films and video games featuring superheroes and martial-arts combatants? Is violent imagery more prev-

1

alent now than in the past? What kind of people are drawn to violent images? What kind of violent images draw them? Is there such a thing as morbid curiosity? Are there equally satisfying substitutes for violent entertainment? What draws our attention to violent media events not intended to entertain? We cannot answer all these questions, but the chapters in this book bring the picture more clearly into focus.

In the initial discussions for this project it quickly became apparent that violent imagery is ubiquitous. There are many realms in which violent images play a role, some of them predictable, like sports and media violence, and a few of them, like religion, quite unexpected.

Obviously a distinction must be made between violence and images of violence, especially staged violence produced for the purpose of entertainment. Psychologists typically define violence as action intended to harm. With such a definition, a boxing match would be regarded as a violent event while a simulated boxing match or a cartoon boxing match would not. When people speak of "violence on television" they generally mean not violence as it is defined here but simulated violence, violent images. Of course, many people are concerned about depictions of violence in news and "reality TV" broadcasts as well. But most of the discussion about violence in the media is about dramatic violence.

We regard violent entertainment as descriptions or images of fighting, bloodshed, war, and gunplay produced for the purpose of entertainment, recreation, or leisure. Violent entertainment includes murder and horror stories; comic books, television programs, films, and cartoons depicting war or fighting; video games with martial-arts and military themes; toy weapons and military matériel; and aggressive spectator sports, like boxing and wrestling. It is difficult to know how to regard books such as this one, intended for an audience that wants to read about violence on an abstract level, with the emotional content dampened. Is this the scholar's horror film?

People voluntarily expose themselves to, and often search out, images of violence. No one, with the possible exception of subjects in a social-psychology experiment, is forced to watch violent films or television programs. What kinds of violent images they seek, why they seek them, and the social and historical context of violent images form the basis of this book.

The trend in film and literature has been to portray violence in increasingly realistic and bloody ways. Does the attraction of violent images, and do the reactions of viewers, differ if the violence is more or less realistic? Many in the audience appear eager to be taken in by dramatic violence; perhaps attraction is enhanced by the viewers' willing suspension of disbelief. After all, most violent images and models produced for entertainment and recreation are not the real thing; they carry clues to their false identity. Just as a baby doll suggests that it is both a baby and not-a-baby, violent entertainment suggests that it is both violent and not-violent. A toy gun must by law carry a brightly colored plug to convey that it is not a gun, but there are other cues to its unreality: its weight, mechanics, place of purchase, packaging, and place of consumption. Films portraying violence often induce reflexiveness in viewers—we become aware of the camera, of the music, or of special effects, and in every case are aware of our status as viewers. Fairy tales, often the grimmest form of entertainment—with witches, child-eating monsters, and evil stepparents—begin immediately with the message that they are unreal: "Once upon a time . . ."

The suspension of disbelief, the eagerness to pretend, may be a requirement for the enjoyment of violent entertainment. It is also a source of pleasure in itself. Fantasy is a source of enjoyment in many forms of play and entertainment. The creation of imaginary worlds may be the most important characteristic of war toys, for example (Mergen, 1982). Does the violence add something further to the attractiveness of stories, legends, rituals, and programs?

In charting the territory of violent imagery, it may be relevant that its producers are not necessarily its consumers. Maria Tatar notes in chapter 4 that children's literature is produced by adults for a child audience. The adults appear to believe either that the violent imagery will appeal to children or that it is good for them, that it will frighten them into obedience. The distinction between the production of violent entertainment and its reception by an audience holds not only for children's entertainment. Dramatic and sports programs for adults are also produced by a small group for mass consumption.

Despite the public controversy over violent entertainment, it is worth noting that nonviolent entertainment, especially film and TV comedies, and nonviolent toys and video games, are far more popular than violent fare. Joanne Cantor (chapter 5) reminds us that not all popular entertainment is violent, and not all violent entertainment is popular.

Many have had the experience in a movie theater of being shocked and puzzled by audience laughter at a gruesome act of violence on the screen. What provokes this laughter—the violence itself? anxiety about violence? sadism? Students in my first-year psychology course used to be shown a film of the notorious experiments by Stanley Milgram in which people are urged to administer painful electric shocks to an innocent victim. At one point in the film a subject expresses concern for his alleged victim, but the experimenter tells him to administer another shock, which the subject does reluctantly. The (off-camera) victim lets out a scream, which invariably provokes laughter from the class. I was myself shocked the first time I heard this but have heard it many times since, always at the same point in the film. Colleagues showing this film to large classes report the same phenomenon. Are the students laughing because the violence is funny, perhaps because it is exaggerated? Is the laughter a sign of discomfort? Does it help release tension evoked by the violence? Those students who laugh during the Milgram film are not, I think, laughing sadistically, expressing pleasure in another's pain. Tatar (chapter 4) describes an episode from the Grimm brothers in which a father eats a stew made from the corpse of his son. "Children may react to this episode with gales of laughter . . . but they are more likely guffawing over an adult's display of unrestrained greed than over the chopping up of the boy's corpse. . . . ," she writes.

Images of violence are sometimes used stylistically to convey countercultural sentiments. Rock bands adopt violent names (such as Sunday Violence), and their fans, like football (soccer) supporters, give the outward appearance of impending violence. Social scientists have focused mainly on the effects of violent films and TV programs on aggressive behavior. J. Hoberman (chapter 6) describes the effect that *Bonnie and Clyde* had on fashion.

These examples illustrate the difficulty of locating the source of pleasure in people's positive reactions to violent imagery. Maurice Bloch and Vicki Goldberg consider violent imagery that is not regarded as entertainment—violent rituals in religious ceremonies and depictions of death and dying in print media. These essays make clear that the attraction of violent images does not necessarily have anything to do with violence, though it may.

What does it mean to say that someone is attracted to violent imagery? Does it mean that he or she finds it pleasurable? Or that it elicits only positive emotions? Based on research by Clark McCauley reported in chapter 7 and on the many studies by Dolf Zillmann and his colleagues (chapter 9), it is clear that one may be attracted to something while at the same time experiencing negative emotions, such as disgust and anxiety. We may be attracted to the scene of an accident, but we don't necessarily enjoy it. The contributors to this book are intrigued by violent imagery, but they do not necessarily find it pleasurable themselves.

"Attraction" is an ambiguous word, for it does not tell us whether the allure lies in the nature of the object or in the eye of the beholder. Are we to explain the appeal of a violent film by analyzing characteristics of the film, the viewer, or the setting in which viewing occurs? Every chapter in this book makes clear that attraction is multidetermined, reflecting the object of attraction, the audience, and the broader context in which the experience occurs. In the concluding chapter, a summary of what we know is examined from these different perspectives.

Several chapters in *Why We Watch* consider the kind of violence that is most appealing. Violent entertainment seems to be most attractive when it contains an engaging fantasy theme in which disliked characters are defeated by liked characters in the cause of justice. Violent entertainment becomes more popular when real violence and war are in the news.

Goldstein, Cantor, McCauley, and Zillmann consider individual differences in the attraction of violent imagery. One group in particular seems most attracted to images of violence—males with a high need for sensation and who are more aggressive than average. But it isn't just "them"—or adolescents, the uneducated, borderline delinquents, or the lower classes—who find violence attractive. Two years ago at a meeting of the International Society for Research on Aggression, one session included a paper on serial killers by a psychiatrist who had interviewed several of them. The room was filled to capacity for this early morning talk. Once the psychiatrist had completed his speech, the room pretty much cleared out. (The second speaker addressed the prevalence of violence in television news, deploring the fact that so many people find such fare attractive!)

The chapters in *Why We Watch* are diverse in subject, perspective, and reliance on "data." We approached this little-explored topic by asking filmmakers and movie critics, literary scholars, historians, sociologists, communications researchers, psychologists, and anthropologists to approach the subject from their own perspectives. The resulting volume contains essays, historical analyses, case studies, and reviews of behavioral-science research. Since violent images can be found in everything from ancient sports to children's literature, from the daily newspaper to the latest Hollywood offerings, chapters examine many domains of culture.

To understand violent entertainment it is necessary to look not only at, but also beyond, the mass media. Depictions of violence, bloodshed, and death are not new, and they certainly are not a product of the electronic age. Interest in blood sports was fervent in classical Greece and Rome, no less than today, as Allen Guttman documents in chapter 1. Historical changes in readers' experiences of death and dying, led by the growth of mortuaries in the nineteenth century, altered peoples' tolerance of images of death. Vicki Goldberg describes our changing mores governing photographic representations of death and bloodshed. The historical theme is continued in my chapter on aggressive play and violent video games, where I note that war toys are among the world's oldest known artifacts. J. Hoberman relates the popular reception of *Bonnie and Clyde* and other violent films of the 1960s and 70s to social and political currents of the times. Maurice Bloch describes how religious ceremonies use violence symbolically to cure the sick, purify the sinful, and mature the young.

Maria Tatar focuses on the socializing functions of horrific children's tales, which give expression to the forbidden, help defeat fear by caricaturing reality, and provide intimate moments between parents and children while scaring the bejesus out of the kids. What kind of media violence is attractive to children? Joanne Cantor presents the results of a survey of children and parents about children's attraction to violent television programs. Clark McCauley studies the sort of violence that people find decidedly *unattractive*. Bloody and disgusting films, devoid of theatrically and special effects, appeal to hardly anyone. This theme is continued in Dolf Zillmann's analysis of the psychology of violent entertainment. It is not necessarily the violence that makes violent entertainment appealing; it is what the violence means to its audience that determines whether it will be entertaining or not. Zillmann summarizes his ambitious research program on entertainment and offers a theory of the appeals of violent entertainment. I have written a final chapter highlighting what we know about the attractions of violent entertainment, and areas where information is inadequate.

1

The Appeal of Violent Sports

ALLEN GUTTMANN

If we define violence as the unsanctioned or illegitimate use of harmful or destructive physical force, which I take to be a reasonable definition, then sports confront us with a paradox: boxing matches and a number of other sports events involve a great deal of interpersonally harmful but nonetheless sanctioned physical force. In sports as in warfare, whose image sports are often taken to be, some forms of interpersonal violence are legitimate. In many sports, physical violence is the core if not the name of the game.

The prestige of a Roman gladiator increased with the number of opponents he slew. The mayhem at a medieval tournament was often more deadly than the carnage of a real battle. (In the course of a tournament held in 1240 near the German town of Neuss, scores of knights were killed [Jusserand, 1901; Keen, 1984].) In our own time, a number of boxers have been beaten to death by opponents who were subsequently judged exempt from legal prosecution for assaults that are severely penalized if committed outside sports' specially privileged time and space. Like gladiatorial combats and knightly jousts, boxing matches are haunted by the specter not only of serious injury but also of immediate death. Yet, these and similarly violent sports spectacles have been enormously popular. Why has this been so? Before I venture a partial and tentative answer to this deceptively simple question, it will be useful very briefly to consider the spectators' *behavior*—as opposed to their *motivations*.

Historical Mayhem

Modern illusions about the dignity and decorum of Greek spectators should be dispelled. Spectators are hardly mentioned in the account of the funeral games for Patroklos in book 23 of the *Iliad*, but Homer does indicate that they were numerous and that they applauded loudly and "thundered approval." Sophilos, a sixth-century-B.C. artist, pictured these Homeric spectators on a vase. Responding to the chariot race, a dangerous sports event that seems to have excited the Greeks beyond any other, the tiny figures are quite obviously screaming their heads off (Weiler, 1974; Yalouris, 1979; Ebert, 1980). It is an oddly familiar sight.

"Olympian" detachment and disinterested curiosity were no more evident at Olympia than on the plains of Ilium. The site was (and still is) fearfully hot and dry in midsummer when the sacred games took place. And the site was crowded with visitors from the entire Greek world, which stretched from the far shore of the Black Sea to the Mediterranean coast of Spain. In the fourth century B.C., the Leonidaion was constructed to house wealthy or politically important visitors to the games, but most of the spectators had to be satisfied with sleeping in tents or with spending their nights under the stars. As late as the first century A.D., after there had been considerable effort to provide some minimal comforts, the Roman stoic philosopher Epictetus used attendance at the games as a metaphor for stress: "But some unpleasant and hard things happen in life. . . . And do they not happen at Olympia? Do you not swelter? Are you not cramped and crowded? Do you not bathe badly? Are you not drenched whenever it rains? Do you not have your fill of tumult and shouting? But I fancy you bear and endure it all by balancing it off against the memorable character of the spectacle" (quoted in Finley & Pleket, 1976, p. 54).

There is abundant evidence for what Epictetus called "tumult and shouting." The *Hellanodikai*, who were in charge of the management of the Olympic games, had to employ assistants who kept athletes and spectators under control. The names of these assistants, *mastigophoroi* (whip bearers) and *rabdouchoi* (truncheon bearers), imply disorderly conduct and the necessity for externally imposed restraint. At Delphi's Pythian games, sacred to Apollo, the spectators were more Dionysian than Apollonian; their drunkenness was such a problem that they were forbidden to carry wine into the stadium (Palaeogos, 1979).

Drawing upon not only Epictetus but also Pausanias, Philostratus, Pindar, Isocrates, Polybius, and a wide range of other ancient authorities, the nineteenth-century scholar Johann Heinrich Krause, who is still the best modern source on Greek spectators, wrote vividly of the visitors to Olympia:

> With what an indescribable enthusiasm those present dedicated them-
> selves to the spectacle, with what a lively sense of participation did
> they share the athletes' feats and enact the outcome of the contests,
> how their spirits were excited by what they saw! They were impelled
> unconsciously to move their hands, to raise their voices, to jump from
> their seats, now with the greatest joy, now with the deepest pain.
> (1972, p. 192)

Sharing vicariously the athletes' fates, the spectators were intensely partisan. Each *polis* honored its winners with material rewards as well as
with statues and victors' odes (Buhmann, 1975; Hyde, 1921; Pleket,
1974, 1975; Young, 1984).

Looking back, the modern Italian historian Roberto Patrucco concludes that the spectators behaved with the uninhibited "human passion" of modern sports spectators (1972, p. 21). M. I. Finley and H. W.
Pleket agree that Greek crowds were "as partisan, as volatile, and as
excitable as at any other period of time" (1976, p. 57).

Whatever minimal decorum was maintained at Olympia seems to
have vanished completely during the chariot races in Hellenistic Alexandria, where Dio Chrysostom condemned the outrageous behavior of
the crowd:

> When they enter the stadium, it is as though they had found a cache
> of drugs; they forget themselves completely, and shamelessly say and
> do the first thing that occurs to them. . . . At the games you are under
> the influence of some maniacal drug; it is as if you could not watch
> the proceedings in a civilized fashion. . . . When you enter the stadium,
> who could describe the yells and uproar, the frenzy, the switches of
> color and expression in your faces, and all the curses you give vent to?
> (quoted in Harris, 1976, p. 89)

Dio's passion matches that of modern journalists excoriating the "mind-
less" behavior of "football hooligans."

One must ask if modern historians have been justified in routinely
citing Epictetus, Dio, and other authors of the first or second century
A.D. as evidence for the habits of spectators who lived five or six hundred
years earlier. After all, it may be that the tumultuous Greek spectators
of Hellenistic and Roman times were quite unlike their fifth-century-B.C.
ancestors. It seems reasonable, however, to conclude in the absence of
any evidence to the contrary that there was continuity rather than dis-
continuity in the patterns of Greek spectatorship. If Greek sports spectatorship was similar to Greek political behavior, the atmosphere at
Olympia was anything but "Olympian."

Roman sports were very different from those of the Greeks. In the
first place, Roman citizens tended to perform physical exercises rather
than to participate in sports. Sport as an activity done for its own sake

attracted them less than exercises performed for some ulterior purpose, usually military. In general, there was hostility to Greek athletics (Friedländer, 1908–1913; Gardiner, 1930; Vogt, 1926; Lindsay, 1973). The poet Horace reacted typically when, in his Second Satire, he scornfully contrasted effeminate Greek sports to rough Roman drill. The emperor Augustus founded several isolympic athletic festivals, but they never became popular. The sports for which the Romans are rightly remembered are gladiatorial games and chariot races, both spectator sports (Balsdon, 1969; Mendner, 1956).

Like the ball games of the Mayans and Aztecs, which ended in ritual sacrifice, gladiatorial combats originated as an aspect of Roman religion. The Greeks of the *Iliad* were content that the funeral games in honor of the fallen Patroklos terminated merely in symbolic death—that is, in athletic defeat—but the Romans celebrated funeral games in which the dead were honored by additional deaths. The first games, held in 246 B.C. by Marcus and Decius Brutus in honor of their deceased father, consisted of three duels (six gladiators) and were held in the cattle market. One can assume that the number of spectators was fairly small. In the centuries that followed, there was an apparently irreversible tendency toward ludic inflation. The number of gladiators continually increased and the facilities available to the spectators grew ever grander. The emperor Trajan is said to have celebrated his victories over the Dacians, at the end of the first century A.D., with combats among ten thousand gladiators, an extravagance surpassed by the naval battle staged by Claudius in 52 A.D. with nineteen thousand combatants (Friedländer, 1908–1913; Ville, 1981).

The Senate, worried about the manipulation of the populace by means of these magnificent spectacles, attempted to limit the number of gladiators at any single set of *ludi* (games) to sixty pairs, but the effort was futile and, in imperial times, emperors (except for the stingy Tiberius) seem to have competed among themselves in staging grandiose spectacles. Since temporary stadia built of wood sometimes collapsed, killing large numbers of spectators, they were replaced by monumental stone structures, the most famous of which is the "Colosseum," more accurately referred to as the Flavian Amphitheater, because it was erected by the Flavian emperor Vespasian and his son Titus. This gigantic structure, finished in 80 A.D., seated fifty thousand. Such stadia provided comforts unknown to Greek spectators. When we read that the arena at Pompeii lured the audience with promises of *vela et sparsiones* (awnings and perfumed sprays), we are apt to think of the luxurious accommodations of the domed stadia of modern American cities (Balsdon, 1969; Auguet, 1972; Hoenle & Henze, 1981).

That many gladiators were professionals is undeniable. Although their legal status was quite low, they unquestionably enjoyed popularity enough for a number of adventurous free citizens to volunteer for the *munera* (gladiatorial games) and *venationes* (combats against wild beasts). The exact proportion of volunteers to slaves and prisoners is uncertain, but incomplete inscriptions referring to the gladiators at Venusia show eighteen slaves and ten free men (Balsdon, 1969). That the spectators preferred free men to slaves or condemned criminals is clear from the remarks of Echion, a character in the *Satyricon* of Petronius, who speaks excitedly of an imminent show with new fights "and . . . not a slave in the batch" (1959, p. 42). Michael Grant's explanation for this preference is simple: "Free fighters were more sought after than slaves, presumably because they showed greater enthusiasm" (1967, p. 31). Georges Ville takes the analysis a step farther and writes that "the public preferred a free gladiator to a slave and a knight or a senator to an ordinary citizen" (1981, p. 262). The plebeian spectators must have thrilled to see the high and mighty brought down to their own level, exposed for once to risks and hazards comparable to those encountered by ordinary mortals.

While most spectators paid for their seats, the poorest of the poor, the *plebs frumentaria* (i.e., those on the dole), had free tickets (Ville, 1981). Neither poverty nor servile status was a bar to enthusiastic fandom. A funerary inscription for the slave Crescens informs the world that he was a Blue and a Thracian, that is, a partisan of one of the two main charioteer teams and of the Thracian style of fighting (Friedländer, 1908–1913). The slave Davus, owned by the poet Horace, appears in the Second Satire, where he marvels "at the posters of athletes straining the muscles in combat" (1959, p. 148). In the same poem we learn that Maecenas, the immensely wealthy patron of the arts, was not above a vulgar curiosity about individual gladiators. A common archaeological find at Roman sites is an inexpensive clay lamp with gladiatorial motifs. Richer folk had *terra sigillata* or bronze statuettes. In the *Satyricon*, Trimalchio has *his* favorite gladiator pictured on silverware. Not even Christians were wholly immune to the appeals of fandom. Saint Augustine's ardent young disciple Alypius suffered a dramatic setback when he ventured into the amphitheater and was overcome: "For so soon as he saw that blood, he therewith drunk down savageness; nor turned away, but fixed his eye, drinking in frenzy, unawares, and was delighted with that guilty fight, and intoxicated with the bloody pastime" (Augustine, 1907, pp. 106–7).

The spectators at the gladiatorial games shared this reaction to blood. While many must have admired the fine points of the highly trained combatants, others seemed to have had eyes only for the outcome of the struggle. They applauded not the skillful use of weapons but rather the victory of their favorite (on whom they often wagered considerable sums of money). Noting this tendency of the *munera* and the *venationes* to become increasingly sensationalistic and perverse, Ludwig Friedländer commented, "Soon bloodthirsty combats and magnificent scenery failed to excite the dulled nerves of the mob, aristocratic or vulgar; only things absolutely exotic, unnatural, nonsensical, tickled their jaded senses" (1908–1913).

Another kind of titillation appeared in imperial times when female gladiators entered the arena (Guttmann, 1991). Two such women are depicted on a stele from Halicarnassus, in Asia Minor (Robert, 1971). Juvenal was, as expected, satirical about the spectacle of "women, breasts Amazon-naked," facing "wild boars at the games" (1958, p. 18), but less moralistic Romans were obviously excited by such sights. In the *Satyricon*, one of Trimalchio's guests complains of a poor gladiatorial show and anticipates a better one with "a girl who fights from a chariot" (Petronius, 1959, p. 43). It seems likely that enthusiasts for this kind of combat experienced an erotic frisson. The poet Ovid urged women to "go and look at the games, where the sands are sprinkled with crimson" (1957, pp. 164–65). The motive here is the chance to display female physical charms ("What are good looks, unseen?"), but the poet clearly assumes that the bloodshed in the arena is no obstacle to amorous dalliance in the stands.

There was very little opposition to the gladiatorial games on the part of pagan moralists. In 55 B.C., when Pompey consecrated the Temple of Venus Genetrix by slaughtering a number of elephants, the dying animals "excited pity by their agonized trumpetings" and "the spectators rose and cursed Pompey for his cruelty" (Jennison, 1937, p. 52), but this was an unusual if not a unique moment of compassion. Most educated Roman spectators seemed to take the deaths of men and beasts for granted. The philosopher-statesman Cicero praised the *munera* because they afforded the spectators an image of fortitude (Hoenle & Henze, 1981). The philosopher-dramatist Seneca was among the handful of pagan moralists who expressed the kind of horror that many twentieth-century critics feel at sports that are far less violent than the *munera*. For Seneca, the arena was the site of cruel and inhuman combats. His comment on the spectators was devastatingly succinct: "In the morning they throw men to the lions and the bears; at noon, they throw them to the spectators" (1917–1925, vol. 1, pp. 30–31).

Christian moralists were, not surprisingly, more sustained and vehement in their denunciations of the games. Tertullian's tract *De spectaculis* set the pattern for subsequent generations of patristic invective and protest. His objections were partly to the violence in the amphitheater and partly to the appalling frenzy of the spectators: "Look at the populace coming to the show—mad already! Disorderly, blind, excited already about its bets! The praeter is too slow for them; all the time their eyes are on his urn, in it, as if rolling with the lots he shakes up in it. The signal is given. They are all in suspense, anxious suspense. One frenzy, one voice!" (1931, pp. 271–73). Salvian, a fifth-century bishop, shared Tertullian's outrage: "There is almost no crime or vice that does not accompany the games. In these the greatest pleasure is to have men die . . . or to have them torn to pieces . . . to the great joy of the bystanders and the delight of onlookers, so that the victims seem devoured almost as much by the eyes of the audience as by the teeth of the beasts" (1930, p. 160).

It was not only the violence and sadism that horrified Christian moralists; they were also shocked by the idolatry of the games. Greek spectators were presumably, except for an occasional skeptical philosopher, worshipers of the Olympian gods, but the Roman Empire included worshipers of Jupiter, Mithra, Isis, and Christ—among others. While Christians, like Augustine's wayward disciple Alypius, were sometimes susceptible to the sadistic appeals of the *munera*, they were repelled by the paganism that was an integral part of the games. Georges Ville has asserted that the games held under Constantine and other Christian emperors were "unrelated to the cult of the gods or the cult of the dead" (1960, p. 289), but Ville's reluctance to take seriously the presence of pagan priests and images seems to be a Christian or secular bias. It is certain that Tertullian and probable that the post-Constantine church fathers were scandalized by the processions of priests carrying images of the Roman gods. Following Tertullian closely, Novatian expressed Christian horror and fear for the spectator's immortal soul when he exclaimed, "Idolatry is the mother of all these games" (1972, p. 171). In Christian tracts like these, protests against violence are mingled with horror at idolatry because, as indicated earlier, gladiatorial violence was, in Roman eyes, not only legitimate but also sacred. After a slave dressed as the god Mercury jabbed a fallen gladiator with hot irons to make certain that death was not feigned, another slave in the garb of Dis Pater dragged the corpse away, after which the dead man's blood was offered to Jupiter Latiaris by the priest who served that deity.

When one ponders the level of violence of the gladiatorial games and the spectators' religious, racial, ethnic, and class differences, it seems almost miraculous that the arena did not explode into disorderly riot. It did—once. The word "Pompeii" summons up visions of volcanic catastrophe, but the wealthy town was also the scene of a disaster that the inhabitants brought upon themselves. The historian Tacitus reports that tumults erupted there during the *munera*, after which the town was for a decade deprived of its right to stage gladiatorial games (1959). This episode of spectator violence was, however, very unusual. There was, in fact, an "almost total absence of documented riots" (Baldwin, 1984).

One explanation for this nonviolent spectatorship is the tightly regulated seating arrangements at Roman stadia. At the gladiatorial games, both communal organization and social hierarchy took spatial forms. In the amphitheaters at Arles and Nîmes, and probably in those of Rome as well, different "tribes" were seated in different *cunei* (wedges) of the stadium (Bollinger, 1969). Augustus had definite ideas about social rank and seating. Everyone, from senator to slave, had his assigned place. Augustus himself was seated, or reclined, on the *pulvinar* (couch) (Suetonius, 1957; Balsdon, 1969; Bollinger; Auguet, 1972). There, bored by the bloody show, he seems to have busied himself with imperial paperwork, but his presence—and that of numerous armed guards—reminded the spectators that external controls were ready to enforce order if internal restraint failed.

Paradoxically, the relatively nonviolent chariot races provoked spectator violence at a level unknown among the fans of the *munera*. In Constantinople, the rioting "circus factions" set the city's wooden hippodrome on fire in 491, 498, 507, and 532 A.D., after which Justinian prudently invested in a marble stadium (Guilland, 1948). In the fifth and sixth centuries, spectator violence in the Byzantine Empire increased to the point where troops were repeatedly called upon to restore a semblance of order. After a victory by Porphyrius in 507 in the circus at Antioch, the jubilant Greens ran wild and, in the course of the riot, burned the local synagogue, a quite typical instance of anti-Semitism (Cameron, 1976; Malalas, 1940). The worst of these many riots took place in Constantinople in January 532 when supporters of the Blues and Greens joined forces. Prisoners about to be executed on the thirteenth were rescued by the mob, which subsequently ignored Justinian's attempts to appease them with the promise of additional games. On the fourteenth the emperor acceded to demands that he dismiss John of Cappodocia and other unpopular officials. By January 18, the still unpacified mob proclaimed a new emperor, to whom a number of senators paid hasty homage. Fortunately for Justinian, his most skillful general, Belisarius, arrived in time to save the day—at the cost of an estimated thirty thousand lives (Cameron, 1976). In comparison with this bloodbath, the worst modern outbreaks of British and Latin American soccer fans seem relatively innocuous.

Although medieval spectators were often unruly and sometimes riotous, the evidence indicates that their disorders never approached the level of tumult and rampage exhibited by Byzantine chariot fans. The reason for this lower level of violence may well be the much smaller scale of medieval sports. The grandest tournaments were diminutive affairs compared with the races in the Circus Maximus or in the hippodrome at Constantinople. The two thousand persons attending the tournament at Sandricourt near Pontoise in 1493 were a mere 1 percent of the Roman crowd that cheered for the Blues and the Greens (Loomis, 1959). A second reason for a lower level of violence may be that the social gap between the participant's role and the spectator's was considerably narrower than in imperial Rome.

For the medieval knight, the line between tournament and battlefield, between mock and real warfare, was thin and often transgressed. "Games resembled war and war resembled games. . . . The union of warfare and games was so close that it is frequently difficult to decide if a given activity ought to be classified under one rubric or the other" (Jusserand, 1901, pp. 12, 18). This was Jean Jusserand's opinion, put forth in 1901. Charles Haskins agreed: "The major sport of the Middle Ages was war, with its adjuncts the tournament, the joust, and the judicial duel" (1927, p. 238). Recent studies of knighthood conclude similarly that "tournaments began as mimic wars in the twelfth century; wars take on the appearance of mimic tournaments in the pages of [Jean] Froissart in the fourteenth century" (Barber, 1974, p. 193). The warlike features of the tournament were especially pronounced in the twelfth century, when the typical tournament was a melee composed of parties of knights fighting en masse, capturing each other, seeking not only glory but also ransoms. Small wonder that a contemporary said of a twelfth-century tournament that "the fracas was such that God's thunder couldn't have been heard" (Meyer, 1891–1904, vol. 3, p. 74). A lapidary modern statement is that the early tournament was "unregulated, it was not a spectacle, and there was little in the way of romantic chivalry attached to it" (Hardy, 1974, p. 96). Combats of this unregulated sort were apt to be deadly. Appalled by the violence of the early tournament, Pope Innocent II condemned the sport at the Council of Clermont in 1130, but this and subsequent bans were ineffective. Priests continued to flock to watch, if not to participate in, tournaments and, in 1471, a tournament was held in St. Peter's Square (Barber, 1974; Hardy, 1974; Krüger, 1985).

With crowds of spectators came the problem of crowd control. Although no sports event of the entire Middle Ages approached the level of violence reached by Byzantine riots, there were frequent outbreaks of violence. The chronicler Matthew Paris wrote in his *Historia Anglorum* of the ill will between the English and their opponents at a tournament in Rochester in 1151. There was "anger and hatred between the English and the foreigners" (quoted in Cripps-Day, 1918, p. 45). At a tournament held at Chalons in 1274, Edward I was illegally seized by the Comte de Chalons, whom he had challenged, and a brawl broke out in which several people were killed (Barber, 1974). When a group of squires held a tournament at Boston Fair in 1288, the fact that one side dressed as monks and the other costumed itself as canons of the church failed to prevent a riot during which the fair was sacked and part of the town burned (Denholm-Young, 1948). "Tournaments were a notable cause of discord and disorder throughout the reign of Henry III" (Barker & Keen, 1985, p. 217). Conditions on the continent were certainly no better. German towns were compelled to recruit hundreds of armed men to contain the violence that threatened always to disrupt the tournament. Augsburg was said in 1442 to have hired two thousand men to keep the peace (Zots, 1985).

To prevent such outbreaks, strict rules were promulgated. The *Sta-*

tuta Armorum published by an English committee of the late thirteenth century reveals a high degree of official worry about spectator violence: "And they who shall come to see the Tournament, shall not be armed with any Manner of Armour, and shall bear no Sword, or Dagger, or Staff, or Mace, or Stone" (quoted in Cripps-Day, 1918, p. xxv). Regulation was ineffective in England and on the continent. As late as 1376, a bloody tumult occurred in Basel when middle-class spectators, trampled by mounted noblemen, responded violently and killed several knights (Wildt, 1957; Schaufelberger, 1972).

In time, as the "civilizing process" brilliantly analyzed by Norbert Elias transformed medieval "expressive" violence into the relative restraint of the Renaissance, tournaments evolved from ludic warfare into elaborately allegorical pageants within which the jousters played a very minor role (Elias, 1969). The perfection of military prowess became ancillary and the tournament became a theatrical production in which fitness to rule was associated with fineness of sensibility. It may seem odd to us, but one of the main themes of the late medieval and Renaissance tournament was the notion that good rulers make good lovers. Whatever the tournament became, it ceased to be the deadly melee experienced by William Marshal.

Telling of the entry of Queen Isabelle into Paris in 1389, Jean Froissart dwelled upon the elaborate pageantry. When twelve hundred burgesses accompany the queen from St. Denis into the city, when damsels chorus their praises, when an allegorical castle is constructed at Chatelet with a figure of Saint Anne lying upon a bed, with twelve young maidens wandering among symbolic animals (a hart, a lion, an eagle), when an effigy of Saladin's castle appears, to be attacked and defended by real knights, it is clear that the demonstration of bellicose prowess with deadly weapons has been overshadowed by the dramatic spectacle in which it has been embedded (Froissart, 1814–1816). At the famous *Pas de la bergère* that René d'Anjou staged at Tarascon in 1449, there was a thatched cottage occupied by a "shepherdess" and knights disguised as shepherds rode forth from pavilions disguised as cottages; the chivalric combat was "entirely absorbed into the fanciful disguisings originally designed as an adornment to it" (Anglo, 1968). René's *Traictié de la forme et devis d'ung tournoy* is a compulsively detailed etiquette book regulating exits and entrances, proper verbal formulas, and appropriate attire. Little is said of the clash of weapons. A modern authority on medieval leisure comments that "René, who adored sumptuous festivals, was essentially interested in ceremony and costume; he regulated the minutest detail; but he did not indicate how the jousts were to be carried out" (Verdon, 1980, p. 179).

Having commented briefly on ancient and medieval spectators, I shall conclude this very selective historical survey with a look at two groups of modern spectators—fight fans and "football hooligans." From

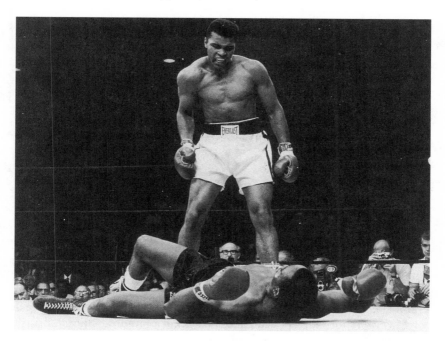

FIGURE 1.1 Muhammad Ali taunting the fallen Sonny Liston. Courtesy of the Bettmann Archive.

the eighteenth century, when pugilism became popular, to the present, when televised bouts continue to draw hundreds of millions of fans, prizefights have been bloody affairs that threaten, always, to conclude with the permanent injury or the death of one of the boxers. Anyone who has been at a match knows that enthusiasts for the "sweet science" are given to shrieking, whistling, stamping their feet, and bellowing their approval and disapproval, but no one seems to have drawn attention to the fact that most of the violence is verbal. The sport is always violent, the fans are usually nonviolent (except, of course, for their verbal incitements to bloodshed).

There have been exceptions to this generalization. In Reno, Nevada, on July 4, 1910, Jack Johnson, the first black heavyweight champion, battered his white challenger, Jim Jeffries, to a bloody pulp. As news of Johnson's easy triumph over the first of the "Great White Hopes" was telegraphed around the nation, the response was violent. Blacks and whites murdered one another in Pueblo, Little Rock, Shreveport, New Orleans, Norfolk, Washington, Wilmington, New York, and a number of other cities (Gilmore, 1975; Roberts, 1983). Scenes of much less bloody jubilation occurred when African Americans celebrated the victories of Joe Louis and Muhammad Ali, but, on the whole, prizefights have *not* instigated in situ spectators to physical violence (although there is some evidence that homicides increase in the aftermath of televised boxing matches [Phillips, 1983; Phillips & Hensley, 1984]).

Soccer football, a sport much less violent than boxing (or rugby or American football), has probably occasioned the most extensive and intensive sports-related violence since the riots of Byzantine circus factions. A pair of examples should suffice. In Lima in 1964, a Uruguayan referee disallowed an equalizing goal toward the end of a Peruvian match against Argentina. The crowd rushed to the seven-foot-high steel-link fence topped with barbed wire and broke through it. Simultaneously, they set fire to the stadium. The police responded by hurling tear gas into the crowd, which intensified the panic. The fans struggled to leave through the stadium's tunnels, but three of the seven doors were tightly locked. Hundreds were crushed to death (White, 1970). In the summer of 1985, English fans took the ferry to Belgium for the European Cup Final (Liverpool versus Juventus of Turin). During the match, they attacked the Italian fans, pushed them up against a brick wall, which crumbled, and pinned others against a fallen fence. The *New York Times* for May 30 reported forty dead and more than a hundred injured. British teams were banned from continental play.

At the University of Leicester, Eric Dunning and a number of Elias-influenced sociologists have applied "figurational sociology" to the analysis of British "football hooliganism." The results of their research, and that of European scholars, like Germany's Gunter A. Pilz, are clear: the typical "football hooligan" is a young, unskilled, unemployed or underemployed working-class male. That corporate managers and mass-media experts have robbed him of what was once felt to be "the people's game" is only one reason for resentment. In fact, the soccer pitch and its surround are a stage for him and his peers to act out, in the form of "aggro," their anger against a society whose evolution has marginalized them (Pilz & Trebels, 1976; Marsh, Rosser, & Harre, 1978; Pilz & Trebels, 1976, 1982; Williams, Dunning, & Murphy, 1984; Dunning, Murphy, & Williams, 1988; Murphy, Williams, & Dunning, 1990).

Some Explanatory Thoughts

To have said this is to have begun the postponed task of explanation. Whether or not a propensity to commit acts of physical aggression is an ineradicable part of "human nature," as Konrad Lorenz and countless others seem to believe, no one can doubt that men and, to a lesser degree, women have a millennia-long history of aggressiveness. It is the cherished belief of many sportswriters that sports and sports spectatorship are a means to rechannel this aggressiveness and to bring it to a harmless catharsis. Here, it seems, we have a simple, satisfying explanation of the

appeal of sports violence, and one with an impressively Aristotelian ge-
nealogy. (It was first set forth in Aristotle's *Poetics*.) Unfortunately, the
theory of catharis, which may indeed be valid for those who experience
"the pity and the terror" of tragic drama, has been thoroughly disconfirmed for the sports spectator. It is worth some time to attempt, yet
again, to slay the theoretical hydra.

Apropos of the alleged catharsis experienced by sports spectators,
there is a rare consensus among non-Freudian social psychologists. This
consensus derives from two types of experiment. In the first type, spectators are tested by pencil-and-paper or projective techniques before and
after they attend sports events. In one study, for instance, obliging American football fans submitted to interviewers who asked them thirty-six
questions from the Buss-Durkee Hostility Inventory. The authors used
the same technique to test spectators at a gymnastics meet. They concluded that there was no support whatsoever for the catharsis theory.
Indeed, the scores tended to show increased rather than diminished aggressiveness after the football game—even when the fan's favored team
won (Goldstein & Arms, 1971).

One of the authors replicated the test with Canadian students who
filled out the questionnaires before and after contests in wrestling, ice
hockey, and swimming. The results once again called into question the
assumption that sports events foster "goodwill and warm interpersonal
relations" (Arms, Russell, & Sandilands, 1977, p. 279; Lennon & Hatfield, 1980; Harrell, 1981). Almost the same results were obtained from
two very similar studies using the Thematic Apperception Test (TAT)
and sentence-completion techniques to test the aggressiveness of football,
basketball, and wrestling spectators at the University of Maryland. Analyzing the data gathered by these projective techniques, the author of
the first study concluded austerely, "The results . . . do not support the
cathartic or purge theory of aggression. Actually, the signficant increase
in the number of aggressive words after the football and basketball contests seem[s] to support the contention that the viewing of violent or
aggressive acts tends to increase the aggressiveness of the viewer"
(Turner, 1968, p. 90; Kingsmore, 1968).

The second type of test, devised by Leonard Berkowitz, involves a
comparison of responses of subjects to violent and nonviolent films. For
instance, the subjects of the experiment see either a travelogue or a
filmed boxing match. They are then tested for their willingness to act
aggressively against another person. This willingness is measured by the
amount of electric shock the subjects *think* they administer to another
person in what they are told is an experiment to test the effects of punishment on learning. (No shock is delivered, but naive subjects are unaware of this happy fact.) Subjects who observe the boxing film are
significantly more willing to administer a dangerously high level of electric shock than are subjects who see films of a travelogue (or a track

meet, a tennis match, a baseball game, and so on) (Berkowitz & Rawlings, 1963; Berkowitz, 1964, 1965; Berkowitz & Geen, 1966; Geen & Berkowitz, 1966a, 1966b; Hartmann, 1969; Geen & O'Neal, 1969; Berkowitz & Alioto, 1973; Goldstein, 1989).

A logical inference from this entire series of experiments is that the alleged catharsis achieved by watching violent sports does not occur. The implications are rather the opposite; aggression can be learned and watching sports is one way to learn it (Bandura, 1973; Zillmann, 1979). As a German scholar concluded after studying 205 soccer fans, "Latent tension is neither repressed [*gebunden*] nor channeled but rather intensified and activated" (Herrmann, 1977, p. 37). Common sense confirms these results. Very little sports-related spectator violence occurs *before* the game, when the fan is supposedly, according to the catharsis theory, most aggressive. The mayhem usually begins in medias res and climaxes after the final whistle has been blown.

Given the persuasive evidence that sports spectatorship *increases* rather than decreases aggressiveness, we can turn the catharsis theory on its head and conjecture that spectators *desire*, consciously or unconsciously, to experience an intensification of aggressiveness. If people really do seek "excitatory homeostasis," as Jennings Bryant and Dolf Zillmann suggested, then the vicarious violence of sports spectatorship is one way to overcome boredom (Bryant & Zillmann, 1984; Zillmann & Bryant, 1986). Their point does not depend upon the common experience of fandom (although it might have) but rather upon laboratory experiments in which, for instance, subjects reported that rough-and-tumble-American football plays were more fun to watch than less violent ones. "Within the rules of the game, the rougher and more violent, the better—as far as the sports spectators employed in this study were concerned" (Bryant, Comisky, & Zillmann, 1981, p. 260). Gordon Russell has reported experiments that suggest that sports violence is *not* as attractive to hockey fans as the owners of the National Hockey League think it is (Russell & Drewry, 1976; Russell, 1986), but the evidence at the box office seems in general to support Bryant and Zillmann. Roughness in the "noncontact" sport of basketball escalated between 1970 and 1990 as the game became increasingly popular with American (and European) spectators.

In a speculative essay entitled "The Quest for Excitement in Unexciting Societies," sociologists Norbert Elias and Eric Dunning conjectured that there is a direct relationship between the routinization of daily life in modern industrial society and the prevalence of rough spectator sports, like soccer, rugby, hockey, and American football: "in the more advanced industrial societies of our time, compared with societies at an earlier stage of development, occasions for strong excitement openly expressed have become rarer" (1970, p. 31). Elias and Dunning emphasize that sports grounds have become a principal venue for the active expression of a variety of otherwise inhibited emotions. If we accept Elias's theory about "the process of civilization" (Elias, 1969; Elias & Dunning, 1986a, 1986b), then it is obvious that a propensity to commit acts of interpersonal expressive violence is precisely what modern society most strongly inhibits and what sports spectatorship most gratifyingly permits—either directly, in the case of fans who run amok, or vicariously, in the case of fans who merely empathize with and take pleasure in the violence they witness. In other words, sports are an especially attractive opportunity for sensation seeking (Zuckerman, 1979). It is doubtful that the vicarious sensations experienced by the sports spectator can be as thrilling or as satisfying as those experienced by the athletes, but the importance of these sensations should not be underestimated.

Sports spectacles are clearly not the only occasions for this kind of release, for sensation seeking—rock concerts come immediately to mind as unintentional invitations to mayhem—but sports events are an especially attractive vehicle for the more or less culturally legitimate indulgence in and expression of strong emotion. One simple reason for this is that sports contests are almost always characterized by suspense, which is not the case with the predictable fare offered by most popular entertainment.

Within the structural framework of a sport's rules and regulations, individual contests are relatively unpredictable, but they are reassuringly repeatable in that there can always be another contest, a new season, a repetition of the unexpected outcome within the familiar format. Psychoanalysts have suggested that this kind of repetition, this combination of variation and sameness, enables sports to function therapeutically. In his essay "The Counter-Phobic Attitude" (1939/1954), Otto Fenichel generalized to all sports the psychoanalytic theories that Helene Deutsch (1926) had suggested apropos of ball games. Like Deutsch, Fenichel assumed that sports are essentially *Männersache* and that the effort to overcome castration anxiety is a prime factor in men's sports participation. The demonstration of physical skills is a mechanism for the mastery of excessive fears, and unconscious desires. Sports provide "functional pleasure," that is, pleasure derived from a dreaded activity that has been repeated until it is no longer feared.

> No doubt there are erotic and aggressive gratifications in sport, just as they are present in all the other functional pleasures of adults. Certainly not everyone who engages in sport is suffering from an unconscious insoluble fear of castration; nor does it follow that the participant sport for which he shows a later preference must once have been feared. But it will generally hold true that the essential joy in sport is that one actively brings about in play certain tensions which were formerly feared, so that one may enjoy the fact that now one can overcome them. (1954, p. 167)

In short, sports allow us "the belated conquest of an unmastered infantile anxiety" (p. 172). Through the mechanisms of identification and empathy, spectators can participate vicariously in the benefits of "functional pleasure."

Identification and empathy are important psychic phenomena. Although sports spectators are unquestionably moved by a variety of motivations, ranging from a disinterested aesthetic appreciation of the athlete's prowess to the crass desire to win a bet, the most avidly, most intensively involved spectators are those who not only empathize with but also *identify* with the athletes. The psychological term "identification" has been criticized because spectators are quite aware of the difference between themselves and their athletic heroes, but "empathy" seems too weak a term to characterize what I have called *representational sports* (Guttmann, 1988). For whatever reason, there is an almost irresistible impulse for sports spectators to feel that the athletes in the ring or on the field represent them.

This feeling is not a recent phenomenon. An anecdote told by the ancient historian Polybius beautifully dramatizes the familiar emotional conflict between sympathy for the underdog and commitment to "the home team." When Aristonicus of Alexandria challenged the mighty Greek boxer Clitomachus, the crowd

> at once took the part of the former and cheered him on, delighted to see that some one . . . ventured to pit himself against Clitomachus. And when, as the fight continued, he appeared to be his adversary's match, and once or twice landed a telling blow, there was great clapping of hands, and the crowd became delirious with excitement, cheering on Aristonicus. At this time . . . Clitomachus, after withdrawing a few moments to recover his breath, turned to the crowd and asked them what they meant by cheering on Aristonicus and backing him up. . . . Did they think he himself was not fighting fairly, or were they not aware that Clitomachus was now fighting for the glory of Greece and Aristonicus for that of King Ptolomy? Would they prefer to see an Egyptian [i.e., an ethnic Greek from Egypt] conquer the Greeks and win the Olympian crown? (Polybius, 1922–1927, vol. 5, p. 509)

This speech by Clitomachus won the spectators over. The demoralized Aristonicus was beaten and the Greeks rejoiced in the triumph of *their* hero.

Modern examples of representational sports are ubiquitous. When Jack Johnson knocked out the "Great White Hope," black America was jubilant (and white America was glum). Whenever Glasgow's Celtics outscore Glasgow's Rangers in a soccer match, Roman Catholics rejoice. Whenever a baseball team wins the World Series, the streets of the city it represents—staid Toronto as well as volatile New York—are filled with shouting, screaming, drinking celebrants. When a team of young Americans defeated the Soviet Union's favored hockey players at the

1980 Olympic Games, the celebrants included not only dedicated fans but also first-time spectators who didn't know the difference between a slap shot and a mug shot. In short, sports spectators feel intensely that *their* race, religion, hometown, or nation is represented in an immensely important competition against some similarly represented rival. Despite its high-minded dedication to rationality, the faculty of Amherst College stands taller (or is somewhat less stooped) when Amherst defeats Williams. In all of these cases, each individual self is part of a collectivity of identically represented selves.

The social-psychological literature devoted to the complexities of this phenomenon is vast (Wann & Branscombe, 1990s, 1993; Branscombe & Wann, 1992a, 1992b; Branscombe et al., 1993; Wann & Dolan, 1994), but two studies can be cited to demonstrate the extremes of harmless and harmful identification with one's athletic representatives. In 1976, a team of six social psychologists published a seminal essay, entitled "Basking in Reflected Glory," in which they showed that students whose team had won a football game tended to wear "school-of-attendance apparel" to their Monday classes (Cialdini et al., 1976). At the other extreme, David P. Phillips discovered not only that there is a statistically significant increase in homicides after televised boxing matches but also that the murders are not, as might be expected, random (Phillips, 1983; Phillips & Hensley, 1984). In fact, the victims tend to be from the same racial group as the defeated fighter, which strongly suggests that the killers are motivated by a sense of empathetic empowerment. Thanks to their representative's success in the ring, they feel that they, too, can do violence with impunity.

Competition is a crucial component of the emotional equation. In a win-or-lose sports contest, more than in most social situations, the collective self is clearly defined against the collective other. This fact helps to explain why "sport generates fanship that is more intense, more obtrusive, and more enduring than it is for other forms of entertaining social activities" (Zillmann & Paulus, 1993, p. 604). It is the intrinsically agonistic character of spectator sports that has always, from antiquity to modern times, made them especially suitable for their representational function. For sports spectators, the appeal of violence is not simply that it happens, that it is an externalized dramatization of the instinctive or learned aggressiveness that all of us seem to harbor within ourselves. The special appeal of sports violence is that those who represent *us* block, tackle, kick, punch, pummel, or pin *them*, whoever they are. And, since it is "just a game," we can reassure ourselves that our emotional binges are harmless. For most spectators, the excitement of sports spectacles is safely vicarious.

Or is it? If sports spectacles provide us with opportunities for the sanctioned vicarious expression of hostility, they are also—for the spectator as well as for the athlete—"a risky venture" (Hirt, Zillmann, Erikson, & Kennedy, 1992, p. 737). Representational sports are not simply a matter of what *we* do to *them*. Since *they* strenuously, and often successfully, do it back to *us*, representational sports are liable to have severe psychic costs. From Roman times to the present, sports history records occasional suicides (by those too emotionally bound to the losers to detach ego from object) as well as murders (by those who cannot bear to see their representatives lose). These responses are also ingredients in the brew of vicariously experienced violence.

Social psychologists are understandably wary of Freud's theories, which are notoriously difficult to verify or falsify, but less positivistic scholars have speculated that sadism and masochism are both involved in the appeal of sports violence. If sports spectatorship is an occasion for the sanctioned expression of sadistic impulses, which seems too obvious to dispute, it is also a site for the enactment of the perverse joys of masochism.

Modern sports spectators rarely admit to the appeal of sports violence that culminates in death, but the experience of the Roman arena should be instructive. Odd as it may seem to us, the gladiator who entered the arena and risked his life in armed combat was "sexually attractive" (Hopkins, 1983, p. 22), an "erotically charged figure" (Barton, 1993, p. 47) whose physical presence excited women of every social class. The word *gladius* (sword) was used in colloquial speech to refer to the penis. And the man with the sword or trident, not the orator and certainly not the poet, was the hero of "the Roman romance with death, unendurably intensified and concentrated" (Barton, p. 47). Indeed, the presence of death seems to have been a crucial factor in the gladiator's erotic appeal. Keith Hopkins remarks that even "the dead gladiator had something sexually portentous about him. It was customary for a new bride to have her hair parted with a spear, at best one which had been dipped "in the body of a defeated and killed gladiator" (p. 22). In the gladiator's courageous death, did the Roman take proleptic pleasure in his own equally courageous demise? To such a question, no definite answer can be given, but the gladiatorial games can be thought of as a magnifying glass that enables us to detect the less obvious sadomasochistic emotions of the modern sports spectator.

As Vicki Goldberg has indicated, photographic images of death have proliferated as the sight of death has become increasingly infrequent in American society. All the more reason, then, to seek in the vicarious enjoyment of sports violence the equivalent of that lost experience. Ernest Hemingway suggested exactly that when he inserted an apparently digressive meditation on the horrors of war into his rhapsodic account of the Spanish bullfight.

That account, *Death in the Afternoon* (1932), can be read as a lay analysis of the sadomasochistic appeal of sports violence. The entire book is an homage to Juan Belmonte and all the other bullfighters, fa-

FIGURE 1.2 Medieval ladies admiring their jousting lords. From the Codex Manesse, courtesy of Universitätsbibliothek Heidelberg.

mous and obscure, who risked their lives in the arena. Of the matador Hemingway wrote, "He is performing a work of art and he is playing with death, bringing it closer, closer, closer to himself, a death that you know is in the horns because you have the canvas-covered bodies of the horses on the sand to prove it" (p. 213). It is the "true enjoyment of killing which makes the great matador" (p. 233). The death of the bull is certain. (If the bull gores the matador, he is nonetheless killed because no matador wants to face an experienced bull.) The death of the matador, which is always possible, unites the two antagonists "in the emotional, aesthetic and artistic climax of the fight" (p. 247).

The erotic frisson experienced by the spectators was better explored by Michel Leiris in *Miroir de la tauromachie* (1938/1981). He described the matador's encounter with the bull as an "erotic activity" (p. 48) as well as a tragic drama and a religious ritual. The entire event is "bathed in an erotic atmosphere" and the bull is "essentially phallic" (pp. 48–49). The movements of the deadly contest symbolize the sexual act. The closeness of the man and the animal is like an embrace; their "coming and going" approximates a "sequence of alternating approaches and withdrawals, like the movements of coitus" (p. 49). With the death of the bull comes the crowd's frenzied ovation, an "ejaculation that has bravos for its sperm" (p. 51). This steamy vision of the bullfight as an orgiastic encounter is illustrated by four drawings done by the author's friend André Masson. Like Pablo Picasso's *Guernica*, which was done at almost exactly the same time, each drawing is a Freudian collage in which images of bulls, matadors, rapiers, and naked women interact and intersect.

With the exception of some important work done in Germany (Hortleder & Gunter, 1986), the triadic association of sports, eros, and violent death has seldom been investigated by serious scholars, but Jennings Bryant and Dolf Zillmann did note, in the conclusion of their essay "Sports Violence and the Media," that the promotional material for a televised sports event included a clip showing accidental death in hydrofoil racing. They wonder if we are involved in a regression toward "gladiator-like combat" (1983, p. 209). The question is a good one. If there has been a "civilizing process" that reduced the level of expressive violence in modern society, it has been less than totally effective. The aficionado of Madrid's bullring is not the only sports spectator who is excited and enthralled by death. Who among the four hundred thousand spectators who gather to experience the excitement of the Indianapolis 500 is unaware of the exciting possibility of a fiery crash? What ringside boxing fan is unaware of the exciting possibility that one of the two physically powerful men—so *alive*—who touch gloves at the start of a bout might, fifteen minutes later, be as dead as the deadest Roman gladiator? Whether we acknowledge it or not, the haunting specter of death is also an aspect—who knows how important?—of the perennial appeal of violent sports.

Note

Several paragraphs of this essay are revised from my books *Sports Spectators* (1984) and *Eros and Sports* (1996).

2

Death Takes a Holiday, Sort Of

VICKI GOLDBERG

The Decline of Death and Ascent of Its Image

In eighteenth-century Europe and England, death was everyone's intimate acquaintance, constantly on view. Child mortality rates were hideously high. Crowded living in unsanitary conditions, malnutrition, famine, disease, and accidents ensured life's unpredictability from day to day. Anyone with a little money then died at home, but the poor, who could not spare a hand from work to tend the sick, sent their relatives to hospitals where atrocious care and rampant infection killed them fast (McManners, 1985, p. 33). The body then went home for washing and laying out, so if you missed the dying you still saw, and most likely handled, the dead.

A Christian death was a public occasion marked by religious ceremony and meant to set an example that would bring the spectator closer to God. Mme de Montespan, who died in 1707, was not so afraid of dying as she was of dying *alone* (Ariès, 1981, p. 18). Most likely she died in a crowd. The last sacrament was ordinarily borne across town to the dying in religious procession, and everyone on the street, of whatever station in life, was entitled to follow the eucharist into the room of the dying and indeed was granted an indulgence for doing so (McManners, 1985, p. 235).

Executions were also public. Well into the nineteenth century, an execution day was a holiday, and schools were let out; it was commonly believed that the sight of punishment would deter future criminals. The bodies were often displayed for a long while, the flesh decaying before people's eyes.

27

The more innocent dead might also be on view. Cemeteries had been attached to churches in residential areas of big cities for centuries, and by the eighteenth century they were literally overflowing. Bodies were tossed into common pits and covered with only a couple of inches of dirt; the process was repeated until the pit was full. When new trenches were dug where corpses had wholly or partially decomposed, bones turned up all the time. These would be arranged in the galleries about the churchyard. Hamlet would hardly have been surprised when a grave-digger came upon Yorick's skull. Though the burial grounds sometimes stank, people frequently played games and hawked merchandise right beside or even atop the dead (McManners, 1985, pp. 304–5).

Late in the eighteenth century, death actually began to recede in many Western countries, if imperceptibly at first, and attitudes to it changed. Life expectancy had begun to increase, in increments too small to be noticeable but possibly intuited nonetheless. Between 1740 and 1749 in France, average life expectancy was 25.9 years; between 1790 and 1799, it was 32.1. (Obviously some lived much longer.) No one knows exactly why, only that it was so. Possibly climate had shifted sufficiently to improve food production; perhaps certain diseases had run their course and become less devastating (see McManners, 1985, pp. 92, 106). Jenner's introduction of the smallpox vaccine, in 1798, offered the first real hope that disease might be conquered.

Over time, social, religious, and medical changes made dying and death gradually withdraw from view; by the mid–twentieth century they became virtually invisible in most large metropolitan centers, especially in America and England. An odd and suggestive aspect of this process is that it roughly coincided with a long increase in *depictions* of death, some driven by new technologies. Though hard proof is lacking, circum-stantial evidence strongly suggests that these two phenomena are related. The diminution of the visible presence of death was not the primary cause of the expansion of depictions, but history and psychology indicate that representation rapidly supplanted actual experience as a new and newly anxious audience sought novel ways to cope with its fears. The increase in representation is more sudden and pronounced and a bit earlier than the most obvious decreases in death's visibility but appears to have received an extra impetus from changes in life expectancy and the vicissitudes of death and dying during the nineteenth century (changes that became more evident as the century progressed), and it both responded to and aggravated new tensions and doubts brought on by these shifts.

The multiplication of portrayals of death in the nineteenth century was accompanied by a turning away from the religious, moralizing rep-resentations of the death of Christ and saints or the lessons taught by *ars moriendi* books to the secular subject of violent death as news and/or a matter of entertainment. These newer accounts and images of death became so numerous in the last century that some found them troubling, and many of the difficult issues raised about the media in our time turn up, at least in miniature, in the infancy of the popular press.

The waning and waxing of death and representations of it were not on precisely parallel tracks nor by any means perfectly synchronized, and one cannot be held strictly accountable for the other. Yet there they are, doing a slightly out-of-step minuet across time: as the dead leave the realm of transcendence to become beautiful dreamers and tame objects, as executions retreat behind prison walls, as the mortal coil gets shuffled off in isolation wards and eventually in faraway nursing homes, the new reproductive media offer more and more realistic or exaggerated visions of how we die.

Death in the Age of Mechanical Reproduction

In the eighteenth century, the popular print, still limited in number, came into its own. The last years of the century saw new and revived graphic techniques, including wood engraving (incising an image on the harder end piece of the wood), which would be vital to the nineteenth-century illustrated press, and lithography. Both permitted much, much larger illustrated print runs. The introduction of photography, in 1839, riveted the eyes of the world on pictures, and by 1851, an easy means of duplicating photographic prints made them cheaper and readily available. Earlier in the nineteenth century, steam-driven presses and machine-manufactured paper made it possible to produce journals by the tens—and within decades, hundreds—of thousands, and more cheaply than anyone could have imagined.

These developments came along as industrialization, capitalism, and social change created a widely expanded audience that was literate and financially comfortable and had a certain amount of leisure time. An enormous working class was newly concentrated in metropolitan areas, literate to a degree, and eager for news, human interest, and entertainment in written and visual—especially visual—form. The makings of a mass audience were at hand.

When executions attracted huge crowds, picture makers came too. Broadside ballads, illustrated with woodcut pictures of crime and punishment, sold well. The images were crude, vigorous—men stabbing women, a woman dashing out a child's brains—and in effect interchangeable. Around 1840, when there was a series of suicide leaps from the same English monument, one enterprising publisher kept on hand blank pictures of said monument so that he could drop in a falling male or falling female body. Often the up-to-date, on-the-spot image of a condemned criminal or a crime was actually a picture made decades earlier to illustrate another dastardly deed (Gretton, 1988, p. 8 and illus. 33; Shepard, 1962, p. 82).

The broadsides, which had a brief but powerful flowering in the first half of the nineteenth century, sputtered out under competition from the illustrated press, which began in the 1840s. Papers like the *Illustrated London News* advertised for sketches from the scene and sent their own artist-correspondents to cover wars and revolutions; sometimes they copied photographs. (Until the late 1880s, there was no practical and inexpensive way to print text and photographs together.) Truthfulness, accuracy, and similitude were implied by pictures from photographs or sketches made on site, though they were not always supplied. When it came to matters of death, people who were no longer seeing quite so much of it up close learned to accept representations that looked real as a substitute for experience.

Even as death seemed to die and be properly buried, it sprang to life on the printed page and in various visual spectacles. Illustration moved in as death moved out. Though the deathbed had ceased to be a public occasion for the community, the deathbeds of great men continued to be so in engravings. Photographers took deathbed pictures of many of the important cultural figures of the century, and these were sometimes copied in the journals.

The serious illnesses of monarchs and major figures had for centuries been closely followed news, and their bodies had lain in state for visitors to pay tribute to, but there were severe limits on what anyone at a distance could see or participate in. Lincoln, Grant, Lord Nelson, and many nineteenth-century statesmen were drawn on their deathbeds before or after their actual deaths, with careful attention to the features of the actual people in attendance, and the pictures were reproduced in a short time for a large audience that in some sense became present at their leader's side. After Lincoln died, his body traveled by railroad to several cities; if the public could not come to the monument, the monument could now come to the public.

The community of mourners who felt present was greatly enlarged, though the immediacy of the experience was diminished. This removal-by-representation prefigured the worldwide attendance at the funeral of John F. Kennedy via TV, as well as the tabloid slab shots, taken in the morgue, of the bodies of Steve McQueen and Elvis Presley.

It was already understood in the mid–nineteenth century that newspapers were replacing the immediate, in-person experience of death. On July 25, 1857, *Harper's Weekly* wrote: "The policy of private executions in an age when the thrilling rhetoric of reporters photographs the details for millions of readers [note the emphasis on realistic visualization before photographs could be reproduced with text], who become spectators in effect, can not now be doubted. . . . The jurists of all countries may well arrive at the conclusion, that the example pondered upon by millions of readers is more powerful than the one gloated over by a few curious thousands of spectators."

Realistic description was keeping even private executions before the public eye. Pictures would heighten the power of the press and compound the issues of public display. The same journal, two years later, trumpeted its own importance and the importance of illustration in general: "The value of the paper can be best realized by supposing that it did not exist, and by trying to conceive how little people would really know of passing events if they had to rely on written descriptions alone" (Dec. 31, 1859, p. 836).

Death was not the only experience that was gradually becoming more mediated than immediate. The post-modernist insistence that real life was being replaced by reproductions gathered force and recognition in the last century. In 1843, Ludwig Feuerbach, speaking of religion, wrote about "the present age, which prefers the image to the thing, the copy to the original, the fancy [sometimes translated "the representation"] to the reality, appearance to the essence," and added that the era was perfectly well aware of doing so (1843/1855, p. 10).

The dominion of illustration was so overpowering that Wordsworth wrote a sonnet in 1846 (published in 1850) inveighing against illustrated books and newspapers in general. He feared that pictures would destroy the hard-won human capacity for thought:

> Now prose and verse sunk into disrepute
> Must lacquey a dumb Art that best can suit
> The taste of this once-intellectual Land.
>
> . . . .
>
> Avaunt this vile abuse of pictured page!
> Must eyes be all in all, the tongue and ear
> Nothing? Heaven keep us from a lower stage!

In 1896, an editor added a footnote saying, "[H]ad Wordsworth known the degradation to which many newspapers would sink in this direction, his censure would have been more severe" (Knight, 1896, p. 185).

Photography explosively heightened this dependence on images. Oliver Wendell Holmes was peculiarly prescient in 1859 when he wrote:

> *Form is henceforth divorced from matter.* In fact, matter as a visible object is of no great use any longer, except as the mould on which form is shaped. Give us a few negatives of a thing worth seeing, taken from different points of view, and that is all we want of it. Pull it down or burn it up, if you please. . . . We have got the fruit of creation now, and need not trouble ourselves with the core. Every conceivable object of Nature and Art will soon scale off its surface for us. Men will hunt all curious, beautiful, grand objects, as they hunt the cattle in South America, for their *skins*, and leave the carcasses as of little worth. (1859, p. 112)

The replacement value and the dominance of the simulacrum were already acknowledged. The eventual substitution of death imagery for the sight of actual death is merely one aspect, if a very important one, of a trend that would in time change the way we experience the world.

Longer Life, Fading Death

As lives gradually lengthened, people grew increasingly attached to life and more frightened of its end[1] (Ariès, 1981, p. 28). The secularization of religious customs, combined with the new strength of family ties that emerged in the later eighteenth century, meant that individual death was retreating from the status of a public ritual—strangers no longer came to the bedside—to that of a private family affair.

Two apparently contradictory attitudes to death developed: the gothic and romantic movements turned it into a lugubrious, morbid, aestheticized fascination, horribly beautiful in its way; and death was made cozily beautiful with a new concept of heaven, where earthly loves continued in snug cottages with married partners (Ariès, 1981, p. 446). The gothic was born in England and the domestic afterlife took strong hold there, but both spread far. The shuddery aestheticization of death was essentially secular, whereas the reduction of heaven to a suburban bourgeois utopia was set in a religious framework; both could be considered imaginative means of coping with heightened anxieties about death.

Life expectancy continued its slow upward climb in the nineteenth century. But statistics like those that indicate slowly declining death rates in England and Wales (see Mitchell, 1962) mask the difference in life expectancy of the various classes. In London in 1830, the average age of death for the gentry, professional people, and their families—the people who would read the illustrated papers when they became available—was 44. For tradesmen, clerks, and their families it was 25, for laborers 22. The reformers were well aware of the discrepancies and in time improved sanitary conditions enough to make a difference. Edwin Chadwick, in his famous report to Parliament in 1842, said that the sanitary reforms he advocated would extend the life expectancy of the laboring class at least 13 years (Morley, 1971, pp. 9–10). In America at the end of the century, the average life expectancy for all classes was 47 (Jackson, 1980, p. 49).

Twenty-two, 44, 47—they do not sound like much to us, but changes in expectations of life, even if only barely perceptible, must make a difference in attitudes to death. And in the later nineteenth century there were some promising medical developments that may well have raised people's hopes beyond the possibilities of the science of the time to fulfill them. By 1858, Pasteur had developed the principle of pasteurization. In 1864, Lister proposed that microorganisms on doctors' hands could spread infection, and in the 1870s and 1880s the microbes responsible for cholera, tuberculosis, rabies, and many other diseases were discovered. Doctors fought Lister's idea hard, but everywhere that it was accepted, mortality rates after deliveries or surgery declined, sometimes radically. Anesthesia was discovered, fever hospitals in London were moved away from residential areas and redesigned to give more air and light and to isolate infectious patients, and Florence Nightingale successfully campaigned for trained nurses, who also improved hospital care.

The result was that people lived somewhat longer and had more hope of doing so, and that many more, rich as well as poor, went to hospitals for treatment, and more died there, out of sight[2] (Rivett, 1986, p. 91). The process of removing death to hospitals has vastly speeded up since the 1930s, but death has been steadily removing itself from view for almost two centuries by the extension of life and the removal of the dying from the home.

The corpse and its care also left home over the course of the nineteenth century. The family had traditionally washed and dressed the body and laid it out in the parlor for friends and relatives to see. By the third quarter of the century, the undertaker began to assume some of those responsibilities. This was partly because life insurance had taken hold, in Britain in the late eighteenth century, in America in the 1840s, and in Europe a little later[3] (Gudmundsen, 1959, pp. 20, 36); people had money for extravagant funerals and undertakers leaped to exploit a growing business. Societies of undertakers were organized in the 1880s, the U.S. College of Embalming was established in 1887 (embalming having begun here during the Civil War), and the funeral parlor replaced the private home's parlor, which was then rechristened the living room.

The dying and dead were slowly fading from the field of view. Cemeteries, which had been attached to churches in town centers, were moved into the countryside. In 1763, when French gravediggers and some residents of houses next to the churchyards died suddenly from graveyard fumes, the Parliament decreed that cemeteries should be moved out of town. This began in earnest when the king issued his own decree in 1776. The Metropolitan Interments Act of 1850 forbade interments in London churchyards or within two hundred yards of any house. English cemeteries in the 1850s, like those of the rural cemetery movement in America, were experienced as delightful places in which the proper burial "must tend to rob death itself of its most repulsive features"[4]—including visibility.

Violent death as an organized spectacle—public execution—was also on its way out. The upper classes mingled with the lower at executions, though it was only the better educated who began to voice their unease in the late eighteenth century. Enlightenment voices declared public torture and execution an "atrocity," and by the first quarter of the nineteenth century, such violent means of death as breaking on the wheel

and quartering had been eliminated altogether. But the people felt entitled to their theater and complained loudly when the guillotine replaced
the gallows because they could not see as well (Foucault, 1977, pp. 55,
58, 59). However, the enormous crowds and unruly celebrations at these
events attracted pickpockets and other criminals and sometimes occasioned riots. Already in the eighteenth century, the authorities began to
see public executions as a threat; eventually they were transferred to the
inner courtyards of prisons.

During the nineteenth century their number declined steeply. When
the century began, England had 160 capital crimes on the books and by
1810 had 320; France had 115. A British citizen could be executed for
stealing five shillings or cutting down a tree as well as for more serious
crimes, though the death penalty was by no means universally applied.
The second decade saw the beginning of a great reformation of the British penal code; this was seen (properly enough) as evidence of an advance in morality and civilization. By 1850 England had fewer than 10
capital offenses, and the punishment of death was rarely imposed except
for treason and murder; in France it was rare, though the Commune
changed that.

Though England did not give up capital punishment until 1969—
more than two centuries after Henry Fielding had called for its abolish-
ment—and France still has not done so, both countries have long since
ceased to make it a public spectacle. By the late nineteenth century the
French carried out their executions at dawn with the crowd held off by
a cordon of police (Kershaw, 1993, p. 74). In the first two decades of
the nineteenth century, approximately twenty-seven hundred people
were executed in England and Wales; in relation to the population, that
was twelve times as many as during the single decade of 1841–1850
(*Illustrated London News*, Aug. 9, 1851, p. 175).

Though public executions were still occasional and riotous spectacles, they were clearly declining. By the 1850s, executions in Germany
and America were carried out in private. Step by step, death was leaving
the home and the public square as efforts were made to draw the curtains of privacy about it. Today in America the issue is not merely
whether we shall have more private executions but whether they should
go public once more, this time on TV.

Death, Fear, and New Responses

Even as death receded, ever so quietly and slowly, from view, nineteenth-
century urban society remained fixated on it while attempting to restruc-
ture its responses and keep the inevitable at a remove. Extended
mourning rituals were often socially, rather than religiously, formalized
and degrees of mourning were prescribed down to the last detail. The
moral and salvific force of what were once personal visits to deathbeds

was transferred to the new literary form of the novel: most of the great books of the age include an extended death scene. Once the cemeteries were shifted away from city centers, the rural cemetery was turned into a delightful garden and the old casual acquaintance with dead bodies was transformed into a spectacle or viewing opportunity. In Paris, people idly dropped in on the morgue, where the door was always open, if they were passing by (Ariès, 1985, p. 211), and the catacombs, where the bones that had welled up from earlier cemeteries were arranged in ranks and galleries, were a popular site for tourists.

Ingenious ways were found to mask the terrors attendant on fixation with death. Hiding death was one way, beautifying it another, taming it yet another. In January 1860, *Harper's Weekly* advertised a chromolithograph of Rembrandt Peale's *Court of Death*, first painted in 1820, for one dollar. "[T]here is not a skeleton or any thing repulsive in the picture," this ad boasted. (Again the word "repulsive"; death was being cleaned up for middle-class consumption.) "It is a work to DELIGHT THE EYE and IMPROVE THE HEART. It can be studied and understood by a child, while its sublime conception affords scope to the strongest imagination." What's more, nothing could be "A more impressive, instructive, or beautiful PARLOR ORNAMENT."

Embalming was one way to hide death with a simulacrum of life, to improve its looks, to render it no longer fearful. There were others. Memorial jewelry, which had earlier been decorated with skeletons and coffins, now held tiny photographs of the departed or even more significantly was made of their hair—an anonymous, unfleshy, undecaying fragment of the body. In mainstream fiction, young heroines died nobly and were assured of an afterlife—Beth in *Little Women*, Little Nell in *The Old Curiosity Shop*, little Eva in *Uncle Tom's Cabin*, the Little Match Girl. In 1858, Henry Peach Robinson, a well-known British photographer, made a famous composite photograph called *Fading Away*, in which a beautiful young woman lies wanly, and beautifully, on a chaise while the family sits by in quiet grief or gazes hopelessly out the window. The image sums up the intensity of family relations and the determination that dying should be well composed, peaceful, and attractive.

In America, postmortem photographs—the next frame in the story, as it were—were popular in many households throughout the century. They were commonly displayed on mantelpieces and parlor tables. (The custom of taking professional photographs of the dead persisted to World War II and apparently till today in some places, but in this century death was no longer publicly acceptable, so the images were usually tucked away in albums [Norfleet, 1993, p. 13].) Postmortem photographers specialized in making the dead look tranquil, in keeping with the new idea of the afterlife as a comfortable bourgeois existence. Southworth and Hawes, the preeminent Boston portraitists, advertised in 1846

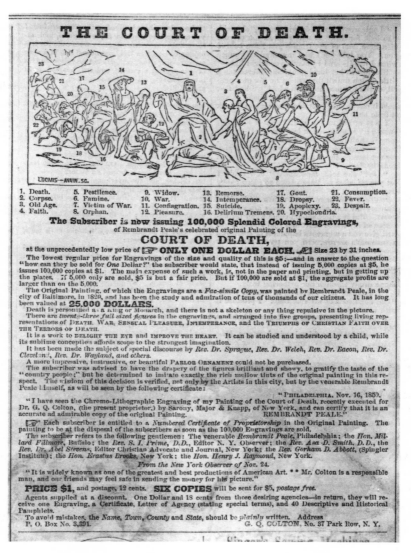

FIGURE 2.1 An era fixated on death tried to tame and conceal its fears and, wherever possible, make life's end attractive. This print of an 1820 painting was advertised in *Harper's* in 1860, when a movement to turn graveyards into delightful places to stroll was in full force.

that "We take great pains to have miniatures of Deceased persons agreeable and satisfactory, and they are often so natural as to seem, even to Artists, in a quiet sleep" (Burns, 1990, n.p.). (One twentieth-century photograph of a dead baby shows the child with wide-open eyes—which have been pasted onto his portrait [Norfleet, p. 97].) It was suggested that cemeteries would be better places to visit if only they were filled with photographs of the dead as they had been in life, and indeed patents for preserving daguerreotypes on tombstones were taken out at least by 1851.

Here Is Thy Sting

As the nineteenth century grew older, its face no longer managed to be quite so pretty all the time. Mme Bovary imagined herself dying in a transcendental swoon when, alas, she merely had flu; later, when she poisoned herself, her death was hideous. Tolstoy's Ivan Ilyich died a lingering, distinctly unromanticized death in which his body became dirty and his fate unimportant to those around him. Death, no longer quite so uplifting, had begun to hide itself away, and attitudes to it changed in many ways. Oscar Wilde said, "One must have a heart of stone to read the death of Little Nell without laughing."

The century's fixation on death, like fixations in general, doubtless indicates intense anxiety. The gradual decline of belief, especially in the afterlife, makes that all the more likely. For many, death became a negation, the dead person a nonentity, a nothing. The Goncourts said, "The dead person is no longer revered as a living being who has entered into the unknown, consecrated to the formidable 'je ne sais quoi' of that which is beyond life. In modern societies, the dead person is simply a zero, a non-value" (Loyette, 1994). Artists like Manet and Degas painted this zero factually and dispassionately. There were several religious revivals during the century, and many people held tightly to belief in a welcoming heaven. Others adopted the Enlightenment notion that immortality resided in the memories of those still here. But once biblical exegesis, Darwin, and modern science got to work they spread wide currents of unease. By 1878, one English funeral establishment offered different forms and colors for funerals depending on whether the survivors believed the dead slept till the Second Coming, went to purgatory, or were totally extinguished[5] (Morley, 1971, p. 31).

The Goncourts, in 1852, declared religious painting "dead with that which has died"—by which they meant faith (Loyette, 1994, p. 30).[6] In 1867 Matthew Arnold wrote in "Dover Beach,"

The Sea of Faith
Was once, too, at the full, and round earth's shore
Lay like the folds of a bright girdle furled.
But now I only hear
Its melancholy, long, withdrawing roar.

Manet's two paintings of Christ in the 1860s do not even make an attempt to inspire religious devotion; he painted them because he thought it an artistic challenge to deal with the traditional iconography. By 1898, an American writer, William Henry Johnson, could say that "the traditional belief is undergoing rapid alteration and, in some quarters, disintegration. Forces are at work which have affected the old dogma more seriously in twenty-five years than all the thought of all the ages since man began to think" (quoted in Farrell, 1980, p. 87).

The prospect of death is newly terrifying if nothing comes after, and in a culture that once felt it had a guarantee of eternal life, blissful or miserable, the undermining and loss of that cherished belief must have created an especially intense anxiety. Photography, which soon after its invention began to represent death, even assayed the afterlife. In the second half of the nineteenth century, what was known as spirit photography claimed to have tapped into the other world, provoking considerable controversy. Portraits were taken of people who wanted to get in touch with deceased relatives; when the pictures were developed, ectoplasmic figures or faces mysteriously hovered above the firm lineaments of the living. These were nothing but double exposures, in which an undeveloped plate with an image of, say, a child, was reused for the current sitter, but many thought they had found the key to the continuing life of those they had lost. (Or to the invisible world of other kinds of spirits, such as fairies.) Arthur Conan Doyle was a firm believer in the power of spirit photography.

The struggle to come to terms with death is built into the human condition. As Freud pointed out, one cannot fully imagine one's own death but always remains a live spectator watching the event in imagination. A terrible need for answers, a deep and implacable denial, and a desperate yearning for mastery buttress our combined fascination, fear, and avoidance of scenes of death.

Death, Violence, and Fascination

In the nineteenth century, as the dead gradually became a less commonplace sight than they had been, as even Christ's death was, in many instances and at least in such countries as England, France, and America, replaced by images of his life as the central religious icons, death was glossed over and negated as far as possible. The sight of death receded faster than the reality, but both were clearly diminishing. I would suggest that the fact that representation so rapidly rose to fill the gap, and that illustrations so often veered toward violence, indicates that the technology and marketing devices of the modern world arrived at the moment to take advantage of (and sometimes exacerbate) the new anxieties of life.

Photography would in time be crucial to the accelerated display of death and violence, but in some cases, such as deathbed and postmortem pictures, it must have aided the mourning process. Photographic images were believed to be entirely truthful and wholly realistic, so that even a wood engraving in a weekly paper that was labeled "after a photograph by Brady" (or whomever) was more *convincing* than the work of the finest artists, if by no means as artistic. This high reality quotient may have made the peacefulness of postmortem photographs more reassuring than they could otherwise have been.

And images, whether photographs, wood engravings, or motion pictures, can offer a kind of ambiguous comfort and control that reality does not, especially for those who look at a picture repeatedly or watch the same film more than once. Having a still picture in hand predicates a kind of control over it, which becomes yet more meaningful when the picture is a photograph, with its credible traces of reality. This may be stared at, queried, turned away from, put away, and later taken out again. It does not call for action, as coming upon a dying man or a murder would, and the spectator determines whether to pay it attention or not.

(There is also a ritual aspect to repetitive viewing of moving pictures. Knowing when the violence and death will turn up allows a certain monitoring of one's own emotions. And since everyone dies only once, watching the same people die over and over tends to erect one poor barricade against the reality of death. Besides, the stars are truly immortal. As Melina Mercouri said of the tragic actors in *Never on Sunday*, after the play they all go off to the beach. Film stars go on to make another film, perhaps to die again.)

Throughout the ages, sculptured reliefs, vase paintings, and murals have depicted death in battles and proclaimed the triumphant brutalities of warrior kings. In the Christian West, Christ's violent death was always visible, at least in church, and the hideous deaths of saints loomed large in paintings, occasionally in sculpture, and, after the fifteenth century, in illustrated hagiographies. The tortures of hell were also generously offered to view. Death in battle never disappeared, but in the postclassical and Renaissance world represented a very small fraction of artistic production. More peaceful endings were provided by scenes of the Virgin's death, by tomb sculptures, and by the *ars moriendi* books.

While the deaths of relatives and strangers might seem random and be hard for the human mind to fathom, Christian depictions of death were purposeful. They carried religious, moral, and instructional messages. Except for the *ars moriendi* books, they concentrated on holy figures who could save the viewer, though he or she was highly unlikely to share the fates depicted.

But mechanically reproduced illustrations in the nineteenth century, far more numerous than any previous pictorial medium, brought to the fore not only more depictions of death but depictions of more secular, violent, and essentially uninstructive death. Aside from respectful death-bed pictures, much of the time death in print and images, from the earliest years of the illustrated press, was ruthless, brutal, vicious—murders, executions, disasters, wars—though not often explicit or detailed.

As actual death was toned down by every means available, *depicted* death swaggered violently onto the stage, and new means and forms were found to keep it before the public eye. Public executions may have been declining, but the journals made sure that whatever there was, even within prison walls, could still be seen. What's more, the illustrated newspaper exponentially increased the number and proportion of depictions of accidents and natural disasters: railroad crashes, shipwrecks, explosions, floods. These had neither religious significance nor salvific force, but since they might happen to anyone, they may well have contributed to general and unspecific increases in anxiety.

Disasters are undeniably news, but in other respects the papers were only responding to a fascination with accounts of violent death that ran alongside the movement to tame and beautify the end of life. The ghosts and ghouls and miasmas of gothic fiction lost their great hold on the imagination in the 1820s, but the gothic fascination with grisly death persisted in waxworks like Mme Tussaud's, where victims of the Terror and criminals painfully executed were simulated as faithfully as possible and the Chamber of Horrors was popular among high and low, men and women. The dioramas early in the century, those fool-the-eye performances in which clever painting and lighting made scenes seem to change and people to advance before the eyes, often included funerals and scenes of dead shades returning.

The most obvious and successful repository of the gothic and romantic fantasy of adventure, struggle, and death was the theatrical melodrama. This was lowbrow hackwork, churned out rapidly to formula, with music underlining the emotions (as in cinema). It appealed mainly to the lower classes, and it appealed to them mightily; these dramas were the narrative counterparts of the broadside ballads. Theater had already begun to feed off the widely popular murder trials of the day. In one instance a play was mounted while the trial was still being conducted. The defense counsel understandably got it enjoined; the curtains were raised once more after the murderer was hanged (Kendrick, 1991, pp. 137, 139). Before the middle of the century, the theater had begun to be domesticated, along with so many other aspects of life at the time: lower-class theater performed fewer melodramas, middle-class theater opted for psychological drama (Kendrick, pp. 120–26).

The passion for crime that gripped the public in the last century is astonishing. Printmakers had been responding to notorious murders with images of them for a couple of centuries, but their production capacity and distribution were limited. In the nineteenth century, various accounts say that well over a million copies of some murder broadsides were sold in England. It so happened that as England in the post-Napoleonic era was enjoying a lengthy peace and simultaneously re-shaping death in the semblance of angelic children and marriages revived in heaven, the country witnessed a startling number of sensational murder cases, culminating in Jack the Ripper.

In 1851 the *Illustrated London News* went so far as to say that thirty-five years of peace in Europe "has allowed no vent for the malignant passions but in those acts which the law undertakes to prevent or to punish" (Feb. 1, p. 86). (In fact, the number of violent crimes had decreased in the eighteenth century and the number of crimes against property had risen as wealth accumulated [Foucault, 1977, pp. 75–76]. Even in the eighteenth century the concentration of people in cities and the growth of broadsheets, popular prints, and newspapers of one sort or another may have made people more conscious of violent crime, as has happened in our own day.)

Do away with war, the British periodical said, and criminals will have to express themselves in their usual ways. Perhaps. Doing away with war, and beginning to push death aside as far as that was possible, seem only to have heightened fascination with the grimmest kinds of deaths, as if there were some level of interest, some level of fear, that had to be satisfied in one manner or another. As it happened, the spate of peacetime murders occurred just as the new popular press swung into high gear; it wasted not a second in bringing murder in all its details into the light of day.

It may be mere coincidence that the penny papers and illustrated journals should have come along at the same time as a slew of murders—or, more likely, it was the print media that made these murders notorious and inscribed them in popular culture for decades.[7] It is no coincidence that the press made much of crime. Up to the 1820s the press was largely political or mercantile and dealt with party issues or such matters as shipping news. A real newspaper as we understand it today chronicles breaking events; crime qualifies in major ways. Criminal trials had already found popular outlets in booklets reproducing the trial transcripts, and some of the new papers continued this tradition. Others bettered it with dramatic and often sensational accounts, and by the time the world's first true illustrated paper, the *Illustrated London News*, appeared, in 1842, some expanded on the tradition with images. The first issue of *L'Illustration*, an illustrated Paris weekly, on March 4, 1843, had accounts of two murders and an assassination; two of the articles were illustrated.

Bad news is good news for a paper. On March 5, 1859, *Harper's Weekly* claimed that their circulation exceeded 75,000 copies. On March 12 they published a big story about Daniel E. Sickles, a member of Congress, who had killed a man he believed was his wife's lover. The story was illustrated with portraits of the three principals as well as

pictures of the Sickles house, the congressman's clubhouse, and an artist's version of the shooting, which took place on the street. On March
19, the front page of the paper proclaimed, "Of the last number of this
journal 120,000 copies were sold." In January of 1862 the same paper
advised its advertisers that "The great exertions made by the proprietors
of HARPER'S WEEKLY to illustrate the [Civil] WAR have been rewarded by
a large increase of circulation." The British and French papers had similar experiences. In 1868, *Figaro* claimed an increased circulation of
30,000 after it provided detailed accounts of the murder of six members
of one family in the French provinces.[8]

Print descriptions of all sorts of crime, especially of gruesome murders, brought people flocking to the newsstands, but illustrations
brought more. The debate about violence in the media today is complicated by the visual nature of so much of our communications systems.
Most of us would testify that pictures are capable of producing more
immediate, visceral, emotional responses than are commonly called up
by the printed or spoken word. No doubt the visual response is more
primitive; at any rate, the eyes believe what they see before the brain
believes what the eyes read or the ears hear.

Violence and Middle-Class Morality

The rapacity with which the press reported crime and the avidity with
which even the gentler sex hung on the details of the trials themselves
or of the journals' reports was offensive to those trying to set moral
standards for the rising middle class. The illustrated papers were trying
to do just that. They believed that the press should instruct and moralize,
and though they printed numerous illustrations of violent death, they
often tried to soften the image by distancing it or omitting details they
were willing to print in the text. They advertised themselves as family
papers, and they spent decades trying to figure out how to deliver the
worst news in an acceptable form.

For reasons that are not clear to me, both the American and British
middle-class illustrated journals—*Harper's, Leslie's,* the *Illustrated London News*—cover murders in some detail in their first two or three decades and then almost stop doing so. Conceivably they found it
impossible to compete with the cheap tabloids and opted for abstinence.
For they disapproved mightily and vociferously of the explicit descriptions of violent crime in the cheap daily papers. In 1866, *Harper's
Weekly* condemned the kind of publicity given to "infamous crime":

> To say, as has been lately gravely asserted, that, because a revolting
> crime has been committed in a city, all the citizens are therefore "com-
> pelled" to listen to the loathsome details, is as ridiculous as to assert

that, because the police may have descended upon a nest of ill-houses in Mercer Street, the public are "compelled" to listen to a minute account of all that was discovered in those houses. That the public will eagerly read such descriptions, and the more greedily in the degree of their prurient detail, is very possible. (Jan. 20, p. 34)

The *Illustrated London News* made similar complaints. *L'Illustration* in 1849 refused to print the debates about an assassination with which the press maintained the public's mournful curiosity. *Plus ça change.* Note that the American paper assumed that people would be offended (if fascinated) by detailed accounts of sex but obviously not by similarly detailed—and by implication similarly prurient—accounts of violence and murder. *Harper's* believed they should be—a losing cause if ever there was one. In this century, this puritan country's film codes have always spelled out limits on violence as well as on sex, but the censors have always been tougher on sex than on mayhem.

By the nineteenth century, Christ's torture and crucifixion had ceased to be a major subject for artists. Manet's dead Christ was said to look like a coal miner, Gauguin's crucifixions were attempts to depict the primitive faith of the French provinces more than images of the sufferings of the son of God. In fact, conscious attempts were made to minimize the impression of Christ's physical torment. In 1850, an English writer remarked on a painting of Christ ministered to by angels after the Temptation: "The painter has attempted to portray divine resignation and exhaustion, free from the more acute bodily suffering under which the Saviour is generally represented" (Hanson, 1966, p. 89). When the last, violent moments of a few ordinary people became increasingly visible in images, they did not promise redemption but did offer a tenuous and temporary security of a sort that was not meaningful in images of Christ: this was not *me*; for this moment at least I have been saved from the particular fate I have just witnessed.

The popularity of images of violent death, then and now, conceivably has something to do with its relative rarity in real life: it is "safer" to fantasize about something unlikely to occur than about death from cancer or Parkinson's. The nineteenth-century journals, incidentally, reported outbreaks of cholera in India and Egypt, often to warn that sanitary measures had best be taken at home because after some months the disease could very well travel. (Would that we had the lag time they had.) But the weeklies did not illustrate the ravages of cholera any more than papers today, which have a good deal less shame, illustrate the incursions of the flesh-eating virus.

The illustrated weeklies may have cut back on murders after a time, but they still published occasional pictures of executions, assassinations, lynchings, and the means of execution in various countries, which kept these events in public view. As various forms of death receded, however

PART OF THE INTERIOR OF THE MAMELON.

FIGURE 2.2 The illustrated papers that began in the 1840s brought home to a newly literate and expanded middle class numerous images of murder and war. Sketch artists were sent to the scene; readers were invited to have a vicarious experience of war's carnage. From the *Illustrated London News,* July 7, 1855.

slowly, various kinds of violent death advanced at their own pace in representation. The journals leaped to illustrate current wars, revolutions, and riots, with their quotas of dead bodies. Sometimes these images contained a shocking amount of death—see a July 7, 1855, illustration in the *Illustrated London News* of the interior of a fort, with corpses everywhere, draped over rocks and breastworks and buried beneath stones. These images were often based on sketches made on the scene and were therefore more truthful than paintings or broadsides. They were still somewhat distanced by the medium, but perhaps less so for the reading public of the time, which had not previously had access to so many eyewitness or near-eyewitness views.

During the American Civil War, photographers took the first widely visible on-the-spot photographs of dead soldiers. Alexander Gardner and Timothy O'Sullivan took pictures of the dead at Gettysburg that were exhibited in Mathew Brady's studio in New York, reproduced, and sold. No one knows how many were printed or precisely what effect they had on the civilian population, but Oliver Wendell Holmes, who had been to the battlefield to look for his injured son, said that looking at the pictures was so like visiting the battlefield that he hid them away (Holmes, 1863, pp. 11–12). The *New York Times*, awed by the faithfulness of photographic reports, speculated about the effects of some wife or mother recognizing her beloved in the image.

These pictures gave the lie to the tradition of battle paintings, as some illustrations, like the interior of the fort mentioned above, had begun to do. Leaders did not always die nobly, nor did lesser men necessarily die bravely in a series of stock gestures. Death in battle did not look so good in the photographs, which nonetheless sold. The bodies had been on the field for two days of rain before the photographers arrived; they were bloated, dark, and stiff. There was an abundance of death in the engraved illustrations in magazines, but in none were the corpses bloated—any more than they are now in printed images of war or even in feature films.

A Question of Class

By the early nineteenth century, class differences in literature and theater were already well established, especially in Britain and America (Kendrick, 1991, pp. 110–11), and the newspapers quickly fitted themselves into these grooves. One of the tasks of defining a paper as middle class was precisely the control and aestheticizing of accounts of murder and vicious crime.

Middle-class illustrations, including pictures of murders, were occasionally gory. In 1857 in America, one Dr. Burdell was viciously stabbed in his home. On February 21, *Frank Leslie's Illustrated Newspaper* had a two-page spread with a picture of the body in a coffin in the room where he was killed; a picture of the doctor's face, complete with wounds, as it appeared in the coffin; a drawing of his sleeve full of blood; one of the heart showing what wounds it sustained; pictures of other rooms; one of a bloody doorknob; and one of sharp instruments. (Even today a slashed heart would probably not appear in the paper; the photographs of Nicole Simpson's and Ronald Goldman's bodies were not shown to the television audience.) The next issue of *Leslie's* had pictures of the coroner's jury as well as an artist's rendition of the supposed manner of the violent attack. And then the paper tried to explain why the public was so wrapped up in this case. Murder is always interesting, it acknowledged, but a recent rash of robberies and disappearances had left the populace so fearful that major crime had become a fixation. Fear breeds more fear, and growing metropolitan centers and rapid communications had heightened the possibilities both for crime and for awareness of it. *Leslie's* said, "It is this feeling of insecurity, this idea that no man's life was secure, that has kept alive the excitement, and made every incident of terrible importance." The paper did not say that its own reports certainly added to the excitement and possibly to

the insecurity. The demand for the issues illustrating "the Burdell tragedy" was so great that *Leslie's* had to electrotype its forms in order to
fill the extra orders (Feb. 21, 28, Mar. 14, 1857).

At the same time, *Harper's Weekly*, which commenced publication
in that year, complained bitterly about the prevalence of murder in the
papers. "Yes *Murder will out!*" it cried on its front page.

> It infects the whole country with a pestilential air; it fills our houses
> with its gloomy horrors; it taints our breath with its poison; it dogs
> our daily walks. . . . You rise in the morning; a word of tenderness and
> love is hardly spoken to the little ones gathered about your knee, when
> with eager excitement, you clutch the morning paper, and you read:
> "THE BOWN ST. MURDER!" "THE BUTCHERY IN OUR CITY!" "INCREASED
> EXCITEMENT!" "HORRIBLE DETAILS!" "DREADFUL MYSTERY!" "EXCITE-
> MENT UNABATED!" "MORE BLOODY GARMENTS!" which stare you in
> the eyes, and fix them in a spasm of concentrated attention on the page.
> The wife appeals fondly to you for a share of the horrors; even the
> little children gape, with open mouths. . . .

Harper's was not even talking about pictures, but, as if it were over a
hundred years later, it was concerned that the press would spur crime
and immunity to it: "[T]his spreading abroad of the information of a
crime, if it does not give rise to a criminal epidemic, which may break
out in similar acts of violence, at any rate so far infects the moral sen-
timent of the community by its contagion as to ferment a taste for the
horrible, and to harden the sensibility of the public conscience to vice."
The paper went on to ask whether there might not be a danger of growing too fond of horrors from seeing so many of them in the papers (Feb.
14, pp. 95–96).

The new newspapers, at once violent and domesticated, defined a
new level of sensationalism: more detailed than that of the broadsides,
somewhat more credible, and apparently slightly more respectable—at
least the journals entered the homes of middle-class families that might
not have been so eager to be seen buying broadsheets. The urban setting
that had spawned a wide middle class fostered new fears—of strangers
on the street and anonymous murderers. What's more, some of the juic-
iest murders were committed by people of fairly good standing, so that
now one had to be afraid of one's own kind as well. All of which fed
the need for more information, more news, more sensational revelations,
more images of violence and death.

But the illustrated papers knew that pictures were all too effective.
Though they castigated the penny journals for reports that went beyond
bounds, the journals were willing to give details in their own text that
they would not permit in illustrations. On November 17, 1855, the *Illustrated London News* published an article called "Horrible Atrocities
in China," about a place where sixty to seventy thousand executions
had been carried out since the previous February. They had received a

sketch and a description of how the executioner would cut his victims in various places before plunging a knife into the heart. He then took down the body, cut off the head, hands, and feet, then removed the heart and liver. This gruesome account was illustrated by a picture of a street with a few people on it and two crosses, which to a casual observer might seem to be local monuments, fixed in the ground—a pleasant enough foreign street scene. A year and a half later, on March 7, 1857, the paper reproduced the letter and, referring to their previous publication, said, "In the Sketch itself, we omitted the live and the dead personages who were portrayed in it, fearing to shock our readers and subscribers by a scene so brutal, so disgusting, and so horrible." The editors added that they hoped to reproduce the sketch exactly in the following issue. By the following week, they had evidently changed their minds.

The Ubiquity of Disaster

The prodigal stream of inventions in the nineteenth century made available a huge supply of murderous images. Not only was the press newly capable of delivering information and images in quantity, but the steam engine that powered railroads and ships carried news with unprecedented rapidity over great distances, and the telegraph delivered it almost instantaneously. Consequently, the daily papers could report not only on distant wars but on far-off disasters—and they did. The illustrated weeklies, which advertised for sketches from any newsworthy scene, received them from the far reaches of the globe.

These papers did not always have images of natural or man-made disasters—sometimes for weeks there would be none—but other times they were served up with some regularity. The *Illustrated London News*, for instance, on July 6, 1850, reported on a "Terrific Explosion at Benares," with an article saying that at least five hundred had been killed and that "limbs and shattered portions of human beings lay strewed far and wide." A sketch of the ruins of the explosion was much calmer, with some distinctly whole bodies lying about, leaving the imagination to fill in the particulars. The July 13 issue carried an image of a wrecked brig at Trinidad (looking, to an unpracticed eye, perfectly fine). The same issue had pictures of a fire at Bristol and one in San Francisco. The July 27 issue had two pictures of a steamboat explosion at Bristol, the August 3 issue a picture of a bull goring a matador in Madrid.

Disasters were not always so plentiful, but fires, floods, shipwrecks, and railway accidents anyplace were generally illustrated within a couple of weeks or more, depending on how far the information had to travel. Often, though by no means always, there would be bodies lying about or being carried off, or a wounded person raising himself up, but no emphasis was placed on gore or details of wounds. Volcanoes, earthquakes, explosions, and building collapses were also occasionally illustrated; they did not happen so often and were not usually so immediately threatening. Anyone could be affected by fire or flood, fires being a particularly great and frequent hazard to life, home, and business. Shipwrecks threatened both travelers and business. The railroads, which had opened up travel to thousands, had scandalous accident records in most countries; passengers might be risking their lives for the chance at an outing.

People needed to know the risks if only to press for higher safety standards, but every report of a railway accident raised the general level of anxiety. It seems likely that the generic anxiety of modern life—the sense we have today, on the evidence of Somalia, Bosnia, Chechnya, bombs at the World Trade Center and the Federal Building in Oklahoma, that the world is rapidly going to hell—was already being nurtured by the newspapers in the nineteenth century.

Life in the eighteenth century had most likely been filled with more-present anxieties, especially as there was so little hope of controlling or conquering disease. But when the daily and weekly news became a necessary adjunct of daily life and steadily presented evidence that crime, torture, and disasters were frequent and widespread, the mind had a much wider territory and greater number of incidents to fear. An odd duality can operate on the reception of such news: What is far away does not directly affect me, which offers a certain reassurance; on the other hand, railway and steamship accidents are generic and may affect me in the future, and if dangers turn up in every corner of the world, I can scarcely feel safe where I am. And the more fearful I am, the more news I need to know, so that I may judge the odds, plan ahead, know where I have to protect myself—and the more palpitatingly I hang on those images of death.

The New Media

The news, which was heavily invested in descriptions and images of violent death from the beginning, has never ceased to be so; the general consensus today is that it has gone ever farther in the same direction. Every new medium has added to the store, from photography to motion pictures to television, video, and now computer games. Photography expanded the range of postmortem pictures, which had previously been limited to a few paintings and prints. A photograph was also proof of death, and a picture of Jesse James's dead body was as important in its day as the famous pictures of a dead Che Guevara or Nicolai Ceaucescu in ours. In the late 1930s and 1940s, Weegee took so many pictures of murdered mobsters for the tabloids that he practically drove himself out of business by oversupply.

By the time cameras were capable of stopping action, murderous action became a major subject. Many of the most famous news photographs of the century have to do with death: Ruth Snyder in the electric chair. (Taken on the sly in 1928—not only were executions off-limits to the public but cameras were not permitted in the chamber. The *New York Daily News* gave its entire front page to the picture.) Piles of bodies in concentration camps. A monk immolating himself in Vietnam. Jack Ruby shooting Oswald. Bobby Kennedy dying on a kitchen floor. General Loan blowing out the brains of a Vietcong suspect on a Saigon street. A dead American dragged through the streets in Somalia. A tangle of bodies thrown into a river and washed down by the current in Rwanda.

When cinema was introduced, in 1895, it laid claim to a more extensive and intimate view of death. One of Edison's kinetoscopes, those brief films viewed individually through an eyepiece, presented the viewer with the execution of Mary, Queen of Scots—not entirely convincing, but she did lay her head on the block, the executioner did swing, and a head did roll onto the ground. The first true narrative movie in history, *The Great Train Robbery* (1903), had several murders. Styles of dying change over time; in this film, all but one of those shot throw their arms up over their heads before falling down, a gesture unknown today.

The cinema moved in close on death in war, avoiding excess gore but not excess death—see *The Birth of a Nation*—and on death at home, often from unnatural causes, such as the girl's death from a beating, the murder of her father by the Yellow Man who loved her, and his subsequent suicide in Griffith's *Broken Blossoms*. *Nosferatu* brought to the screen the apparent terror of not quite dying that has raged at various times in the last century. Gangster films in the 1930s made multiple deaths something of a commonplace. Like the nineteenth-century melodrama, these sometimes borrowed from actual and recent crime accounts—*Little Caesar, Scarface*—so that the audience came anticipating a heightened emotional impact from a story that had already elicited a strong response. Pulp fiction of the time, usually detective stories, was also full of violent deaths. Westerns, too, served up large helpings, and World War II films kept the heroic death on view.

In the years after the war, when the audience had become acquainted with the real thing, violent death on-screen began to change. In the 1950s, some of the exaggerated violence and death that had been the domain of adolescent boys and lower-class types edged into mainstream movie houses. Late in the decade, partially in response to the threat of the atom bomb, the science-fiction film was crossbred with the horror film, and new ways to die were invented—in the jaws of monsters, in the embrace of a protoplasmic blob of vegetable matter. The industry has become ever more inventive about means of death as film technology and special effects advance, so that now men may die from alien creatures bursting out of their breasts or from powerful rays that make them simply disappear.

More common forms of violent death turned more explicit and gruesome in the 1960s. *Psycho*, in 1960, came in close on a vicious stabbing, the camera changing angles so rapidly that the audience was continually off balance—and seldom aware that they never saw the knife entering flesh. *Bonnie and Clyde*, in 1967, riddled its protagonists with so many bullets at the end that they performed a virtual dance of death. In *Bullitt*, the following year, a shot blew an informer off his feet and jammed him up against a wall in a spurt of blood—or more precisely, a plastic bag full of fake blood—assisted by lurch cables. In *The Wild Bunch* (1969), the big killing scene orchestrated a veritable deluge of death, with bodies flying through the air and blood in quantities unseen before. The progress of death on-screen—including the television screen, in both action series and nightly news—between that film and *Natural Born Killers* and *Pulp Fiction* is surely well enough known to need no introduction.

It is not enough for someone to picture more, and more violent, death; someone has to want to look at it. James Twitchell has written that the audience for violence in general is an audience of adolescent boys. There have been more of them since the baby boom, they have more disposable cash, they see films more than once, and they need to learn the mythic lessons that action and horror films teach (1989, esp. pp. 182, 200). That is probably true, but it does not explain why adults also patronize such films—and read such fiction and see many more images of violent death in the papers and on TV and read many more obituaries than teenagers do—or why such films play so well abroad.

The adult audience after World War II had a new fear of death: the bomb. In 1953, the U.S. secretary of defense announced officially, for the first time, that America and the USSR each had the capacity to wipe out the entire human race. Rather suddenly in the 1960s, people who were already trying to find ways to live with terror of that magnitude were confronted with a devastating series of assassinations. The most violent films have never eclipsed the Zapruder tapes, which were so explicit that many frames were never shown. Adults also witnessed Oswald's murder on TV, no doubt a first, and also a last, such sighting for millions. Television sales vaulted upward in the late 1950s and early 1960s, so images of the death of Medgar Evers, RFK, and Martin Luther King were more widespread than such images had ever been.

During the first four or five years of the Vietnam War, death was implied often enough by scenes of bombing, patrols, and burnings, but there was not so much killing on the screen. Around 1968, as the media themselves began to turn against the war, the imagery of death heated up: General Loan, My Lai, Larry Burrows's photos of bloody soldiers in color in *Life* magazine. Real death in terrible circumstances was all around. The audience was effectively primed for violent fictional deaths, which at least offered the solace of *being* fictional. Action films and special effects made falls from high buildings and death in car chases so acrobatic, so fantastic, that one could admire the skill of the actor or the technician and keep the terror of death at some distance.

The Death and Resurrection of Death Itself

Obviously the fascination with death is multidetermined. One other factor takes us back to the beginning of this essay: death was disappearing from view, and, in the twentieth century, rapidly. In 1935, sulfa, the world's first anti-bacterial-infection drug, came on the market. Penicillin, discovered in 1928, commenced commercial sales in 1945. A treatment for tuberculosis was discovered in the 1950s, the first polio vaccine in 1955. Between 1945 and 1955, mortality from influenza and pneumonia fell by 47 percent and from syphilis by 78 percent, and death from diphtheria almost disappeared (Shorter, 1987, pp. 5, 37, 44, 45). Life expectancy, which had been climbing throughout the century, continued to do so. People died—or rather, passed away—in hospitals, and soon in nursing homes, often at great, invisible distances from families and friends.

By the 1950s in America and England, and to a somewhat lesser degree in other Western countries, death had just about vanished from view. For a while, there was a peculiar fantasy that maybe we had it beat, and there was a tacit social compact not to discuss it, not even quite to believe in it. But of course it does not work that way, and we need to know, or think we need to know, what it is, how it looks, what it does to us, what we can do about it. Images step up and offer their services. Geoffrey Gorer, in "The Pornography of Death," his seminal essay of 1955, said, "While natural death became more and more smothered in prudery, violent death has played an ever-growing part in the fantasies offered to mass audiences . . ." (p. 51).

I would say that's right. But I would also say that it is not new, only larger and bolder. Images began to fill in, to substitute, to heighten the terror and often, at the same time, to calm the nerves by their sheer improbability, over a century before Gorer wrote. They began their dance with death long before that, but they hit their stride almost as soon as mass reproduction and a mass audience began to take shape, at the moment that death began to shift from ritual to news and entertainment.

Notes

1. See Ariès, 1981, p. 28, on the general conception of a "tame death" and a resignation in the face of death that persisted into the eighteenth century. He

suggests that the terror of death did not manifest itself until life became more precious.

2. The annual reports of London's Local Government Board show not only a marked decline in smallpox deaths among the London poor between 1871 and 1881 but also an increase in the percentage of deaths in hospitals over deaths at home. In 1871–1872, the total number of dead equaled 9,742, of which 6,509 had died in private houses. In 1881, the death total was 2,371; 797 had died at home (Rivett, 1986, p. 91).

3. On January 8, 1853, the *Illustrated London News* wrote that "Life Assurance" was important, but only 240,000 people had taken it out. That is already a large-enough number to swell the tide of fancy funerals, and if this paper was urging people to buy insurance, presumably the matter was a topic of some interest.

4. *Illustrated London News*, July 24, 1858, p. 77. On the Metropolitan Interments Act, see Morley, 1971, p. 50.

5. Though the general decline is unmistakable, religious belief and its diminution are notoriously difficult to pin down and vary from place to place and time to time. See, for instance, McManners, 1985, p. 440, on the "de-Christianization" of death rituals in France in the late eighteenth century, and Pelling, 1964, for a brief discussion of the decline of religion in large cities in England in the nineteenth century, especially among the working classes, although Scotland, Wales, and Ireland, as well as smaller English towns and rural areas, remained more religious.

6. Loyette cites Jean-Paul Bouillon, (Ed.), *La critique d'art en France, 1850–1900: Actes du colloque de Clermont-Ferrand 25, 26 et 27 mai 1987* (Saint-Etienne France: CIEREC, 1989), p. 51 n. 26.

7. My thanks to Joel Wallman for reminding me that these crimes might scarcely have existed for the public, or for history, had it not been for the press.

8. *Harper's*, March 5, 1859, p. 1; March 12, 1859, pp. 168–69; March 19, 1859, p. 1; January 4, 1862, p. 2. *Figaro* cited in *Harper's* October 30, 1869, p. 698.

3

Immortal Kombat:
War Toys and Violent Video Games

JEFFREY GOLDSTEIN

Attractions of War Toys and Violent Video Games:
Jurassic Park Meets *StreetFighter II*

The second most profitable item on the entertainment agenda in 1993 was the film *Jurassic Park*. Its financial success was exceeded only by a video game with violence as its theme. "One single game—*StreetFighter II*—made $1.5 billion last year [1993]. Nothing, not even *Jurassic Park*, touched that success in the entertainment business," said screenwriter Michael Backes (quoted in Covington, 1994). Nineteen ninety-three also saw two versions of the video game *Mortal Kombat* in the shops: the original version, sold by Sega, with its notorious decapitations and blood-dripping spinal cords, and a sanitized version in which the violence was toned down, offered by Nintendo. Although there were more Nintendo than Sega game systems present in U.S. households, the bloody Sega version of *Mortal Kombat* outsold the less violent version by about 7 to 1.[1]

There appears to be a ready market for violent entertainment. Perhaps there always has been. Playing at and with images of war and violence is nothing new. It is certainly not a product of the electronic or television age. In this chapter we consider the appeals of playing at and with violence and war. In considering not only the passive witnessing of violence but also its mock reenactment in play, this chapter has a slightly different vantage point than the remaining chapters in this book. We begin with play fighting and go on to toy soldiers, war toys, and video games with violent themes. The pronounced sex differences in this kind of play are examined to better understand its appeal to some youngsters, particularly boys.

Aggression and Play Fighting

Sometimes I accompany teachers to the playground during recess to watch elementary-school children at play. Boys are seen running, chasing, pretending to shoot one another or to be shot, or they stand face-to-face as they go through martial-arts movements. Girls, more often than not, do not participate in this highly active, raucous, almost anarchic play. Instead, they stand mostly in small groups talking animatedly, their conversations punctuated by shrieks and laughter.[2] When asked to describe what they see, the teachers invariably say that the boys are aggressive and the girls are "nice" and not aggressive.

In many respects, the boys' play resembles real aggression, which also involves running, chasing, and fleeing. But there are differences between play fighting and real fighting, notably in facial expressions, the longer duration and repetition of play fighting, and the fact that the boys remain together once these play episodes have run their course (Boulton, 1991; Costabile et al., 1991; Fry, 1990; Pellis & Pellis, 1996; Smith & Boulton, 1990; Wegener-Spöhring, 1994). The main difference—the defining feature of aggression, which is absent from aggressive play—is the intent to injure another person.

The boys recognize these differences and are cognizant that they are playing, not fighting. In fact, if some boys fail to observe this distinction—fighting while their counterparts are pretending to fight—they will be excluded from subsequent play (Willner, 1991). Boys generally agree that play fighting can become real fighting, particularly when accidental injury occurs. This happens only occasionally, according to many studies (Fry, 1990; Humphreys & Smith, 1984; Pellegrini, 1988; Sutton-Smith, Gerstmyer, & Meckley, 1988).

The girls standing and chatting on the playground, in contrast to the boys whose play is more active, may be engaged in aggression if their behavior is designed to injure someone. Social ostracism and gossip are often used by girls to hurt other girls, and thus constitute a form of aggressive behavior (Bjorkvist, Lagerspetz, & Kaukiainen, 1991; Bjorkqvist & Niemela, 1992). What at first sight appears to be aggressive boys and nonaggressive girls may, in deed and in consequence, be the other way around.

Attitudes toward War Toys and Aggressive Play

Critics tend to focus on the similarities and overlook the distinctions that make *aggressive behavior* and *aggressive play* independent. Many studies fail to distinguish aggressive play from aggressive behavior. For example, Sanson and DiMuccio (1993) claim that children who viewed an aggressive cartoon and then played with the associated aggressive toys were more aggressive than other children. However, the researchers fail to distinguish between pretending to shoot someone (aggressive play) and trying to injure someone (aggressive behavior).

Societal attitudes toward war play are, and apparently always have been, ambivalent (Beresin, 1989; Goldstein, 1995; Twitchell, 1989; Wells, 1913). Aggressive play, including war play and video games with violent themes, elicits two major reactions from adults (see Smith, 1994). Opponents argue that war play impoverishes the child's imagination, fosters imitative violence, perpetuates war, and is unseemly (Carlsson-Paige & Levin, 1987; Miedzian, 1991). Proponents of this sort of play argue that it is a natural, even inevitable aspect of boys' play. They point out that the young males of all primate species engage in play fighting. Furthermore, this sort of play heightens imagination, teaches role taking, and affords the child an opportunity to try to come to terms with war, violence, and death. Proponents argue also that war play reflects adult behavior and values.

Parents and teachers who view children's play from a distance seem less often to make a distinction between play fighting and real fighting. In a study of English and Italian parents' attitudes toward war play, parents did not consistently see aggressive play and aggressive behavior as different. Attitudes toward war play in the home are diverse, although parents seem most concerned about war play in girls (Costabile, Genta, Zucchini, Smith, & Harker, 1992).

Men and women differ in their interpretations of rough play. According to studies by Kathleen Connor (1989), women are more likely to interpret rough play as aggression, while men are more likely to see it as play. Connor videotaped 4- and 5-year-olds playing with toy trucks, dolls, and crayons (neutral toys) or with GI Joe, Rambo, guns, and grenades (war toys). Fourteen of these play episodes were shown to university students, who classified each as "play" or "aggression." Men and women viewed 10 of the 14 episodes differently. For example, in one incident, two boys and a girl are playing with toy guns. They decide that shooting a "dead" person with his own weapon restores him to life. In the incident, a "dead" boy is shot and revived in this way. Seventy-five percent of the men viewed this as playful, compared to only 38 percent of the women. "Aggression is in the eye of the beholder," writes Connor; women in comparison to men are more likely to label an episode as aggression.

Women who as children had engaged in aggressive play were more apt to interpret the episodes as play than as aggression. Likewise, parents with firsthand experience of video games have more favorable attitudes toward them than do adults with no experience (Sneed & Runco, 1992).

Perhaps the Connor study shows only that men and women differ in their use of the word "aggression." But it does not matter if her results reflect "only" differences in vocabulary, since play that is labeled aggression will be treated differently than play not so called. For example, men will be more likely to allow the play to continue, while women may be more likely to try to stop it. Still, perhaps it is a mistake to regard aggressive play and aggressive behavior as completely independent. Surely the similarities between them are not accidental; one must have something to do with the other. What is the relation between war play and war? Between aggressive play and aggression?

The World at War Play:
Relations between Violence and Aggressive Play

> And sometimes for an hour or so
> I watched my leaden soldiers go,
> With different uniforms and drills
> Among the bedclothes, through the hills.
>
> —Robert Louis Stevenson,
> "The Land of Counterpane"

Toy soldiers are among the oldest known toys, excavated from ruins throughout the ancient world, in Syria, Egypt, and Asia (Fraser, 1966; Foley, 1962; Mergen, 1982; Twitchell, 1989; Wells, 1913). Miniature soldiers and miniature weapons are thought to have been used to teach future generations of warriors the art of war. "Where girls had their dolls, the boys also had their soldiers," wrote Antonia Fraser (p. 51). "The lands and islands of the Mediterranean have all provided evidence of the ancient making of model warriors in metal or clay, and tiny Roman war-like figures have been found in Spain, Germany, Britain and even Abyssinia."

Of course, toys and games bear some relation to the culture of which they are a part. "In a martial era boys will inevitably turn to soldiers," writes Fraser. "Children's toys often reflect a nation's concept of a hero, and children as far back as in Greek times have had a predilection for war games as illustrated by [a] clay war chariot from Athens" (Fraser, 1966, p. 47).

Although they have long since lost their military association, playing cards, chess, and checkers began as games of military strategy. Playing cards originated in ancient India and were designed to teach military tactics to young nobles. Unlike chess, checkers, and backgammon, which were also developed to teach military strategy, playing cards have two different red armies and two different black armies, allowing for more intricate maneuvers as well as a greater number of possible participants in the game (Reid, 1993).

The highest level of symbolic aggression is found in games in which one opponent directly attacks another, such as by capturing or neutralizing an opponent's piece (as in checkers, chess, or the Japanese game go). "Only a few games other than organized sports have retained overt aggression, such as 'King-of-the-mountain' and 'Flinch' (the latter involves one person hitting another if the other moves in response to the pretend action of hitting)" (Reid, 1993, p. 327). According to Loy and Hasketh (1992), competitive play among nineteenth-century Plains Indian boys helped to prepare them for their future role as warriors. In the modern world, too, bellicose cultures permit or encourage warlike play (Keefer, Goldstein, & Kasiarz, 1983; Roberts & Sutton-Smith, 1962; Sipes, 1973).

War Play during Times of War

Although war toys made of clay and wood are ancient artifacts, we must speculate on their use and popularity. Mass-manufactured tin soldiers may have begun with the exploits of Frederick the Great, King of Prussia from 1740 to 1786, which, according to Foley (1962), "captured the imagination of the whole world" (p. 62). Tin soldiers were produced in Nuremberg from 1760 on. German manufacturers, such as Johann Hilpert and Ernst Heinrichsen, emerged as Europe's first mass producers of toy soldiers. In the nineteenth century the major toy supplier was Germany, whose wares included fully modeled three-dimensional lead soldiers produced by the firm of George Heyde. The French firm of Mignot turned out a similar product, which found a ready market in Britain.

Toy soldiers became popular in Europe after the introduction of professional standing armies. By the early nineteenth century, new metals and cheaper production considerably widened the toy-soldier market. There was a substantial output of toy soldiers in late Victorian and Edwardian Britain (1875–1910). Among those who participated in the craze for toy soldiers were Robert Louis Stevenson, Jerome K. Jerome, G. K. Chesterton, H. G. Wells, and Winston Churchill.

What of the relationship between toy soldiers and militarism? Brown (1990) has written a history of toy soldiers, focusing specifically on nineteenth- and early-twentieth-century Britain. He believes that war games contributed to a buildup of aggression that resulted in enthusiasm for World War I. He identifies two ways in which toy soldiers and war were linked at the turn of the century. First, toy soldiers formed part of a continuum of militaristic influences to which boys were exposed. Implicit in simulated battles played with toy soldiers are "the ideas of enemy and conflict. Here perhaps the toys may have contributed to that build up of aggression which, in some commentators' views, explains the rush to the colours in 1914" (p. 248). Brown's second argument is that toy soldiers were insidious because they "helped to reinforce a particular view

TABLE 3.1 Correlations among War Toys, War Movies, and Militarization

	War Movies	War Toys
Militarization	.83	.74
War Movies		.64

Adapted from Regan, 1994, p. 52.

of the nature of war." Was it to this romanticized, heroic version of war, he asks, that the volunteers of 1914 thought they were going? Brown adds, "In the last resort, it is impossible to prove conclusively that playing with toy soldiers had any influence at all on subsequent behavior. . . . Nor was any relationship necessarily a straightforward causal one. Some individuals doubtless took to the soldiers because their enthusiasm for martial matters had already been fired by other aspects of contemporary militarism."[3]

Interest in war toys and war movies is correlated with heightened public support for military expenditures, according to a study by Patrick Regan (1994), who examined the prevalence of war toys, war movies, and militarization within the United States for the years 1900–1985. War toys were measured as the proportion of military toys in the Sears catalog and war movies as the proportion of U.S. films with war themes. Militarization was regarded as the percentage of the labor force involved in the production and preparations necessary to wage war. The main findings appear in table 3.1, which shows strong relationships among the three measured variables.

According to Regan, "toys, movies, and the education system help to form mental images of the dominant norms within the society" (p. 48). He says not that the creation and manipulation of these symbols is responsible for these dominant norms, "but rather that they are part of the process in the militarization of society" (p. 52).

The studies by Brown and Regan both demonstrate a relationship between war and war toys. This, as both note, does not imply causality. Offerings of war toys and war movies rise and fall with militarization, perhaps reflecting the attitudes of the people who choose them, or who choose to produce them.

There is at least one study showing a causal relation between war and war play. Shortly after the bombing of Pearl Harbor, Hawaiian schoolchildren began to play more war games and make more toy weapons (Bonte & Musgrove, 1943). Girls, too, took part in this play, making buildings to be "bombed" and playing the roles of military nurses.

The salience of war influences the propensity for war play, as these studies illustrate. If children are first "primed" by listening to aggressive stories, they are more likely to choose toy weapons for play (Jukes &

Goldstein, 1993; Lovaas, 1961). The reasoning underlying this research is that exposure to violence activates aggressive associations and images. These, in turn, heighten the preference for further exposure to violence (Berkowitz, 1984). Lovaas (1961) found that an aggressive prime influenced the aggressive toy preferences of 5-year-olds. Children who viewed a violent television program chose to play with an aggressive toy; those who had seen a nonviolent program preferred a nonaggressive toy. Priming also affects preference for violent film entertainment (Langley, O'Neal, Craig, & Yost, 1992). One study reported an increase in attendance at violent films by University of Wisconsin students following the murder of a student on campus (Boyanowsky, Newtson, & Walster, 1974). There is also anecdotal evidence to support the priming position. During the Persian Gulf War, sales of replica missiles skyrocketed, though the market for these expensive models consisted mainly of adults (Goldstein, 1994).

Video Games with Violent Themes

The most recent—though certainly not the last—manifestation of violent toy play are video games with aggressive themes.[4] Video games occupy an interesting position among the various forms of entertainment considered in this book. They fall somewhere in the middle of a continuum from passive viewing of violence, as in film or spectator sports, to active reenactment of violence, as in aggressive play.

Based on a content analysis of the then best-selling video games, Malone (1981) concluded that video games are attractive (to boys) to the extent that they contain the following characteristics:

uncertainty
speeded responses
multiple levels of difficulty
sound effects
feedback/scoring, and
gradually revealed hidden information.

Although these are structural, not content, qualities of video games, violence may be featured in many of these ways. Indeed, it is difficult to think of potential video games that meet these criteria that do *not* rely upon shooting, intercepting, chasing themes. Nevertheless, many or all of these features can, in principle, be achieved without violent images.

One difference between violent video games and violent images on television and in film is that video-game players, in contrast to television viewers, exert *control* over what takes place on the screen (Goldstein, 1994, 1995). They are participants in a quasi-interactive system that allows them to regulate the pace and character of the game. This, in turn, gives them increased control over their own emotional states during play. A substantial body of research demonstrates that perceived control over events reduces the emotional or stressful responses to those events (e.g., Cortez & Bugental, 1995; Langer & Rodin, 1976; see Cantor, this volume).

A study at the University of Utrecht (Goldstein, Claassen, van Epen, de Leur, & van der Vloed, 1993) found attenuated emotional reactions to violent imagery when viewers had control over the images. Students viewed a 10-minute violent scene from a film (*Rambo*) with or without a remote control in their hands. They then completed a mood adjective checklist measuring their emotional states immediately after viewing. Those who had control (although they rarely used the remote-control device) experienced less negative reactions to the violence than those without (the remote) control. Because video-game players have more control than, say, TV viewers, perhaps the effects of violent images are reduced. An alternative explanation for these findings is based on Bem's self-perception theory (1972): those with the remote control rarely used it and therefore may have concluded that the violence could not have been very disturbing. Whatever the correct explanation, the violence in video games may have different consequences than the violent images found in other media.

Explanations for Aggressive Play

How has children's perennial interest in aggressive play and war toys been explained? Table 3.2 contains a distillation of the various accounts that have been offered. For the sake of convenience they are divided into three categories: biological/physiological, psychological, and social/cultural. These are neither exhaustive nor mutually exclusive. All three levels of influence can occur simultaneously and may interact with one another. Furthermore, not all of these have been studied closely or at all (Goldstein, 1995). They are offered here to demonstrate the diversity of positions about the appeal of one sort of violent entertainment: aggressive play. Where possible, I cite evidence that bears on the utility or validity of an explanation.

Biological Foundations of Play Style and Toy Preference

Some theories of rough-and-tumble and other forms of aggressive play are based on the idea of energy regulation. For example, Herbert Spencer (1891) wrote that "surplus energy" not needed for more serious pursuits is burned up in play. This idea is still found in the use of school recess to allow children to "blow off steam" after sitting through their lessons (Pellegrini, 1989). Recent versions of this position are based not on the discharge of "energy" but on the regulation of "arousal" of one sort or

TABLE 3.2 25 Reasons for Play with War Toys

Biological/Physiological

1. To discharge energy
2. To achieve a desired level of arousal/stimulation/excitement
3. "Hard-wired" tendency to practice adult skills and roles
4. Hormonal and genetic influences

Psychological

5. To engage in fantasy/imaginative play
6. To experience "flow"
7. In response to priming/salience of violence
8. To come to terms with violence, war, death
9. To achieve a desired emotional state
10. To experience and express intense emotions
11. To see justice enacted
12. To control and resolve conflict satisfactorily
13. To practice strategic planning
14. To set goals and determine effective means for accomplishing them; to gain a sense of mastery
15. To experience intimacy

Social/Cultural

16. Direct modeling by peers or family
17. Indirect modeling: influences of media, marketing
18. To belong to a group
19. To exclude oneself from a (negative reference) group (e.g., parents, girls, boys who disapprove of these games)
20. Rewards and encouragement for such play
21. Salience within a culture of war, violence
22. To wield power; to affect others
23. To elicit a predictable reaction from parents/teachers
24. To sample a variety of adult roles
25. As a reflection of cultural values—dominance, aggression, and assertion

another (Apter, 1992; Barber, 1991; Burghardt, 1984; Zillmann, this volume).

The different activity levels of boys and girls may help explain their play styles and toy preferences. Children with a high need for movement and activity may play with traditionally masculine toys because these permit highly active play. The strong differences between males and females in the appeal of violent entertainment can be explained on the basis of their differing needs for arousal and excitement (Eaton & Enns, 1986; Maccoby & Jacklin, 1974).

Boys, who in most situations are restrained in their public display of emotion, may also find violent entertainment an appropriate medium for the experience and display of strong emotions. This should not be confused with catharsis, which is the purging of emotion. In the guise of aggressive play, boys can shout, express passion, and share these intense experiences with their peers. Perhaps males can overcome the social pressures on them not to be emotional or intimate with other males only in a hypermasculine context, like aggressive play and games.

THE PRACTICE HYPOTHESIS

The philosopher Karl Groos (1898) viewed play as preparation for adulthood. In a safe setting, the young of many species, including humans, practice roles and learn skills that they may need to succeed later in life. This is known as "the practice hypothesis." It is supported by observations that children's play reflects activities and roles found in the larger adult society (Fry, 1990; Parker, 1984; Roberts & Sutton-Smith, 1962; Sipes, 1973).

How do the youthful participants in rough-and-tumble play know that it is play and not to be taken as aggression? According to ethologists and others who study play in situ, there are nonverbal signals or cues that "this is play" (Bateson, 1955; Boulton, 1991; Fry, 1990; Smith & Boulton, 1990). Facial expressions, the duration and repetition of the activity, the wish to remain together following aggressive play all signal that it is something other than true aggression. The message communicated by these cues, that the activity is not to be taken seriously, appears also to be important in our enjoyment of other forms of violent portrayal—films, television programs, and video games, for example. (See chapters by Hoberman, Tatar, McCauley, and Zillmann in this volume.)

Humphreys and Smith (1984) observe that "the most likely original function of human rough-and-tumble play . . . is as practice for fighting and hunting skills. This is the only hypothesis which has so far provided a convincing explanation of the forms of the activity and the appreciable sex differences" (p. 262). Since that was written, studies have reported a link between prenatal exposure to sex-linked hormones and the play and toy preferences of boys and girls.

SEX DIFFERENCES IN AGGRESSIVE PLAY: BOYS R US

Boys as young as 2 years of age show a preference for tanks, planes, toy guns, and male action figures (Almqvist, 1989; Singer & Singer, 1990). Interviews with a (nonrepresentative) sample of 5- and 9-year-old German schoolchildren found that 76 percent of the boys owned toy guns, compared with 29 percent of the girls (Wegener-Spöhring, 1989). In a 1994 U.K. survey, 13 percent of boys said they liked violent themes in video games (Phillips, Rolls, Rouse, & Griffiths, 1995). A second English survey found that 44 percent of boys and 11 percent of girls preferred video games with violent themes (Cumberbatch, Maguire, & Woods, 1993). If an aggressive theme, like blasting an enemy, is added to a video game, its popularity increases among boys but decreases among girls (Malone, 1981; see Cantor, this volume).

Someone once said that if you gave dolls to 100 boys and footballs to 100 girls, within the hour most of the boys would be kicking the dolls around the room and the girls would be nurturing the footballs. Is there any truth to this ugly tale?

Although sex differences in rough-and-tumble play and preference for aggressive toys are reliably found, the reasons for these differences are in dispute. Explanations span a wide spectrum—from prenatal exposure to hormones (Meyer-Bahlburg, Feldman, Cohen, & Ehrhardt, 1988; Berenbaum & Hines, 1992) to social modeling (Shell & Eisenberg, 1990) and marketing/advertising influences (Karpoe & Olney, 1983; Kline & Pentecost, 1990; Schwartz & Markham, 1985).

Specific toy preferences have been related to prenatal exposure to hormones. Both boys and girls exposed prenatally and in early postnatal months to high levels of androgens, the male hormones, showed greater preference for traditionally boys' toys at ages 3 to 8 years (Berenbaum & Hines, 1992; Berenbaum & Snyder, 1995). Studies by Meyer-Bahlburg et al. (1988) have documented the relationship between prenatal exposure to the synthetic female hormone progestogen and rough-and-tumble play in both sexes. Early exposure to progestogen is related to reduced levels of aggressive play.

Even if there are biological bases of toy play, however, this does not preclude a host of psychological and social influences. We consider some of them below.

Psychological Explanations for Aggressive Play

Historian Bernard Mergen (1982) says that the creation of imaginary worlds is "the most important characteristic" of war toys (p. 164). To the extent that war toys stimulate imaginative play, they are related to a variety of positive cognitive and social skills (Singer, 1994).

Flow

Intense, repetitive play may result in an altered state of consciousness, referred to as "flow" by Csikszentmihalyi (1990). Perhaps play scripts are so often repeated because their familiarity has a different "feel" from other, more improvised play. Active play that occurs during flow states is experienced as more positive and desirable (Goldstein, Cajko, Oosterbroek, Michielsen, Houten, & Salverda, 1997; Stein, Kimiecik, Daniels, & Jackson, 1995; Turkle, 1984). Aggressive play may be repeated because it lends itself to this experience. This interpretation still does not explain what there is about specifically aggressive or war play that makes it such a common vehicle for the experience of flow. The use of imagination or of repetitive acts is not limited to play with war toys but can be stimulated by any toy and by many sorts of play. So the question remains why war play is particularly appealing to some boys at some times.

Salience of Violence

Two school teachers in Hawaii reported an increase in war play shortly after the bombing of Pearl Harbor. Bonte and Musgrove (1943) attribute their students'—both boys and girls—greater interest in war play to the heightened anxiety brought on by the bombing.

But it does not take a Pearl Harbor to make war and violence salient to children. Brian Sutton-Smith (1988) has said that boys learn at an early age that it is men who fight and die in all those wars and crimes that fill the news, the papers, and the screens large and small. In their aggressive war play they try to envision what lies in store for all too many of them (Lahey, 1996).

Relative to other children, aggressive boys prefer aggressive toys (Jenvey, 1993; Watson & Peng, 1992). In a study of 7- and 8-year-old English schoolchildren, Jukes and Goldstein (1993) found a correlation of +.63 between aggression (as measured by questionnaire) and preference for war toys. The correlation for girls was not statistically significant.

These findings are consistent with research by Lefkowitz, Eron, Walder, and Huesmann (1977), also with children of about this age. Although a relationship was found between boys' aggression and violent television program preference, Lefkowitz et al. did not find a similar relationship for girls. They suggest that this is due to social pressures that discourage girls from watching violent television. Similar forces may deter girls from playing with aggressive toys.

The relationship between play with aggressive toys and level of aggressive behavior says nothing of cause and effect. Nevertheless, it provides one answer to the question of which children most like this sort of play, even if it does not tell us why.

AGGRESSIVE ENTERTAINMENT AND THE
SEARCH FOR JUSTICE

Aggressive/war play may be an attempt by children to achieve a complete or satisfactory resolution to conflict, which in real life, is so difficult to achieve. This type of play, if it is not prematurely terminated (for example, by teachers or parents, or by the accidental injury of a playmate), plays itself out, so to speak—it lasts until children mutually agree to terminate it. This allows for a "peaceful" resolution to conflict, a sense of closure, and often an enactment of the child's sense of justice, with evildoers receiving their just desserts. De Waal (1989) has observed a similar sort of peaceful resolution of conflict among primates.

The idea that justice may lie beneath an attraction to violence has been tested, not with toys or video games, but with violent films (Boyanowsky et al., 1974; Langley et al., 1992; Wakshlag, Vial, & Tamborini, 1983). In a replication and extension of these studies, we[5] asked 30 university students to read one of three newspaper articles: (1) an article about a violent crime with a just resolution (arrest and confession), (2) one about a violent crime without resolution (unknown assailant escaped), or (3) a noncrime article. Students then selected from a list of films with accompanying descriptions those films they would most like to see at that moment. There was a significant preference for films depicting successfully resolved violence after subjects had first read a newspaper article about an unresolved violent crime. If we can extrapolate from these findings, children select scripts for their play that enable them to enact conflict and aggression that end in ways that are satisfying to them. Although this simple study bears replication, it suggests that perhaps not all the motives for aggressive play stem from aggression or negative emotions. Instead, there may be positive reasons behind such play—the wish to see justice restored or to be reassured that good prevails over evil. Likewise, many children may use aggressive play not as a way of being antisocial, but as a way of joining in intense and satisfying activities with their peers.

Social Bases of Aggressive Play

The often horrified reactions of adults to unseemly or aggressive play may reflect what Norbert Elias (1969) refers to as "the civilizing process." Violence is increasingly removed from public view, and what violence remains is less tolerable to people. (See Goldberg, this volume.)

Children's identities are made known to their peers by the clothes they wear, the toys they play with, and the music they listen to. Children use sex-typed toys to identify with a particular group, to distinguish themselves from others, and to elicit predictable reactions from others, particularly approval or disapproval from parents and teachers (Goldstein, 1995).

Early exposure to particular hormones influences children's play styles and toy preferences. So, too, does early exposure to the behavior of parents, siblings, and peers. Sex-stereotyped play increases with age, reflecting mainly parental and peer modeling (Moller, Hymel, & Rubin, 1992; Parten, 1933; Rheingold & Cook, 1975; Zammuner, 1987).

Whether a toy is perceived as appropriate for a boy or a girl is determined partly by the child's same-sex peers. In a study by Shell and

FIGURE 3.1 *Kinderspiele* (Children's games), painted in 1560 by Pieter Bruegel, shows many varieties of horseplay and rough-and-tumble. Courtesy Kunsthistorisches Museum, Vienna.

Eisenberg (1990), 4- and 5-year-olds viewed a toy as a "boys' toy" if they previously observed mainly boys playing with the toy and as a "girls' toy" if girls were seen playing with the toy. Children, particularly boys, tend to avoid the toy preferences of age-mates of the other sex (Ruble, Balaban, & Cooper, 1981).

When children choose toys considered appropriate for their sex, playmates of the same sex are more likely to approach them (Eisenberg, Tryon, & Cameron, 1984; Moller et al., 1992). Indeed, among the reasons for making these toy choices may be the desire for peer approval, the wish to avoid negative reactions from peers, and the desire to engage in further interactions with same-sex peers (Cooper, Hall, & Huff, 1990; Shell & Eisenberg, 1990).

Parents are also sex-role models for their children. According to Catherine Garvey (1991), sex-typed toy preferences are due to "parents' influence as models and to their approval or support of children's interest in sex-stereotyped objects" (p. 54). Many studies report that parents are likely to purchase sex-stereotyped toys for their children, particularly if the parents themselves hold traditional sex-role attitudes (Eckerman & Stein, 1990; Rheingold & Cook, 1975; Zammuner, 1987).

Adults pass their own attitudes on to children along with the toys they give them. As these attitudes change among parents, they are reflected in toy purchases for their children (Singer & Singer, 1990).

Conclusions

Toy soldiers and weapons are as old as any known toys. Aggressive play and military toys are ancient; they certainly are not a product of the modern age. Even though they may be regarded as universal, the popularity of war toys and aggressive play themes changes with changing circumstances. They are to be found especially in cultures where war and aggression are prevalent. The relationship between adult culture and children's play is not necessarily a causal one. Both war and war play may reflect the prevailing values of the cultures in which they flourish, values that stress aggression, assertion, and dominance.

Aggressive and war play are found mainly among boys. Attitudes toward and views of aggressive play vary with the sex and childhood experiences of the observer. Those who played with war toys as children, for example, are less opposed to them than those who lack such experience. The latter group, of course, consists disproportionately of women.

Many interpretations of aggressive play are possible, ranging from biological necessity to social by-product. We are not in a position to choose one from among them and proclaim it as the explanation for aggressive play. We can, however, point to the plurality of influences that appear to give rise to and sustain periodic interest in aggressive play.

Of the more than two dozen explanations for the appeals of aggressive play shown in table 3.2, we have discussed about 20 here. There is little to go on besides speculation for many of them. For example, in their war play children may make elaborate strategic plans for attack and defense, and for some children this may be an appealing feature of such play. But there is virtually no research on this subject and no theory that addresses the attractiveness of strategic planning. Likewise, there is nothing but anecdotal evidence to support explanations about the exercise of power or the sense of competence to be gained from war play.

On the basis of the weight of evidence alone, one would have to favor the biological explanations—the practice hypothesis in particular—and the social modeling and imitation positions. However, like the drunk who looks for his lost keys under the lamppost because the light is better there, psychologists tend to study what has been studied before. So basing conclusions on the sheer quantity of evidence alone may be inadequate.

Children play with toy weapons for many reasons, many of them having nothing to do with aggression or war, although war and violence may temporarily enhance or dampen enthusiasm for such play.

Notes

1. *Mortal Kombat* 2 was on the shelves in time for Christmas 1994. This time around Nintendo chose not to dilute the violence and to compete head-to-head with Sega.

2. Iona Opie (1993) observed similar sex differences on the playground, although she notes that girls fight too.

3. Concerning Brown's point that enthusiasm for war may have contributed to an interest in toy soldiers, Jukes and Goldstein (1993) did not find heightened interest in war toys by boys during the Gulf War. However, this may have been due to the very high level of interest in war toys that predated their study.

4. The first published experiment of virtual reality I have seen is an experiment on the effects of violent virtual reality games (Calvert & Tan, 1994).

5. Jeffrey Goldstein, Carla Claassen, Elsbeth van Epen, Wieger de Leur, and Gert van der Vloed.

"Violent Delights" in Children's Literature

MARIA TATAR

"Children don't read to find their identity. They don't read to free themselves of guilt, to quench their thirst for rebellion, or to get rid of alienation. They have no use for psychology. They detest sociology" (Singer, 1994). These words reveal just how repellent the notion of bibliotherapy was to Isaac Bashevis Singer, who believed that children read because they love stories and are fascinated witnesses to what is enacted in them—especially when it takes the form of "violent delights," to use Shakespeare's oxymoronic formulation. Singer rightly stresses fascination over function, but his evident disdain for considering the sources and implications of that fascination speaks volumes about our cultural unwillingness to consider the degree to which that fascination is a product of adult calculation and has been instrumentalized by adults. The cultural stories to which we have exposed children over the centuries—those that have real staying power—are more than pure entertainment devoid of psychological weight or social significance. The stakes are always high when words and images prove so riveting that a child remains wide-eyed at story time or is unable to put a book down.

Violence as a Laughing Matter

Few scholars, researchers, or parents will contest the notion that children are fascinated by violence, whether it takes the form of Bugs Bunny in a pot of boiling water, Snow White opening the door to an old hag handing out red apples, or Max squaring off with the Wild Things. But this fascination with catastrophic events, with perilous encounters, and with seemingly mortal combat does not necessarily correlate with a *need* for displays of violence. When Bruno Bettelheim's influential study of fairy tales was translated into German, its title was changed from *The Uses of Enchantment* to the more programmatic *Children Need Fairy Tales (Kinder brauchen Märchen)*. Bettelheim, who stresses that Pollyannaish protagonists and sunny plots make for real trouble in children's literature, endorses violent representations in children's books and believes in their therapeutic benefits. While Bettelheim's anecdotal evidence often succeeds in persuading us on an intuitive level that it makes sense to expose children to the impassioned conflicts and emotional tangles of fairy tales, there is no documented, clinical evidence whatsoever in his book demonstrating an individual or global human need for reading about violence.

In many ways, the original English title for Bettelheim's volume is even more revealing than its German counterpart. The phrase "the uses of enchantment" tells us something about what is at stake in Bettelheim's account of how fairy tales guide the child "to relinquish his infantile dependency wishes and achieve a more satisfying independent existence" (Bettelheim, 1976, p. 11). No good tale goes unpunished by Bettelheim; each has an incisive lesson and a pointed moral for the child. The subtitles for each interpretive exercise are telling: "The Queen Bee" is really about "Achieving Integration"; "Brother and Sister" tells about "Unifying Our Dual Nature"; "The Goose Girl" teaches about "Achieving Autonomy"; and "The Three Languages" offers lessons on "Building Integration." Fairy tales, it would appear, have more than a therapeutic purpose. Not only do they help volatile, unstable children master their "unruly" emotions and turn them into "healthy" adults; they also are powerful tools in socializing children and enlisting their consent to developmental paradigms that lead from childish dependence to adult autonomy.

Bettelheim's analysis of "Hansel and Gretel" reveals how heavily *The Uses of Enchantment* is funded by a belief in the aggressive drives of the child. The Grimms' tale of siblings in the woods is cited as a story that enacts the child's need to "overcome and sublimate his primitive incorporative and hence destructive desires" (Bettelheim, 1976, p. 160). Hansel and Gretel, like all children, are carried away by "uncontrolled craving" and give in to "oral regression," "cannibalistic inclinations," "gluttony," "untamed id impulses," and "uncontrolled voraciousness" (pp. 161–62). Their story, by staging destructive inner desires, has a powerful therapeutic effect, allowing the discharge of "primitive" emotions. For Bettelheim, the children hearing the story or reading it, like the children within the story, will not only miraculously purge themselves of all their violent, unmanageable personal feelings but also achieve astonishingly successful social integration: "Having overcome his [*sic*] oedipal difficulties, mastered his oral anxieties, sublimated those of his cravings which cannot be satisfied realistically, and learned that wishful thinking has to be replaced by intelligent action, the child is ready to live happily again with his parents" (p. 165).

That Bettelheim's views have become the prevailing orthodoxy on fairy tales is symptomatic of our cultural willingness to embrace the view that "delinquent and violent tendencies" are part of human nature and that children, in particular, must learn to manage this innate behavior (Bettelheim, 1966, p. 189). But just as there is no clinical documentation proving that children discharge hostile and aggressive feelings when exposed to fairy tales, there is no hard evidence for the view that children have an "innate tendency to act aggressively" (Bettelheim, 1966, p. 187). What Bettelheim's *Uses of Enchantment* does allow us to see, however, is the remarkable appeal of violence for adults: the way in which adults instrumentalize narrative violence in order to discipline and socialize children in the name of guiding and healing them.

It would, of course, be naive to suggest that the violence in our cultural stories for children is there only because it has a pragmatic edge for adults. In almost all cases, the violence in these tales is psychologically overdetermined and motivated by multiple plot considerations. As Perri Klass asks in an analysis of Disney films: "Do we really want to protect our children from being saddened or scared or even upset by movies—or by books? Do we want to eliminate surprise, reversal, tragedy, conflict and leave children with stories in which they can be smugly confident that the good will always be rewarded and the bad always punished?" As Klass emphasizes, stories without villains and without dramatic conflict make for predictable, flat, and boring reading with no educational or entertainment value whatsoever (1994, p. 20).

We now know that the stories collected between the covers of the nineteenth-century folktale anthologies produced by the Brothers Grimm in Germany, by Alexander Afanasev in Russia, and by Joseph Jacobs in England had their origins in an irreverent folk culture that set itself in conscious opposition to the official ecclesiastical and feudal order. The narrative excesses of folk raconteurs often took the form of comic exaggerations, burlesque humor, and a form of earthy realism that depended on violence for its full effect. By overdoing it in the realm of narrative, these tellers were able to undo—if only temporarily—some of the real-life effects of being the underdog. When folktales moved from the workroom into the nursery, they lost most of their bawdy humor but retained the grotesque excesses of earlier days and presented a world in which villains are regularly decapitated or boiled in oil and giants are slain or tricked into cutting the throats of their children.

Fairy tales may now belong to the culture of childhood, but they have always been of adult making. The violence in the tales is driven by the psychological needs of the adult or by the narrative exigencies of the plot, not by the supposedly anarchic, innately aggressive nature of the child. Still, the violence is not without a certain appeal for the child. To understand its hold on the child's imagination, it is important to distinguish between burlesque violence, which depends for its effect on distortion and exaggeration, and retaliatory violence, which turns on the notion of physical punishment. Children often respond with undisguised glee to both—a witch's preparations for a cannibalistic feast or the whacks inflicted on a villain's backside by a magic cudgel can be equally hilarious. But in many cases what they are responding to has more to do with the tale's staging of surreal excess rather than with physical violence. Consider the episode from the Grimms' "Juniper Tree" in which a father greedily devours a stew made by his wife from the dismembered corpse of their son. Children may react to this episode with gales of laughter, as one professional raconteur reports, but they are more likely guffawing over an adult's display of unrestrained greed than over the chopping up of the boy's corpse to prepare a stew (Mönckeberg, 1972, pp. 14–15). At a recent viewing of *Pocahontas*, what audibly captured the attention of the children in the audience was not the preparations for battle between the bloodthirsty British and the Indians, but the wanton gluttony of the racoon Miko.

When children are authorized to write their own fairy tales, they are at pains to avoid retaliatory violence and to produce happy endings for the entire cast of characters. Heads rarely roll, witches are not sent down hills in barrels studded with nails, and no one dances to death in red-hot iron shoes. Usually it is only imaginary creatures, such as dragons, who are put to death. In her extensive study of children's refashionings of fairy tales, Kristin Wardetzky observed that the children whose narratives she studied invented "comparatively harmless demises. . . . Not a trace of sadistic blood-curdling revenge, no perfidious cruelty, no aggressive retaliation" (1990, p. 164). These youthful tellers (all were in the age range of eight to ten years) did not invest their stories with issues of separation and autonomy—what was at stake was the resolution of conflicts and the reconstitution of a stable and harmonious family. For them, it was less important to kill monsters than to befriend them and to persuade others to accept them.

Pedagogies of Fear

Violence in children's literature has two entirely distinctive aspects that must be separated out and designated as its production and its reception. First, there is an author or agent of representation responsible for the violent event in the text. Then, there is the reader or recipient who responds in some way to the constructed violence. As it happens, the author/agent is in virtually every instance an adult, for children's literature is a form of cultural production controlled almost entirely by adults.

Adults are the authors, illustrators, editors, distributors, publishers, and (until the child reaches a certain age) the buyers. The implied recipient is always the child, for children's literature is designed both *for* the child as audience and *for the sake of* the child. Yet no other body of literature is also so openly funded by difference: the ideological, generational, and cognitive gaps between adult and child are vast. And no other body of literature also constructs itself so emphatically as champion or coconspirator of its audience even as it resolutely aims to secure control of it through its relentless efforts to beguile the child outside the book by teaching a lesson to the child inside the book.

John Locke, whose philosophy of education has been seen in the first instance as laying the groundwork for truly "enlightened" and "progressive" practices, remained untroubled by the way in which a desire to befriend the child could serve as a pretext for governing the child. He urged parents to "settle your authority" over children, to become their "lords" and "absolute governors" (1693, p. 30), for only by instilling "fear and awe" could parents secure the true "love and friendship" of their children, which would, in turn, secure the child's willing submission to the adult's educational program. Even as Locke was writing with passionate eloquence about the horrors of tyranny, of absolute monarchy, and of government without consent, he argued convincingly that children, who are born "without knowledge or understanding," must submit to patriarchal authority and subordinate themselves to their parents. While Locke recommended restraint when it came to physical punishment, he had no trouble endorsing the notion of using "fear and awe" to instill obedience to parental rule and thereby to educate children to the state of equality to which they are born.

The mentality of being cruel only to be kind had informed—in a far less sophisticated form—much of children's literature from its inception through the early twentieth century. What but a pedagogy of fear could be at work in James Janeway's *A Token for Children, Being an Exact Account of the Conversion, Holy and Exemplary Lives and Joyful Deaths of Several Young Children* (1672/1977)? In his vignettes, Janeway gave prolonged accounts of children on their deathbeds, reciting Scripture and urging others to follow them to the grave. To ensure that his readers understood that they too were candidates for an early death, Janeway addressed them with a barrage of questions reminding them of their mortality: "Did you never hear of a little Child that died? & if other Children die, why may not you be sick & die? and what will you do then, Child, if you should have no grace in your heart, and be found like other naughty Children? How do you know but that you may be the next Child that may die? and where are you then if you be not God's Child?" For the terrorized child-reader, Janeway offered salvation in directives instructing the child to engage in abject self-mortification: "Get by thy self, into the Chamber or Garret, and fall upon thy knees, and weep and mourn, and tell Christ thou art afraid that he doth not love thee."

From our perspective, Janeway's book seems perversely cruel in its elaboration of the physical sufferings and spiritual ecstasy of dying children. Yet historians of children's literature are quick to defend the book as a source of "comfort and consolation" to seventeenth-century boys and girls (Jackson, 1989, p. 25). To be sure, messages about the snares of mortal existence and the superiority of the afterlife must have been important for children living in an era of civil war, plague, and natural disasters. For the child who had witnessed the death throes of disease-stricken family members and friends, who had lived through the Great Fire of 1666 that decimated London, or who had seen people collapse on the streets only to be picked up by the dead carts, a volume like Janeway's must have offered invaluable solace. Still, it is important to emphasize that Janeway's work had a remarkably emphatic disciplinary edge. Its "comfort and consolation" came with a price—one exacted at the expense of the children, who were urged to avoid play and spend their time weeping, praying, reading Scripture, and who sometimes aspired to imitate more than the religious engagement of the book's model children. "Their premature eminence, suited to my own age and situation, strongly excited my emulation," William Godwin wrote in recalling his own childhood reading of Janeway's case histories. "I felt as if I were willing to die with them, if I could with equal success engage the admiration of my friends and mankind" (Paul, 1876, pp. 7–8).

Janeway's *Token for Children* seems relatively benign when compared with what is perhaps the most enduringly popular children's book in German-speaking countries: Dr. Heinrich Hoffmann's *Struwwelpeter* (1845). The verses of *Struwwelpeter* also unfold events ending at the grave, but the deaths recounted are anything but joyful. There is the case of Conrad the Thumbsucker, whose thumbs are lopped off by a tailor with gigantic shears. In one colorful illustration, blood drips from the mutilated hands, and the final page of the story shows Conrad with both thumbs missing. Disobedient Pauline plays with matches despite the warnings of her two feline companions, who are depicted at the girl's grave, mourning her foolishness as much as her death. And "Suppen-Kaspar," who refuses to touch his soup, wastes away, and ends up in the cemetery, with a soup tureen marking his grave. While many adult readers will shake their heads in disbelief as they contemplate the image of the anorexic Kaspar and his gravestone, William J. Bennett seems to have found the story so edifying that he included it in a section on self-discipline in his *Book of Virtues* (1993). "The Story of Augustus, Who Would Not Have Any Soup" is designated by Bennett as a tale "in which we see the inevitable result of not eating enough of the right stuff" (p.

FIGURE 4.1 A fleet-footed tailor lops off the thumb of the delinquent Conrad, who has insisted on sucking his thumb despite his mother's prohibition. The tailor ensures that the boy will no longer disobey his mother by slicing off the other thumb as well.

45). Here is the ending that is designed to instill "discipline" in the child-reader:

> Look at him, now the fourth day's come:
> He scarcely weighs a sugarplum;
> He's like a little bit of thread,
> And on the fifth day, he was—dead!

That *Struwwelpeter* is not in the least exceptional in its overt sadism becomes evident from surveying children's literature in the eighteenth and nineteenth centuries. Cautionary tales abound, as in Richard Johnson's *Juvenile Rambles* (1786), which recounts how Dicky Flight steals from an orchard, flees when caught, and breaks his leg, which has to be amputated: "he died before it was well." *The Adventures of Master Headstrong, and Miss Patient* (c. 1802) allows its protagonist to survive, but not before subjecting Master Headstrong to a variety of tribulations at the end of which he is obliged to swallow the black waters of Repentance. Then there are the extraordinary numbers of storybooks in which children go up in flames. William Darton's *Little Truths, for the Instruc-*

FIGURE 4.2 The illustrations for "The Story of Soup Casper" graphically reveal the consequences of stubbornness in a child. A well-nourished Casper wastes away and finally expires because of his strong will.

tion of Children (1802) has the illustrated story of Polly Rust: "*Yes: she was one day left alone, and I think, playing with the fire; her clothes were burnt off her back, and she so scorched as to die the next morning in great pain.*" Or there is Augusta Noble, who walks carelessly with a lighted candle and is found "in a blaze, from head to foot," in *The History of the Fairchild Family* (Sherwood, 1828). *Rhymes for the Nursery* (1808) emphasizes the prolonged pain caused by playing with fire:

For many months, before 'twas cur'd,
Most shocking torments she endur'd;
And even now, in passing by her,
You see what 'tis to play with fire!

(Taylor & Taylor, 1835/1984, p. 238)

The consequences of playing with fire are such that the child both inside and outside the book will find it impossible to forget the lesson inscribed in the tale. Even when a child survives a fire, as does Harry in Catherine Sinclair's nineteenth-century classic *Holiday House*, a severe punishment substitutes for the burn marks that would have made it impossible to forget the perils of playing with fire: "Harry must sleep all night to-night in the burned nursery," Uncle David declares, "having no other covering than the burned blankets, with large holes in them, that he may never forget THE TERRIBLE FIRE!" (1864/1985, p. 28).

Cruel as these stories may seem to modern-day sensibilities, they were not entirely without merit, for they offered a program for survival in an era when open fires and flames put children at nearly constant risk. Yet much as the pedagogical function may have made sense and may still make sense today, it has what we would consider a needlessly sadistic edge to it. Today we may worry about toddlers putting metal objects into electrical outlets, yet we do not produce storybooks showing them being electrocuted. For Jacqueline Rose, who is more concerned than any other critic about the "impossible" relationship between adult and child, the development of narrative in children's books "has gone hand in hand with an apparent reduction in its pedagogic function and an increasing stress on the child's own pleasure" (1984, p. 62). In this view, the appeal of *representing* violence in children's stories has diminished over the centuries, with the result that twentieth-century Anglo-American and Continental writers of children's stories are less invested in teaching children lessons than in providing them with pleasurable delights. This does not, by any stretch of the imagination, erase the issue of securing control over the child—the end may remain much the same even if the means have changed. From Rousseau's educational program for Emile, we know the degree to which adult tutors can perceive themselves as benevolent agents serving the interests and desires of the child even as they create a network of surveillance that subjects a child to the violence of ruse rather than to the violence of physical force (Starobinski, 1971). As Alan Richardson has pointed out, "an affectionate relationship between parent and child" can be an "even more effective and durable form of discipline" than coercion, for it facilitates the internalization of habits and values (1994, p. 48).

From Locke and Rousseau we have learned something about the way in which the violence of physical force inevitably backfires. Writing about the futility of corporal punishment, Locke noted: "The child submits, and dissembles obedience, whilst the fear of the rod hangs over him; but when that is removed, and, by being out of sight, he can promise himself impunity, he gives the greater scope to his natural inclination; which by this way is not at all altered, but on the contrary heightened and increased in him; and after such restraint, breaks out usually with the more violence" (1693, p. 34). Similarly, children who are read stories designed to frighten them into good behavior rarely buy into the adult agenda and may be more likely to give free reign to the transgressive impulses represented in a story than to curb them. "Follow children learning their fables," Rousseau advised adults, "and you will see that when they are in a position to apply them, they almost always do so in a way opposite to the author's intention, and that instead of looking within themselves for the shortcoming that one wants to cure or prevent, they tend to like the vice with which one takes advantage of others' shortcomings" (1763/1979, p. 115). By engaging in a deconstructive analysis of La Fontaine's fable "The Fox and the Crow," Rousseau demonstrates how the text subverts the very terms it establishes and encourages the children reading it to deride the crow and to identify with the cunning fox.

Violent images in children's literature represent, for adults, a quick fix. What faster and more efficient way to modify the behavior of children than to frame stories that threaten capital punishment for one offense or another? Yet the disciplinary intent of violent images can backfire by producing images that appeal to a child's "naturally" unruly and transgressive spirit and to a child's appetite for the grotesque and macabre, thereby intensifying the appeal of the very behavior it was meant to restrain. Take the case of Anthony Greedyguts, in *The Friends* (1801), who "loved eating much better than reading; and would prefer a tart, a custard, a plumcake, or even a slice of gingerbread, or an apple, to the prettiest, and most useful little book you could present him with." At a single sitting, we learn, he ate a dozen penny custards and "thereby gorged his stomach, and threw himself into a mortal fever" (Pickering, 1993, p. 7). What child will read this account and feel restraint about overindulging in sweets? The recital of the treats seems more likely a stimulant to the appetite than the mortal fever is a deterrent to indulging in cakes and custards.

For children, the elaboration of a vice and its consequences can be funnier than it is frightening. From the context in which Anthony Greedyguts appears, it is clear that the nineteenth-century author of his story had no subversive intent—the text is framed as a cautionary tale, not as a send-up of object lessons. While the child reading the story at the time of its publication, in 1801, might not have been able to evade fully the disciplinary energy of the text, the child schooled in Lewis Carroll or Edward Lear will already have taken important tutorials in defusing the coercive power of adult messages in children's books. As we

move from Janeway, Bunyan, and Watts to the latter part of the nineteenth century, we see the disciplinary gap between adult and child nar-
rowing, with the adult author lining up with the child against a regime
of productive labor and discipline. In order to appreciate the satiric wit
directed by Lewis Carroll at the world of official culture, it is not always
necessary to know his Puritan intertexts. But those who have read Isaac
Watts's "Against Idleness and Mischief" and know his lines about the
"busy bee" and how it improves "each shining hour" by gathering honey
"from ev'ry op'ning flow'r" will more fully understand how the following verses from *Alice in Wonderland* undermine a pedagogy of fear with
burlesque humor:

> "How doth the little crocodile
> Improve his shining tail,
> And pour the waters of the Nile
> On every golden scale!
>
> "How cheerfully he seems to grin,
> How neatly spreads his claws,
> And welcomes little fishes in,
> With gently smiling jaws!"

(Carroll, 1992, p. 16)

In writing the poem about the predatory crocodile, the author of
Alice in Wonderland positioned himself as coconspirator with the child
against adult cultural sentences. While Watts was intent on impressing
children with the way that "Satan" finds mischief for "idle hands," Carroll was determined to dismantle that piece of adult wisdom by revealing
the absurdity of enshrining industry in and of itself as a virtue.

Twentieth-century authors have gone Carroll one better by self-
consciously declaring themselves to be squarely on the side of children.
Roald Dahl perceived the key to his success as an author of children's
books to be his ability "to conspire with children against adults" (Tatar,
1992, p. 237). Maurice Sendak found that, as a "former child," he was
in the best possible position to write children's books—his allegiance to
the child, rather than to the adult, could not be declared more succinctly.

An adult author's declaration of loyalty to the child does not necessarily take the terrifying sting out of representations of violence, particularly when a child is the target of the violence. In fact, it becomes
clear that adult authors—even in their most violently disciplinary moments—never construct themselves as anything but champions of the
child. Much as children may laugh their heads off (along with Willy
Wonka) as they witness the fate of Augustus Gloop, the "greedy boy"
of Roald Dahl's *Charlie and the Chocolate Factory* (1964), they will
also find the description of the "powerful suction" that pulls him into
the mouth of a factory pipe and shoots him to the Fudge Room fright-

ening. And who can fail to be unnerved by the way in which the narrator reassures the reader that Augustus is unharmed even as he places him in constant mortal danger? Consider the song of the Oompa-Loompas about Augustus:

> But don't, dear children, be alarmed;
> Augustus Gloop will not be harmed,
> Although, of course, we must admit
> He will be *altered* quite a bit.
> He'll be *quite* changed from what he's been,
> When he goes through the fudge machine:
> Slowly, the wheels go round and round,
> The cogs begin to grind and pound;
> A hundred knives go slice, slice, slice;
> We add some sugar, cream, and spice;
> We boil him for a minute more,
> Until we're absolutely sure
> That all the greed and all the gall
> Is boiled away for once and all. (p. 85)

That Willy Wonka declares their song to be "nonsense" does not in any way alter the dreadfulness of these images. Indeed, the uncertainty about the fate of Augustus Gloop is further underscored by the exchange between Charlie and Grandpa Joe at the end of the chapter:

> "Are the Oompa-Loompas really joking, Grandpa?" asked Charlie.
>   "Of course they're joking," answered Grandpa Joe. "They *must* be joking. At least, I hope they're joking. Don't you?" (Dahl, 1964, p. 86)

To keep us in further suspense, the next chapter begins with Wonka's halfhearted assurance that Augustus Gloop will survive: "He's bound to come out in the wash. They always do" (p. 86).

While it may be appealing to witness the torments of Augustus Gloop, who has been described as "enormously fat" with "great flabby folds of fat" bulging out from his body and a face "like a monstrous ball of dough," it is unclear that Dahl's story is any less disciplinary in its ultimate intent than many earlier cautionary tales. After all, unruly children, like the greedy Augustus Gloop, the spoiled Veruca Salt, the gum-chewing Violet Beauregarde, and the compulsive television watcher Mike Teavee, all receive their deserved punishments in the end, while the saintly Charlie Bucket gets the ultimate reward of owning a candy factory. Like Locke, who focused on correcting bad habits so that the child would ultimately internalize adult behavioral codes and no longer require supervision, Dahl seems intent on changing habits that are repulsive to the adult.

Charlie and the Chocolate Factory reveals how extremes can meet when it comes to representations of violence. The children's book writ-ten with a subversive intent and aimed at celebrating burlesque humor can have the same *effect* as the book written with the express purpose of reinscribing cultural norms and socializing unruly children. The range of responses to Dahl's stories is broad—some children will find the im-ages of Augustus Gloop hilarious, others—like many adult reviewers of the book—will find them unsettling, disturbing, and disagreeable (Cam-eron, 1972). To some extent, this range of responses was a product of calculation: Dahl emphasized time and again that the complex interplay of pleasure and pain engaged the energies of all good writers and created interesting textual effects for readers. His casual observations about the appeal of his own books and those of others—when pieced together—go far toward explaining what makes violence so fascinating for chil-dren.

Torture and suspense, according to Dahl, are the most effective means of casting a narrative spell on readers: "By creating suspense, the writer is simply playing upon the subconscious masochistic instincts of the reader. He is torturing him. And if the torture is expertly applied, the reader will cry out: 'I can't stand it, not for another moment! Oh, isn't it wonderful!'—and he will read on" (Warren, 1994, p. 26). For Dahl, this mingling of pleasure and pain has an especially strong prag-matic edge for child-readers, for it keeps them hooked on books and away from the television set (think of Dahl's endless denunciations of television watching in both *Matilda* and *Charlie and the Chocolate Fac-tory*). More important, however, the violence to which the character in the book is subjected comes to be repeated on the reader of the book. When a sympathetic character is placed in jeopardy, Dahl writes, "anx-iety and apprehension are created in the reader's mind" and are pro-longed "to the point where the narrative becomes *painful* to read" (my emphasis). Through identification, the reader comes to feel the agonies experienced by characters in the book, yet remains safely ensconced in a chair, experiencing the pleasures of the witness/survivor.

Dahl believed in the cathartic pleasures of narrative violence, but—despite his obvious flair for surreal violence—he could not resist taking the moral high ground and declaring his allegiance to a pedagogy of fear: "Children love to be spooked, to be made to giggle. They like a touch of the macabre as long as it's funny, too. They don't relate it to life. They enjoy the fantasy. And my nastiness is never gratuitous. It's retribution. Beastly people must be punished." Narrative suspense, ca-thartic pleasure, and surreal comic effects are all part of the delicate weave that constitutes the appeal of violence for children. But since giggling, being spooked, and enjoyment carry little weight for adults, violence comes to be seen as part of the moral calculus of children's narratives.

Framing Violence

To a great extent, a child's response to violence in a story is determined by context. Nowhere is this more clearly evident than in the reading of stories to children in the age range of three to seven, where the same printed text can yield very different results. Imagine one adult reading the Grimms' "Little Red Riding Hood" to a child. This reader has a great deal of faith in cautionary tales and finds that they provide children with important developmental lessons. Thus Reader Number One will accentuate the words of Red Riding Hood's mother, who lectures her daughter on everything from the merits of rising early to curbing curiosity: "Get an early start, before it becomes hot, and when you're out in the woods, be nice and good and don't stray from the path, otherwise you'll fall and break the glass, and your grandmother will get nothing. And when you enter her room, don't forget to say good morning, and don't go peeping in all the corners."

This same reader will place great stress on the heroine's final thoughts to herself: "Never again will you stray from the path by yourself and go into the forest when your mother has forbidden it." Reader Number One will never stop to interrogate the fact that Little Red Riding Hood meets the wolf and gives him instructions on how to get to Grandmother's house long before she strays from the path or that the mother, in the barrage of instructions given to her daughter, neglected to give her the one piece of information she really needed: If you see a wolf, run for your life. Instead, this reader will validate the lessons enunciated in the story and will reinforce them by creating an atmosphere of nervous anxiety about the devouring of grandmother and child. Charles Perrault, who, to his credit, delivered a consistent and logical message (It is dangerous to stop and listen to a wolf, i.e., a stranger), did not include a rescue scene in his version of the story. His Little Red Riding Hood, who is "gobbled up" by the wolf, might well be appealing to Reader Number One, who is intent on mobilizing the story into service as a warning to little girls about wolves—both the "noisy" kind and the even more dangerous "tame, obliging and gentle" ones.

The violence in "Little Red Riding Hood" can be constructed as terrifying rather than entertaining by a reader invested in the pedagogy of fear. Let us assume a second reader, one who is intent less on teaching lessons than on simply reading a cultural story with the child. Reader Number Two may dwell on the wolf's desire for a good lunch and emphasize his greediness by rubbing her hands as she recites the lines "This tender young thing is a juicy morsel. She'll taste even better than the old woman. You've got to be real crafty if you want to catch them both." The exchange between the wolf and Red Riding Hood about "big ears," "big hands," and a "big mouth" can offer the opportunity for role-playing, with the reader as wolf and the child as Red Riding Hood.

It goes without saying that fears about the heroine's being devoured can easily be defused through a playful reenactment of the scene. The wolf, for all his cunning, can also be portrayed as a buffoon by imitating his loud snores as he sleeps in Grandmother's bed. This reader would probably find Perrault's version less appealing than an oral story recorded by the French folklorist Paul Delarue called "The Story of Grandmother" (Zipes, 1993, pp. 21–23). In that tale, the heroine escapes by telling the suspiciously hairy grandmother that she has to go outdoors to relieve herself. The wolf's suggestion that the girl can do it in the bed and his impatient question about whether she is "making a load" once she gets outside are further comic touches to a story full of scatological humor. Inspired by rewritings of "Little Red Riding Hood" ranging from Thurber's heroine (who takes an automatic out of her basket and shoots the wolf dead) to the heroine of one of Dahl's *Revolting Rhymes* (who ends up with a beautiful fur coat), these readers can modify details, propose alternate scenarios, and recraft the tale.

What we have are two very different scenes of reading, scenes that make it evident that the act of reading aloud to a child is tantamount to interpretation—more than that, to a rewriting of the printed text. Addressing the question of violence on the page or on-screen usually presumes a stable text; in the case of fairy tales read to children, that text is destabilized by its performative aspect, by the interpretive theater created when the adult reads the story to the child. Both the appeal of the violence and its effect on the child are determined to a great extent by context, by the way in which the violence is framed by the adult reader. But what holds true for fairy tales read to preschoolers can also obtain (if to a lesser degree) for books read by school-age children. How third graders, for example, respond to the represented violence often depends on how they are trained as readers by their adult mentors.

Constructing Childhood

Readers who construct a disciplinary gap between themselves and the children to whom they are reading or to whom they talk about stories are clearly very different—in intent if not always in effect—from those who try to close that gap by transforming violent terrors into violent delights. Because this gap is so crucial to an understanding of how violence can be instrumentalized in children's literature and why it might appeal to the child, I want to pause for a moment to consider how childhood has been constructed over the centuries and what it is that separates the child from the adult.

There is a world of difference between children and adults. But defining that difference, or rather those differences, and determining the degree to which they are transhistorical or culturally specific is not an easy task. In this context, I will not attend to the obvious physiological differences between children and adults, including the notion of infantile weakness that was so important to Rousseau as a marker of childhood. Knowledge, carnal or cognitive, is traditionally seen as the great divide separating children from adults. For James Kincaid, author of the controversial *Child-Loving*, the "acknowledged difference" between adults and children, the rupture that has divided them for the last two hundred years, is "heavily erotic": "The child is that species which is free of sexual feeling or response; the adult is that species which has crossed over into sexuality" (1992, pp. 6–7). It is hard to believe that Kincaid could make this assertion without acknowledging how Freud long ago undermined that division when he declared that children have an "aptitude"—"innately present" in them—for "sexual irregularities." For Freud, children are in fact so charged with sexual energy that, until they develop a sense of "shame, disgust and morality," they can be easily led to engage in "polymorphously perverse" practices. Thus for Freud the real difference between children and adults has less to do with sexual response—"innately present" in both—than with a lack of shame about sexuality in the young (1905/1962, pp. 87–88).

For most pre-Freudian thinkers, the gulf separating children from adults had more to do with a lack of education and experience than of shame or guilt. Locke saw the child as a tabula rasa, a "white Paper," on which culture inscribes its civilizing sentences. For Rousseau, "Everything that we do not have at our birth and which we need when we are grown is given us by education" (1763/1979, p. 38). In a more contemporary vein, Neil Postman, who argues that the gap between children and adults is rapidly closing owing to the indiscriminate technological dissemination of information, finds that "one of the main differences between an adult and a child is that the adult knows about certain facets of life—its mysteries, its contradictions, its violence, its tragedies—that are not considered suitable for children to know" (1982, p. 15).

What makes all these definitions of difference interesting is their investment in finding deficiency in the child. Children lack strength, a sense of shame, experience, and knowledge. From there we could go on to speak of other absences: manners, culture, decorum, tact, and so on. If children are not defined by lack (childish "innocence" is the idealized version of the deficiencies), then they are creatures of sinful excess. Whether we ponder Calvinist notions of Original Sin and the child as having a "corrupt nature" and "evil disposition" or Freudian notions of the child as "polymorphously perverse" and as a carrier of transgressive desire and murderous hostility, children are perceived as needing civilizing restraint and rehabilitation.

Rather than identify the child as marked by lack or excess, I want to reformulate the question about critical differences between adult and child. Instead of questioning how the child fails to measure up to an adult standard, I want to consider what children have that adults are missing. Here again, I will leave aside the question of what George Bernard Shaw felt it was such a crime to waste on children and focus on the mind rather than the body. Exuberance, energy, mobility, irrepressibility, irreverence, curiosity, audacity—these are traits that we are right to envy of youth. But they are also the very characteristics that make the child intractable—resistant to the civilizing powers of the adult world. The boundless transgressive energy of children will forever confound and vex adults as they set about the task of socializing the young.

Curiosity, because it drives children to push the limits of what is permitted to them and to ignore prohibitions, may promote transgressive behavior, but it also fuels development. John Locke had the wisdom to recognize that curiosity in children represents "an appetite after knowledge, and therefore ought to be encouraged in them, not only as a good sign, but as the great instrument nature has provided, to remove the ignorance they were born with, and which without this busy inquisitiveness will make them dull and useless creatures" (1693, p. 88). In other words, what we condemn as a form of excess (curiosity, audacity, disobedience) is in fact exactly what the child needs to compensate for lack (ignorance). Without curiosity about the world, about all the things from which children are shielded, the child is condemned to remain forever a child.

There was a time, according to one historian, when children were sheltered neither from the facts of life nor from the hard facts of violence and death. Philippe Ariès has argued that "an awareness of the particular nature of childhood, that particular nature which distinguishes the child from the adult," simply did not exist before the Renaissance (1960, p. 128). Ariès may not be completely correct in declaring that childhood, as we know it, is an invention of later centuries, but it is clear that the cultural gap separating children from adults was not nearly as great in, say, the thirteenth and fourteenth centuries as in the eighteenth or nineteenth. Schools, for example, have played a powerful role in segregating children from the culture of everyday life by delaying their routine integration into the adult world of work.

As the cultural gap between child and adult widened from medieval times to the nineteenth century, a body of literature targeted exclusively for children emerged. Missing from that body of literature were adult "secrets"—the stories of incest, murder, rape, and human sacrifice that made children's Bibles, along with folktales, such riveting, if also terrifying, fare for children of an earlier age. Interestingly, sex, more than violence and death, became the real taboo subject of children's literature. Whether we look at eighteenth-century retellings of biblical stories for children or nineteenth-century revisions of folktales, we find that ribald episodes, along with allusions to transgressive sexuality, discreetly vanish while violence, particularly when directed at curious, disobedient children, escalates.

A look at the publication history of the *Nursery and Household Tales* collected by the Brothers Grimm reveals just how easy it was to turn bawdy stories meant to entertain into tales designed to impart lessons. The Grimms' collection, which was revised heavily as it became increasingly evident that the book was being read to children rather than scrutinized by scholars, included in its first edition the story of Hans Dumm, who has the power to impregnate women simply by wishing them to be with child. Wilhelm Grimm transformed the story "The Frog King or Iron Heinrich" from a tale replete with sexual innuendo to a story about the importance of obeying fathers and keeping promises. In one version collected by the Grimms that never made it into print, the princess dashes the hapless frog of the story against the wall: "He falls down into her bed and lies there as a handsome young prince, and the king's daughter lies down next to him." In the "official" version read by children today, the frog is transformed into a prince as soon as he hits the wall or is kissed by the heroine, and the happy couple does not retire for the evening until wedding vows are exchanged.

When the violent act of the princess is uncoupled from its erotic consequences, it produces an effect that is highly unpredictable. The princess's mounting sense of frustration and her unbecoming expression of disgust build to a climax that turns a fit of passionate violence into a moment of comic salvation. When nineteenth-century collectors of fairy tales became aware of the commercial potential of children's literature, they divested the tales of all erotic components and, whenever possible, added lessons, even when they did not square with other messages sent by the text. In practice, this meant that violence could appear to be wholly gratuitous (as in "The Frog King or Iron Heinrich") or it could be motivated as a disciplinary measure (as in the story of "Mother Trudy" where a girl is turned into a log and thrown into the fire as a punishment for her curiosity).

We know from Iona Opie's study of playground culture (1993) that children, when left to their own devices, create a folklore that relies heavily on scatological and sexual humor—in part to promote solidarity among themselves, in part because of their curiosity about the world of adult secrets. What is disturbing about efforts to strip violence of its burlesque features and to invest it with disciplinary power is the way in which it creates a divide between adult and child—a divide that shields the child from knowledge of the body and declares any jokes about biological functions to be taboo. When our cultural stories are rewritten in such a way as to "protect" the child, they often end by doing violence to the child's legitimate sense of transgressive curiosity and by declaring war on all those unruly impulses that go by the name of childish behavior. It may be that those rewritings, however disciplinary they may be, retain a hold on the imagination of the sensation-seeking child. Yet it is important to remember that the violence emanates from an adult source and that children find nearly all displays of excess exciting, though not necessarily attractive. As Roald Dahl has observed in the context of remarks on violence in "the old fairy tales," "When violence is tied to fantasy and humor, children find it . . . amusing." They find it compelling even when that violence, in an effort to produce a docile child outside the book, is trained on the body of the unruly child inside the book. Rather than channeling our efforts into ways of instrumentalizing narrative violence and placing it in the service of a pedagogy of fear, we need to think about interrogating (with the child) the attractiveness of violence. Once violence—whether it includes assaults on the body, violations of the body, or the dissolution of the body—becomes a routine topic deprived of its transgressive charge for children, it may also become so demystified that it loses some of its charm for both adults and children.

Children's Attraction to Violent Television Programming

JOANNE CANTOR

Mighty Morphin Power Rangers is the most recent example of an extraordinarily popular children's television show that features violence.

> "Mighty Morphin Power Rangers" . . . is the hottest kids' television show on earth, broadcast in nearly 40 foreign markets, watched by 70 percent of British kid viewers and 75 percent of kids watching in France. . . . The Power Rangers . . . preach cooperation and mutual respect, and generally have excellent manners. They also spend much of each show karate-chopping, kicking, elbowing, punching, and shooting their enemies with powerblasters. . . . Sixteen factories working around the clock to produce Bandai Power Ranger toys are still not meeting the demand. (Winerip, 1995, pp. 77–78, 80)

The controversy this program has provoked worldwide over whether it is stimulating children to fight with each other and even whether it was responsible for a child's death in Norway (see, e.g., Ho, 1994) has reinvigorated the ongoing debate about the contribution of televised violence to the aggressive behavior of children. But this debate, which has circulated at least since the advent of television, may not be as interesting as the more perplexing and intriguing question of why such programs attract and delight huge audiences of children again and again.

The fact is, of course, that we cannot determine whether or why violence is attractive by looking at the popularity of a single show. The response to any program is inevitably the product of many of its features working together. If violence were a necessary and sufficient condition for popularity with children, all popular programs would be violent and all violent programs would be popular. A more reasonable question to ask is whether violence is an important feature in the attractiveness of programs to children. And if we conclude that there is something about violence per se that is attractive to the child audience, we should ask what it is about the violence that draws children to it.

Certainly these are difficult questions to contemplate from a social-science perspective. Research on motivations for viewing and the gratifications obtained by exposure to entertainment is in its infancy compared to the long tradition and volumes of research on the *effects* of exposure to television. What is more, the media's effects on overt behavior are much more readily observable than the individual's motivations for exposure. Because of this, and perhaps because the question of why children are attracted to violent television has not been at the center of the public's attention, there are relatively few data that can be brought to bear on this issue. Yet these questions need to be addressed by social scientists, given the frequency with which speculations regarding the issue enter the public debate. For example, it is often argued by producers of violent children's programming that they are merely giving their audience what it wants, and some apparently think that violence is the most reliable way to attract child viewers. Moreover, opponents of the view that television violence causes children to become aggressive argue that it is children who already are aggressive who prefer to watch violence. The opposing viewpoint frequently advanced by critics of children's fare is that children don't seek out violent content, that it is action, not violence, they seek and enjoy watching. Very few data are available on which to evaluate the validity of these contentions.

In this chapter I am concerned with two major questions: First, what evidence is there that media violence is attractive to children? And second, assuming that violence is to some degree attractive, what accounts for children's willingness, even eagerness, to experience violence through the media?

In addition to citing already published data, I present relevant findings from two recent surveys. The first involved a random sample of 281 parents in the Madison (Wisconsin) Metropolitan School District who had children in kindergarten or second, fourth, or sixth grade during the spring of 1994 (Cantor & Nathanson, 1997). Among other questions, parents were asked about their child's interest in four different aggressive program genres and to name their child's favorite programs, as well as to indicate whether and why they restricted their child from viewing any programs, to rate their child's aggressiveness level, and to indicate whether their child had ever been frightened by something seen on television.

The second survey was conducted independently by Lisa Bruce (1995a) in the spring of 1994. It involved 314 sixth, seventh, and eighth graders in two schools in central Milwaukee and a third school in the

Milwaukee suburbs. Among other questions, these children were asked about their degree of interest in violent programs, as well as their exposure to violence in their own lives, their level of traumatic anxiety symptoms, their level of concern about violence, their exposure to advice against viewing violence, their tendency to empathize with characters in violent shows, and the gratifications they received from viewing violence.

The two surveys are not directly comparable, because one interviewed children and the other talked to parents about their children. Moreover, they do not contain any of the same questions, and, in particular, their measures of attraction to violent TV are very different. Furthermore, the Madison survey represents a rather homogeneous middle-class, overwhelmingly Caucasian population. The central-city Milwaukee sample, in contrast, was predominantly nonwhite (76 percent African American and 11 percent Hispanic) and involved mostly children from disadvantaged and often dangerous neighborhoods. My approach here is to make the best sense of the data currently available and to suggest studies needed to reach conclusions with more confidence.

Evidence for the Attractiveness of Violence

There are at least three related but distinct senses of the notion of attractiveness of media violence. One is *enjoyment*, often measured by observing a viewer's facial expressions or attentiveness. A second is *selective exposure*, or how much a viewer's knowledge that a program contains violence increases his or her interest in seeing it. As Zillmann argues in this volume, selective exposure is not identical to enjoyment; for example, one might be compelled by "morbid curiosity" to get a glimpse of the gory remains of an accident victim and yet find the experience highly unpleasant. Finally, the attractiveness of media violence might refer to its *genre popularity*, or its drawing power compared to other types of programming. This is typically assessed through audience-size measures such as the Nielsen ratings.

There is no definitive line between attractiveness and lack of attractiveness. Attractiveness is a matter of degree. The question of how attractive media violence is can be answered only in a comparative sense, and choosing the appropriate comparison object becomes an important issue. One question is whether a program with a lot of violence is more attractive than one with less, other things equal. However, in most research on this topic, programs with a lot of violence are compared to programs with less violence or no violence, but these programs differ from each other in a multitude of other ways as well. In addition, it must be remembered that media violence always occurs in a context, and it seems clear that the contextual features associated with violence are important determinants of selective exposure, enjoyment, and popularity.

What does research say about the attractiveness of television violence to children?

Enjoyment: How Do Children Respond While Viewing Violence?

Do children enjoy viewing violence? Of course they do; at least some of them enjoy some types of violence some of the time. More useful are more specific questions, such as, Does the addition of violence to a program enhance children's enjoyment? and, Do increases in levels of violence in a program produce greater enjoyment? The critical studies have yet to be done. Only one study of enjoyment manipulated the level of violence displayed within a show while leaving everything else constant, and this was conducted with adults as participants. Diener and DeFour (1978) varied the amount of violence in one episode of the series *Police Woman* by creating an altered version in which almost all of the violence was omitted. When they showed these two versions to groups of undergraduates, the violent (intact) version was liked somewhat more than the nonviolent version but the difference was not statistically significant. The authors concluded that "the networks apparently could reduce the incidence of portrayed violence substantially and lose few or no viewers" (p. 339).

The other studies of children's enjoyment of violence compared responses to programs that differed in many ways in addition to their amount of violence. Diener and Woody (1981) reported a series of three studies in which both undergraduates and a community sample ranging from children to the elderly viewed intact episodes of crime series that had earlier been rated by coders on their amount of violence, conflict, action, and realism. Participants saw programs that had received high or low ratings on these attributes. In two of the three studies, there was no significant difference in liking for programs rated high versus low in violence. In the third, although adult viewers liked low-violence programs significantly more than high-violence programs, the children showed a trend in the opposite direction. In addition, one of the studies found that programs high in conflict were liked significantly more than low-conflict programs. Moreover, the viewers perceived the high-conflict programs to be more violent than the low-conflict programs, in essence indicating that they preferred the programs they perceived as more violent. In spite of these somewhat inconsistent findings, the authors contended that their results "destroy[ed] the argument that . . . viewers like and actively seek out violent content."

There are no studies that observed the effect of varying levels of violence in the same program on children's enjoyment. In their research for the Surgeon General's Report, Greenberg and Gordon (1972a, 1972b) reported that boys found violent clips more enjoyable than a set of arbitrarily chosen nonviolent sequences, but these programs differed in innumerable ways. A study by Lagerspetz, Wahlroos, and Wendelin (1978) suggests that different types of violence may produce different types of emotional reactions in children. These researchers reported that preschool children typically showed facial expressions of "joy" while watching cartoon violence but showed negative affect while watching realistic physical violence. Such findings suggest that the context or format of violence is a determinant of children's emotional responses. Given that the two types of presentations differed in a multitude of ways, however, it is premature to make any conclusions about differences between specific genres on the basis of this one study.

The most frequently cited study on children's reactions while viewing violence was conducted by Potts, Huston, and Wright (1986). In an attempt to determine whether it is action or violence that draws children to programs, they chose a group of programs to systematically vary the level of violence and action. They defined violence as the incidence of physical and verbal aggression between characters, and action as characters "moving at human running speed or faster." On their only measure of attraction, visual attention to the screen, they found that preschool boys' attention was significantly higher for high action than for low action. Moreover, although high-violence programs received slightly more attention than low-violence programs, the difference was not significant. On the basis of this nonsignificant difference, Potts et al. concluded that "violence is not necessary to hold the interest of the child audience. . . . [E]liminating violent content reduces the likelihood of stimulating aggressive behavior without losing the audience appeal of a program." These researchers base their conclusion on a questionable measure of attraction: the amount of time the child's eyes were on the screen. This measure may simply reflect the child's need to visually attend to high-action sequences in order to follow them. It may have little or no relationship to enjoyment of what is being seen.

To summarize the findings on enjoyment, only one controlled study has been conducted, and it produced nonsignificant findings. In the remaining studies, violence was associated with greater liking, less liking, and no significant relationship. The only firm conclusion to be drawn, then, is that it is premature to draw any conclusion about the effect of violence on children's enjoyment.

Selective Exposure: Does Violence Increase Audience Size?

Although it is popularly asserted that violence is so prominent on television because it increases the size of the audience, there has been little research on this issue. The typical approach has been to relate audience-size measures (such as Nielsen ratings) to various measures of violent content in programs or movies. The results of this work have not been consistent.

For example, Diener and DeFour (1978) measured violent content, the amount of physical and verbal aggression, in individual episodes of crime series. They then correlated the amount of violence with the Nielsen rating of that series the next time it aired and found no significant relationship between the two measures. Such studies of viewership, however, should consider such well-known confounding variables as time of broadcast and the popularity of lead-in programs. It should also be pointed out that *no other feature* of these programs—including the presence of drama, action, or humor—was significantly related to their Nielsen ratings either.

A different type of study, and one that may support a positive relationship between violence and audience size, was based on Belgian television data. Herman and Leyens (1977) found that over a three-year period, movies broadcast with violence advisories earned significantly higher audience shares than those broadcast without advisories. This finding suggests that information that a movie will be especially violent attracts a larger audience for that movie. This study also showed that movies with advisories warning of sexual content had larger audiences than movies without advisories. Therefore, the findings may mean that both sex and violence attract larger audiences, or they may simply mean that viewer advisories promote interest in movies. In addition, this study again did not control for other contributions to a movie's audience size, such as the popularity of lead-in programs or the way the movie was advertised.

Recent work by Hamilton (1994) eliminated some of the methodological problems of these earlier investigations. He looked at the Nielsen ratings for prime-time movies broadcast on network television between 1987 and 1993 and determined the factors that made significant contributions to the movies' ultimate audience size, incorporating each movie's scheduling, the rating of the show preceding it, and the manner in which it was described and categorized in *TV Guide*, among other factors. Consistent with the notion that violence attracts viewers, Hamilton found that descriptions in *TV Guide* that involved "murder" or "family crime" themes were significant positive predictors of a movie's overall Nielsen score (adding .47 and 1.00, respectively, to the movie's rating). On the other hand, *TV Guide* descriptions that involved the theme of murder were a significant *negative* predictor of ratings among children aged 2 to 11 and teens aged 12 to 17 (losing .36 and .45 of a ratings point, respectively).[1] In addition, when the impact of a movie's assignment to a genre was assessed, both "crime-drama" and "mystery" genres were associated with decreases in ratings among children and teens. In contrast, two other genres that may be suggestive of violent content were positive predictors of the size of the child audience: "science fiction," for both children and teens, and "adventure," for children only. Finally, the "fantasy" genre increased both child and teen audience size (adding 3.24 and 1.15 ratings points, respectively), and the "comedy" genre was also positively related to audience size in these age groups. This study, then, provides evidence that information about the violent content of movies may attract a larger adult audience, but it seems to reduce the size of the child audience at least as often as it increases it.

Of course, ratings data, by their very nature, reflect attractiveness only to the extent that viewers are making their own choices of what to watch. This study leaves unclear whether children and teens were less interested in viewing various types of violence or whether their parents were restricting them from access to content that the parents deemed inappropriate. A different conclusion about children's selective exposure to violence might be inferred from Bruce's survey of children in the Milwaukee area. Bruce asked her respondents, "Would you watch a television program if you knew it contained a lot of violence?" Fully 82 percent replied in the affirmative, with 24 percent responding "definitely yes," and 58 percent responding "probably yes."

In sum, the data on selective exposure present as muddy a picture as the data on enjoyment. The studies report variously that violence increases, decreases, and exerts no significant effect on selective exposure to programs.

Genre Popularity: Are Violent Programs Children's Favorites?

Current Nielsen ratings of programs popular with children also provide a mixed picture of the popularity with children of violent shows. Stipp (1995) recently presented Nielsen data on the popularity of programs with two-to-eleven-year-olds in the United States. Portions of his data are presented in table 5.1. A glance at the upper half of the table, indicating the most popular Saturday-morning programs, suggests that programs that draw the greatest number of children are predominantly of the action/violence type, particularly in cartoon form. Out of context, these data appear to provide powerful support for the argument that the best way to attract a child audience is through violent programs. However, the bottom half of the table, listing the most popular children's programs overall, shows that the most watched programs are almost exclusively family-centered situation comedies. Moreover, all of these nonviolent programs received higher viewership ratings than any of the Saturday-morning violent cartoons. The highest rated violent cartoon, *Spiderman*, came in eighteenth in the overall rankings. Converting the Nielsen ratings to viewer numbers, a minute of the top-rated sitcoms is

TABLE 5.1 Children's Most Watched Programs: Nielsen Ratings for Children Aged Two to Eleven, February 1995

Program	Type	Rating
Saturday Morning		
Spiderman	Cartoon	8
X-Men	Cartoon	8
The Tick	Cartoon	7
Animaniacs	Cartoon	6
Power Rangers	Action	6
Eek the Cat	Cartoon	5
Aladdin	Cartoon	5
Ninja Turtles	Cartoon	5
Bugs Bunny/Tweety	Cartoon	5
Carmen Sandiego	Cartoon	5
All Times		
Step by Step	Sitcom	14
Boy Meets World	Sitcom	14
Home Improvement	Sitcom	14
Hanging with Mr. Cooper	Sitcom	13
Family Matters	Sitcom	13
Full House	Sitcom	13
Me and the Boys	Sitcom	13
Simpsons	Cartoon	12
America's Favorite Home Videos	Variety	10
Fresh Prince	Sitcom	10

Note: A ratings point for these data is equivalent to approximately 380,000 child viewers. Data reported by Stipp (1995).

seen by an average of 5.3 million child viewers, whereas a minute of the top-rated action cartoons is seen by an average of 3 million youngsters.

It could, of course, be argued that the reason for the greater popularity of prime-time sitcoms is that the potential audience is larger during prime time and that parents are more likely to be co-viewing or supervising children's viewing during the evening. As program schedules are currently fashioned, there is little opportunity to observe the critical comparison, as first-run family-oriented situation comedies and action cartoons rarely compete head-to-head. Although the contribution of parental co-viewing and audience availability cannot be ruled out, the data in table 5.1 clearly contradict any notion that violence is the only way to attract a substantial child audience.

The data we recently collected in Madison are consistent with the notion that although violent programming is popular with young viewers, situation comedies are equally or more popular. For example, in this random phone survey of parents, *Mighty Morphin Power Rangers* was spontaneously listed by 26 percent of the parents of kindergartners and second graders as one of their child's favorites. On the other hand, the program mentioned most frequently as a favorite was not a violent program at all, but the family-oriented sitcom *Full House*. According to parents, this nonviolent sitcom was among the favorite programs of 33 percent of the children in these age groups.

Taken together, these data suggest that one thing that shows attracting the largest Saturday-morning child audience have in common is violence. However, substantially larger audiences of children are attracted during prime time by situation comedies depicting family interactions. In evaluating the popularity of violent programming, it is important to keep in mind that there are other types of offerings that are even more popular with children.

Although much more systematic research needs to be done to clarify the issue, research seems to indicate that to different degrees, violence is an important component of mass-media programming that children like to watch. The variety of findings with regard to this issue seems to be in part due to the fact that violence may or may not be attractive depending on other things. There is some evidence in these data that the attractiveness of violence varies by the type or format of violence. And as we will see in the next section, it also varies according to other characteristics of the program and the nature of the audience. In order to understand the appeal of violence, then, a more important and clearly a more difficult task is to determine, not whether, but *why* children are attracted to media depictions of violence, and under what circumstances they find them enjoyable. Perhaps this question could be phrased more specifically: What aspects of mass-media violence attract what types of children to it?

Possible Reasons Children Choose to View Violence

Of the various rationales that have been forwarded to explain why media violence is attractive to children, I will explore what seem to be the most prominent and most plausible. I will stress the degree to which each of them can find support in the data currently available.

To Be Aroused

One prominent explanation is that children view violence on television because it is arousing; that is, the viewing of violence increases the child's emotional arousal. There is a good deal of evidence that the viewing of either violence or the threat of violence reliably increases sympathetic activation, particularly increasing heart rate and blood pressure in adults (see Zillmann, 1971, 1991). The impact of media violence on children's arousal level has been documented in studies that measured heart rate and skin temperature (e.g., Wilson & Cantor, 1987; Zillmann, Hay, & Bryant, 1975).

But beyond the fact that violence increases arousal lies the question of why viewers, and particularly children, should seek entertainment choices that produce this effect. Zillmann and Bryant (1994) argue that television's capacity to increase arousal accounts for viewers' selective exposure to television in some situations. They argue that people are motivated by a hedonically based drive toward excitatory homeostasis. Thus, for example, people who are bored or feel understimulated should be most receptive to programming that produces excitement.

It seems relatively easy to argue that children will be a prime audience for the arousal-enhancing, exciting aspects of media violence. As any parent will attest, children are characterized by high activity levels. In a study by O'Brien and Huston (1985), for example, both boys and girls were shown to prefer toys that allowed moderate to high activity levels. Perhaps one reason children enjoy active pursuits is that they experience the arousal that comes with such pursuits as pleasurable. Perhaps they enjoy viewing violence for the same reason.

Another reason to expect viewers to be drawn to violence for its arousal-inducing capabilities can be derived from Zuckerman's (1979) "sensation-seeking" motive. Zuckerman argues that individuals vary in their need for arousal and that those with a relatively great need will tend to seek out arousal-inducing activity. He also asserts that, as a general rule, sensation seeking increases through childhood, peaks in adolescence, and then declines with maturity. Thus, children are expected to be high sensation seekers. One set of findings consistent with the notion that arousal is an important component of viewers' attraction to violence is that among adolescents and adults, attraction to horror films (inarguably rife with violence) is positively associated with one's rating on the sensation-seeking trait (Edwards, 1984; Tamborini & Stiff, 1987; Zuckerman & Litle, 1986).

The Milwaukee-area survey asked the children to what extent they agreed with the statement "When I see something violent on television, it makes me feel excited." Thirty-four percent of the students in the sample agreed with this statement, with 7 percent agreeing "strongly." To determine the degree to which this outcome of viewing violence is associated with being attracted to violence, Bruce's "interest in media violence" measure was correlated with this measure of excitement from viewing violence. The correlation was positive and significant ($r=.39*$).[2]

These latter findings are consistent with a recent study by Johnston (1995), who gave adolescents a questionnaire about their motivations for viewing graphic horror and performed a factor analysis on the responses. The motivation that she observed to be the most strongly predictive of positive affect while viewing horror was termed "thrill watching" (e.g., "I watch because I like to be scared").

To Experience Aggression Vicariously: Empathy with Whom?

Another possible reason for children to be attracted to programs depicting violence is that children enjoy vicariously participating in aggressive behaviors, behaviors that they either are too small and weak to perform successfully or are in the process of being trained to inhibit (see Goldstein, chapter 3 in this volume). It is sometimes suggested that children feel empowered by imagining themselves in the role of the aggressor, usually the "good guy," and that this accounts for a substantial portion of the appeal of violent programs.

There is not much published data on this issue. However, in Bruce's Milwaukee survey, she asked the children to report on how often when viewing a violent television show they imagined or pretended that they were (a) a person in the show who gets hurt by someone violent (i.e., the victim), (b) a person in the show who is violent (i.e., the aggressor), and (c) a person in the show who catches the "bad guy" or who helps the victim (i.e., the "good guy"). Of these students, 48 percent responded that they ever empathized with the victim, and 45 percent reported ever empathizing with the violent person. Slightly more (59 percent) said that they ever pretended to be the "good guy."

These empathic processes were differentially related to interest in viewing violent television programs. Only imagining oneself as the aggressor was positively correlated with interest in viewing violence ($r=.20^*$). As might be expected, empathizing with the victim was negatively related to interest in viewing violence ($r=-.14$), but perhaps surprisingly, empathizing with the "good guy" was also negatively related to Bruce's measure of attraction to violent TV ($r=-.15$).

In contrast to these empathic responses to viewing violence, a seemingly detached stance while viewing was much more strongly related to interest in viewing violence. A sizable minority (39 percent) agreed with the item "I enjoy watching people fight and hurt each other on violent television shows," and this item was strongly correlated with interest in viewing violence ($r=.50^*$).

These latter findings are consistent with data from the Johnston (1995) study on adolescents' motivations for viewing horror. In Johnston's analysis, the "gore-watching" motivation (e.g., "I like to see blood and guts") was the only measured motivation that was a positive predictor of "identification with the killer." Gore watching was negatively associated with "identification with the victim." Taken together, these data suggest that enjoyment of highly violent shows is related to the enjoyment of violence per se and empathy with the aggressor rather than to empathic responses toward the hero or victim.

To Defy Restrictions: The "Forbidden Fruit" Hypothesis

Another possible explanation for children's attraction to media violence is that because parents often restrict access to violent TV shows, the shows come to appear more valuable. This explanation has sometimes been referred to as the "forbidden fruit" effect and has been related to Brehm's (1972) theory of psychological reactance. Both the Madison and Milwaukee surveys contain data relevant to this point.

The Madison survey asked parents to indicate whether they thought a violence advisory label would make their child more eager or less eager to see the program. Contrary to the notion of the attractiveness of "forbidden fruit," the overwhelming majority of parents expected either that their child's interest would be diminished or that the advisory would have no effect. Parents were also asked to indicate whether they restricted their child from viewing any programs, and if so, to indicate why they restricted the programs. It was therefore possible to distinguish between parents who restricted their children from viewing violent shows (44 percent) and parents who did not (56 percent). The results indicated that children of parents who restricted violent programs were no more interested in any of the four aggressive program genres asked about than were children of nonrestrictive parents.

In the Milwaukee-area survey, there were three questions that might be considered to be related to the notion of the attractiveness of "forbidden" violent television. Children were asked to indicate whether any of the following types of people had ever talked to them about why they should not watch too much violence on television: (a) a teacher or school counselor, (b) a parent or other adult family member, or (c) a doctor or nurse. When these responses were related to the child's interest in viewing violence, the data again did not support the reactance notion. An index of advice against viewing violence was created by assigning a value of 1 for each yes answer for the three sources of advice and summing the responses. This index was uncorrelated with the child's interest in viewing violence ($r = -.01$, ns).

It's a Male Thing: Gender Differences

A fourth popular explanation for the attractiveness of media violence relates to the role of violence in *gender-role socialization*. Although it is a truism that violence is much more a male than a female activity, a variety of theorists argue that the gender differences in aggressive behavior are more strongly attributable to socialization pressures than to biological differences (see Baron, 1977; Frodi, Macaulay, & Thome, 1977; Johnson, 1972; Zillmann, 1979). Goldstein (chapter 3 in this volume), in contrast, cites evidence that there may be an important hormonal component to gender differences in aggressive play. Whatever the origin of these differences, male children and adults are readily seen to engage in more violence than females, and they are also taught that violence, although it must be controlled to a great extent, is more appropriate for their gender. It may be argued that little boys are attracted to violence in the mass media because they learn very early that it is their domain and that it is a way to distinguish themselves from little girls.

Little boys have repeatedly been shown to be more interested in aggressive toys than little girls are (as discussed in chap. 3). Consistent with the literature on attraction to violent toys, attraction to violent programs seems to be strongly sex-linked. For example, Lyle and Hoffman (1972) found that among the three-to-five-year-olds they interviewed, three times as many boys as girls named a violent cartoon as their favorite. Donohue (1975) found similar gender differences among African-American elementary-school children.

A recent study by Collins-Standley, Gan, Yu, and Zillmann (1995) looked at gender differences in two-to-four-year-olds' preferences for fairy-tale books with covers suggesting violent, scary, or romantic content. The data revealed increasing gender differentiation in choice of violent books over the age groups, with boys significantly exceeding girls in their interest in violence in the four-year-old group.

The data recently collected in Wisconsin also support the notion that boys are more interested than girls in violent television. In the Milwaukee-area sample, interest in watching violence was significantly stronger for boys than for girls ($\overline{X}$= 3.2 vs. 2.9 on a 4-point scale).[4]

When Madison parents were asked about their child's interest in viewing various genres of television shows containing violence—classic cartoons, such as *Bugs Bunny*, action cartoons, such as *Teenage Mutant Ninja Turtles*, live-action adventure shows, such as *Power Rangers*, and reality-based action shows, such as *Rescue 911* and *Cops*—there were some sex differences in attraction to these genres. Parents reported that their sons were significantly more interested than their daughters in two of the four types of programs. Boys significantly exceeded girls in their interest in action cartoons (2.5 vs. 1.6 on a 4-point scale) and live-action shows (2.6 vs. 1.9).[5] The two sexes did not differ in their interest in classic cartoons and reality-action shows, however.

Another indicator of differences between boys and girls on the Madison survey was observed in the question on the effect of violence advisories. Although the majority of parents said that an advisory would not make a difference in their child's interest in a program, more boys than girls were expected to have their interest stimulated (boys, 20 percent; girls, 14 percent) and more girls than boys were expected to be turned away by the advisories (boys, 16 percent; girls, 28 percent).[6]

A confounding factor, or one that may exaggerate the sex differences in attraction to violent programs, may be that most violent programs feature males as the violent characters. Research indicates that children pay more attention to same-gender characters and remember more of their activities (e.g., Maccoby & Wilson, 1957; Maccoby, Wilson, & Burton, 1958). Anecdotal reports that *Power Rangers* is one of the few violent programs that have a large following among little girls are consistent with this notion, since this is one of the few programs in which the female main characters are as violent as their male counterparts.

It's a Youth Thing: Age Differences

Various theorists have speculated that interest in media violence is strongly determined by age as well as gender. For example, the main thesis of James Twitchell's *Preposterous Violence* (1989) is that interest in vicarious participation in violence is at its height among adolescent males. He argues that adolescence is the time when boys must struggle to bring their aggressive urges under control and to ready themselves for the responsibilities that go along with being an adult male. I would argue, however, that the male preschool child goes through somewhat similar socialization struggles involving the control of his aggressive impulses as he experiences the newfound freedom associated with developing strength and the ability to move about on his own. If, as Twitchell argues, adolescent males are the primary audience for horror movies and slasher films, it also seems that preschool and early-elementary-school boys are the primary audience for action-adventure-type television, at least in its popular cartoon form.

Although one might argue that there is a stage of childhood in which interest in media violence reaches its peak, it seems more likely that the age of maximum interest will differ as a function of genre. Twitchell's notion that interest in media violence peaks in adolescence is consistent with the data from the Milwaukee area. Using grade in school (sixth through eighth) as a surrogate for age, Bruce found that interest in violent television was positively related to age ($r=.14$).

The data from Madison reveal, however, that different genres of violent TV are associated with different patterns of viewer interest as a function of age. Figure 5.1 shows the mean interest levels in four violent program genres as a function of grade level. As can be seen from the figure, interest in reality-action shows increases with age, whereas interest in action cartoons and live-action shows exhibits a predominantly decreasing trend with age. Finally, interest in classic cartoons shows a curvilinear relationship with age. These genres vary in predictable ways

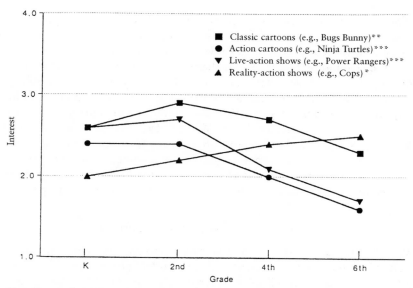

Note: Interest Scores Range From 1, "not at all interested" to 4, "extremely interested."
For the main effects of grade, $*p<.05$, $**p<.01$, $***p<.001$.

FIGURE 5.1 Interest in violent genres as a function of grade (Madison sample).

in terms of content, and I will return to some of these typical differences later in the discussion.

To Witness Behavior Like Their Own: The Role of Viewer Aggressiveness

Another commonly held view of the attraction of violence is that *violent people are attracted to programs depicting behavior that is characteristic of themselves.* This rationale is consistent with the notion that television violence does not increase aggression but that children who are already aggressive like to witness other people behaving violently. Much of the correlational data linking the viewing of violence to violent behavior is ambiguous in this regard, having been measured at only one point in time.

One of the most frequently cited proponents of the claim that aggressiveness promotes violence viewing is Fenigstein (1979). Fenigstein proposed that "aggressive thoughts or actions set in motion certain psychological processes, such as the need to understand one's behavior" (p. 2308). Other theorists have argued that aggressive people want to witness other people behaving violently to justify their own actions and to perceive them as more typical. Research finds that individuals high on personality measures of aggressiveness, or those who have just engaged in tasks involving aggression, choose to view more aggressive programming and enjoy it more (Diener & DeFour, 1981; Fenigstein; Langley, O'Neal, Craig, & Yost, 1992).

A relevant study conducted with children was reported by Atkin, Greenberg, Korzenny, and McDermott (1979). In a longitudinal study of children in fourth, sixth, and eighth grades, these researchers reported that physical aggressiveness measured during the first wave of the questionnaire, based on children's responses to hypothetical vignettes, was significantly correlated with the viewing of programs involving physical aggression one year later, and remained a significant predictor even after controlling for earlier program exposure.

The study of children's interest in violent fairy tales discussed earlier (Collins-Standley et al., 1995) also reported an association between aggressive disposition and interest in violence. There was a positive association between the degree to which children were rated as "aggressive" by their caretakers and their choice of violent fairy tales during the experiment.

The survey on the Madison sample included a question about the parent's judgment of his or her child's level of aggressiveness. To determine whether parents' reports of their child's aggressiveness related to their perceptions of their child's interest in violent programs, children who were rated as not at all violent were assigned to a low-violence category and all others to a high-violence category. As might be expected, the distribution across these cells was different for boys and girls. For boys, 37 percent were assigned to the low-violence category and 63 percent were assigned to the high-violence category. For girls, 68 percent were considered low on violence and 32 percent were considered high on violence. Although these data are completely ambiguous regarding whether aggressiveness leads to violence viewing or vice versa, they do support a positive relationship between the child's level of aggressiveness and his or her interest in some types of aggressive programs—but not others.[7] An analysis of interest in classic cartoons revealed an interaction between gender and violence level. Rated aggressiveness in boys was unrelated to their interest in classic cartoons (the mean for both groups was 2.6). However, more aggressive girls were considerably more interested in classic cartoons than their less aggressive peers (3.1 vs. 2.5, respectively). Children's rated aggressiveness was also significantly related to their interest in action cartoons. Children who were rated by their parents as aggressive were said to be significantly more interested in this genre than those who were rated as nonaggressive (2.5 vs. 1.7, respectively). In contrast, children's aggressiveness was not significantly related to their interest in live-action violent shows or reality-action shows.

To Learn about Their Environment: The Role of Exposure to Community Violence

An alternative to the hypothesis that children like to witness behavior that is similar to their own could be that *children for whom violence is a significant part of their environment are more interested in viewing violence*. There are a variety of reasons that such an interest might exist. One possibility is that children enjoy entertainment programs that are related to their lives and that "resonate," so to speak, with their experience. Another reason could be that children have an instrumental approach to media viewing, and try to expose themselves to media from which they can learn important lessons relevant to their own problems.

These rationales lead to the expectation that children who have a good deal of experience with violence in their lives will be more attracted to media violence. Williams (1989) reports that African-American and Hispanic teenagers comprise 60 percent of the audience for American horror movies and that African American and Hispanic homes with teenagers are three times as likely as Caucasian households to rent horror movies. Goldstein (1986) also noted this phenomenon, remarking upon the predominance of young African American males standing in line to see *Mark of the Devil*, a movie advertised as the first film to be rated V for Violence ("due to the horrifying scenes, no one admitted without a vomit bag," claimed the advertisement). Williams cites Children's Defense Fund statistics that African American children are three times as likely as Caucasian children to be victims of child abuse or to be murdered as teenagers, and argues that it is certain minority groups' exposure to violence that draws them to horror movies. Consistent with the appeal of violence for those who live with violence, Frost and Stauffer (1987) found that inner-city subjects were more likely to support increased production of violent films than were suburban college students. It must be acknowledged here, however, that African Americans expose themselves to more mass media in general than do Caucasians (e.g., Roberts & Bachen, 1981).

Bruce's Milwaukee-area study provides much data relevant to this issue. In her survey, central-city children expressed more interest than their suburban counterparts in viewing very violent programs (3.1 vs. 2.9 on a 4-point scale).[8] Moreover, the children's scores on a set of six items adapted from the National Institute of Mental Health (NIMH) *Survey of Children's Exposure to Community Violence* (Richters & Saltzman, 1990) were significantly correlated with their interest in viewing violent television programs ($r=.13$, $p<.05$). In addition, exposure to community violence correlated significantly with reports of experiencing positive emotions while viewing violence ($r=.25^*$) but was uncorrelated with experiencing negative emotions ($r=-.06$, ns). (See McCauley's chapter in this volume for a discussion of the independence of positive and negative emotional responses to violence.)

To explore the reasons that exposure to violence might predict attraction to television violence, Bruce assessed the relation between exposure to real-life violence and various "gratifications" received from television violence. Exposure to violence was positively correlated with the following gratifications from viewing violence (rank-ordered by strength of the correlation): "Violent shows make me think about things in my own life" ($r=.37^*$), "I like to talk with friends about the things on violent television shows" ($r=.27^*$), "I can learn to protect myself by watching television violence" ($r=.26^*$), and "I enjoy watching people on violent shows fight and hurt each other" ($r=.22^*$).

To Calm Themselves: The Role of Viewer Apprehensions

Another reason for the attraction of violence often advanced is that people expose themselves to violence *to help them cope with their apprehensions and fears about violence in their own lives.* Orbach, Winkler, and Har-Even (1993) contended that children who are frightened by a scary story voluntarily expose and reexpose themselves to the story as a way of learning to master their fears, supporting what they call the "repetition-compulsion" hypothesis. Orbach and his associates' Freudian notion does not presume that the fictional story will project a happy ending, but seems to rely on desensitization by repeated evocation of an emotion. In Orbach et al.'s study, children who were exposed to a truncated version of a frightening fairy tale without the happy ending reported more anxiety than children exposed to the complete fairy tale. Moreover, although the amount of anxiety experienced was not significantly related to desire to hear the story a second time among children who had heard the complete story, the amount of anxiety the truncated story induced was a positive predictor of the child's interest in hearing the story again. This finding seems a bit puzzling at first. An alternative explanation might be that the children had already learned the schema for children's stories, including the fact that they have happy endings. Therefore, they may have been motivated to rehear the story, expecting that the second time they would hear the "proper" resolution. It makes sense, then, that children who had become more anxious upon hearing the truncated story would be more motivated to hear the happy ending.

Most rationales linking the attraction of violence to anxiety reduction, in fact, do involve the assumption that reassuring outcomes to the violent episode are essential. Goldstein (1986) argued that "perhaps witnessing fictional violence can help a person cope with the real violence to which he is exposed; one might learn from the film's characters that violence can be overcome, that it is not really to be feared" (p. 46). Similarly, Boyanowsky (1977) suggested that frightened viewers antici- pate that a film related to the feared outcome will provide information about the threat and how to cope with it. Boyanowsky, Newtson, and Walster's (1974) finding that the attendance of female college students at the violent movie *In Cold Blood* increased 89 percent during the week after the brutal murder of a coed has been interpreted as consistent with this reasoning.

Zillmann (1980) proposed a related argument when he contended that apprehensive individuals selectively expose themselves to suspense- ful (usually violent) programming because the typical plot of such tele- vised fare involves the successful restoration of order and justice at the end of the program. He argued that anxious individuals may be under- going a self-administered desensitization procedure when they expose themselves to dramatic depictions of suspenseful, violent presentations that portray a just resolution.

All of the above rationales lead to the expectation that children who are more anxious should selectively expose themselves to violent content as a means of coping with, or mastering, their anxieties. On the other hand, the opposite relationship could reasonably be expected—children who are easily frightened or highly anxious about violence might come to selectively avoid violent programs to avoid experiencing the negative emotions associated with exposure (see Cantor, 1994).

An experiment by Bryant, Carveth, and Brown (1981) provides data relevant to this issue, although it was conducted with college students. The students were divided into high-versus low-anxiety groups based on personality measures. Students in these groups were then randomly as- signed to view either "light" or "heavy" doses of television for a period of six weeks. Half of the heavy viewers watched action-adventure pro- grams that regularly offered a clear "just" resolution, and the other half viewed shows in which there was a preponderance of crimes for which the evildoers went unpunished. The results revealed that subjects in the high-anxiety group somewhat decreased their anxiety level after the heavy viewing of adventure programs depicting justice. In contrast, highly anxious subjects who underwent a diet of programs depicting injustice showed a dramatic increase in anxiety levels. More important, students who had received heavy doses of justice-restoring drama se- lected to view significantly more action-adventure programs after the experiment was over than those who had been on the other viewing regimens.

The findings of Bryant, Carveth, and Brown (1981) seem to suggest that crime drama depicting the restoration of justice may provide an anxiety-reducing function for anxious individuals and that these individ- uals may selectively expose themselves to such materials for their calming qualities. Both the Madison and Milwaukee studies contain data relevant to this issue. However, they yield what appear at first glance to be contradictory results.

TELEVISION-PRODUCED FRIGHT AND ATTRACTION TO
VIOLENT PROGRAMS

In the study conducted in Madison, there were no questions about the child's general anxiety level or apprehensions about violence. However, there was one related question: parents were asked whether anything on television had ever disturbed, upset, or frightened their child so much that the effect was still there after the program was over. Forty-three percent of the respondents answered this question in the affirmative, and we therefore explored whether children who had been observed to experience a fright reaction were more interested in watching the various forms of violent programming than those who had not shown such a reaction.

Consistent with the reasoning that anxious children would be more interested in viewing violence, children who had experienced a fright reaction from TV were more interested than their less reactive peers in three out of the four violent genres described. Although there was no difference between the two groups in their interest in classic cartoons, children who had been upset were significantly more interested than their less reactive peers in action cartoons (2.3 vs. 1.9), in live-action shows (2.5 vs. 2.1), and in reality-action shows (2.4 vs. 2.1).[9] It is interesting to note that all three genres for which this effect was observed typically depict the triumph of good over evil. Action cartoons and live-action dramas have well-delineated "good guys" and "bad guys" and feature the heroes triumphing in the end. Moreover, reality-action shows exhibit a similar tendency. As Oliver (1994) has recently reported in a content analysis of reality-based police shows, such as *Cops*, these shows grossly overrepresent both the occurrence of violent crimes and the proportion of crimes that are solved. In contrast to these genres, classic cartoons typically portray a series of aggressive activities and pratfalls, with no concept of "good guys" and "bad guys," and no provision of justice or of good triumphing over evil.

TRAUMATIC ANXIETY AND ATTRACTION TO
TELEVISION VIOLENCE

The data on the children in the Milwaukee area present a much different picture, although it must be kept in mind that Bruce's measures of anxiety and attraction are very different from those used in the Madison survey. In focusing on inner-city children, Bruce was primarily interested in studying the type of severe anxiety that is related to "post-traumatic stress disorder" (American Psychiatric Association, DSM-IV, 1994; see also Bruce, 1995b). Therefore, she had her respondents fill out a series of fourteen items adapted from the NIMH *Checklist of Child Distress Symptoms* (Richters & Martinez, 1990) to assess the degree to which they experienced various acute anxiety symptoms, such as hypervigilance, nightmares, and the intrusive recurrence of disturbing thoughts. Contrary to the Madison findings and contrary to the rationales that postulate a positive association between anxiety and attraction to violence, interest in viewing very violent programs was negatively related to anxiety scores ($r = -.12$, $p < .05$). Furthermore, anxiety was positively correlated with reports of feeling negative emotions while viewing violence ($r = .25^*$) and unrelated to feeling positive emotions while viewing it ($r = -.03$, ns).

Bruce also explored the relationship between anxiety and reported gratifications received from viewing violence. Anxiety was positively correlated with children saying that violent programming makes them think about things in their own lives ($r = .38^*$).

CONCERN ABOUT VIOLENCE AND ATTRACTION TO VIOLENT TELEVISION

One reason these findings are so contradictory to the notion that anxiety increases interest in media violence may be that the anxiety measure Bruce used taps very high levels of anxiety, bordering on pathological levels. In addition, the items do not relate specifically to anxiety about violence. Bruce's questionnaire also contained another set of seven items, tapping what might be considered a less intense "concern about violence." These items asked about the probability that the child would be hurt by violence, the perceived seriousness of the consequences of violence, the perceived difficulty of protecting oneself from violence, and the frequency of thinking or worrying about violence.

In contrast to the measure of severe anxiety, this measure of concern about violence was unrelated to interest in viewing violence ($r = -.04$, ns). It was, however, strongly related to feeling negative emotions while viewing TV violence ($r = .33^*$) and negatively related to feeling positive emotions while viewing violence ($r = -.21^*$). Consistent with the notion that anxiety might fuel an interest in the restoration of justice, however, concern about violence was strongly correlated with feeling good when seeing the bad guys get caught ($r = .27^*$).

THE IMPORTANCE OF SEEING THE BAD GUYS GET CAUGHT

Because most rationales related to the use of media violence for anxiety reduction involve the element of seeing justice restored, it is interesting to explore the degree to which interest in television violence is related to interest in seeing the villains brought to justice. The overwhelming majority of children in the Milwaukee-area sample agreed that they enjoyed seeing the "bad guys" get caught (57 percent agreed and another 22 percent agreed strongly). However, in contrast to the earlier mentioned gratification, enjoyment of watching people fight and hurt each other, which was strongly correlated with interest in viewing violence, this item was *negatively* related to interest in violent television ($r = -.19^*$). In other words, although enjoyment of watching the bad guys get caught is a typical attraction of violent content, those who enjoy the just resolution more are less likely to say they would watch a show if they knew it would be very violent.

Comparing the Predictive Power of Various Rationales

After considering eight plausible reasons for the attractiveness of violence and reading this array of sometimes contradictory data, the reader might wonder what conclusions this chapter could possibly provide. Most rationales for the attractiveness of violence have received some support. One approach to choosing among them is to analyze the relative strengths of various antecedent variables in predicting the dependent variables of attraction to violence in the Madison and Milwaukee surveys. In order to compare the contributions of various predictor variables, regression analyses were performed using only antecedent variables. Variables that involve responses *while viewing* violent content, such as arousal, empathy measures, and gratifications, were not included because their high correlations with the dependent variables might be due to the fact that they are indeed partly synonymous with the dependent variable. In other words, feeling excited while watching violence is in some sense another measure of attraction to violence.

To determine the relative contribution of various antecedent variables to the measure of attraction to violent TV for the Milwaukee-area sample, a hierarchical multiple regression analysis was performed using the following variables in the following steps: (1) gender, (2) grade, (3) the index of advice against viewing violence, (4) exposure to community violence, and (5) both traumatic anxiety and concern about violence. The results of this analysis are shown in table 5.2.

This regression analysis revealed that, as expected from the correlations reported earlier, neither concern about violence nor advice against viewing violence were significant predictors of interest in violent TV. Gender was the strongest predictor, contributing 6.3 percent of the variance, with males more strongly attracted. Grade predicted 2.3 percent of the variance, with attraction increasing with grade. Even after controlling for the effects of gender and grade, exposure to community violence was a positive predictor of interest in viewing violence, accounting for 1.7 percent of the variance. And even after the impact of this

TABLE 5.2 Hierarchical Regression Analysis for Variables Predicting Interest in Viewing Very Violent Programs (Milwaukee-Area Sample)

Step	Variable	B	SE B	Beta	Delta R^2	Significance
1.	Gender[a]	.34	.08	.25	.063	***
2.	Grade	.12	.05	.15	.023	**
3.	Advice	−.01	.05	−.02	.000	ns
4.	Violence exposure	.02	.01	.13	.017	*
5.	Anxiety	−.02	.01	−.18	.020[b]	*
	Concern	.01	.01	.06		ns
Full Equation:						
	Gender	.30	.08	.22		***
	Grade	.12	.05	.14		*
	Advice	−.01	.05	−.01		ns
	Violence exposure	.03	.01	.20		**
	Concern	.01	.01	.06		ns
	Anxiety	−.02	.01	−.18		*

[a]Coded as Male=2, Female=1.
[b]When entered by itself on the last step, the R^2 for Anxiety remained the same.
*p.05; **p.01; ***p.001.

and all the other variables was removed, anxiety was negatively correlated with interest in viewing violence, accounting for 2.0 percent of the variance. What this suggests is that exposure to real-life violence contributes to interest in viewing violence, but after controlling for exposure to violence, high levels of anxiety are associated with reduced interest in viewing violence.

A similar hierarchical regression analysis was performed on the Madison data to determine which antecedent variables best predicted interest in the four TV-program genres. First, interest in classic cartoons was predicted by variables in the following steps: (1) gender, (2) grade, (3) whether or not the parent restricted violent programming, and (4) both whether the child had had a fright reaction to television and the child's aggression level. In this analysis, the only significant predictor was grade (Beta=−.15, $p<.05$). Interest in classic cartoons was negatively related to grade in school, with grade contributing 2.3 percent of the variance.

Because the other three genres—action cartoons, live-action shows, and reality-action shows—are theoretically similar, in that they all depict violence in the context of justice restoration, a regression analysis was performed on a combined index of interest in the three genres, using the same five predictor variables in the same order. Table 5.3 shows the results of this analysis. As can be seen from the table, gender contributed 9.6 percent of the variance in attraction to these genres (with males

TABLE 5.3 Hierarchical Regression Analysis for Variables Predicting Interest in Viewing Justice-Depicting Genres (Madison Sample)

Step	Variable	B	SE B	Beta	Delta R^2	Significance
1.	Gender[a]	.53	.10	.31	.096	***
2.	Grade	−.14	.04	−.19	.036	***
3.	Violence restricted	.05	.10	.03	.001	ns
4.	TV fright	.34	.10	.19	.067	***
	Aggressiveness	.18	.06	.17		**
Full Equation:						
	Gender	.46	.10	.27		***
	Grade	−.12	.04	−.16		**
	Violence restricted	−.04	.10	−.00		ns
	TV fright	.34	.10	.19		***
	Aggressiveness	.18	.06	.17		**

[a]Coded as Male=2, Female=1.
[b]Entered on the last step, TV fright was associated with Delta R^2=.037; entered on the last step, Aggressiveness was associated with Delta R^2=.025.
**$p<.01$; ***$p<.001$.

showing greater interest), and grade contributed another 3.6 percent (with interest decreasing with grade). Parental restriction of violent television was not a significant predictor, but both fright reactions and aggression level were positively related to interest, and contributed significantly even after all other variables were accounted for. When each was added on the last step, having had a fright reaction to television contributed 3.7 percent of the variance and aggressiveness contributed 2.5 percent.

Making Sense of the Consistencies and Inconsistencies

Almost all the rationales advanced for the attraction of violence have received some support here. The only exception is the "forbidden fruit" hypothesis. Although there is intuitive appeal to the notion that children have a special interest in media violence because they are repeatedly barraged with messages telling them that it's bad for them, neither the Milwaukee nor the Madison data provided support for the notion.

The remaining rationales were all supported to some extent, although the amount of data available on which to evaluate them varies. The notion that violence is attractive because it is arousing is a viable one. Previous research shows that children do react with increased arousal to media violence. Moreover, research on sensation seeking links this variable to interest in the highly violent horror genre. Finally,

Bruce's data revealed that interest in viewing TV violence was strongly correlated with feeling excited while viewing.

The rationale regarding vicarious participation in aggression received some support in Bruce's data. However, the findings showed that the only empathy measure that was a positive predictor of attraction to violent television was empathic participation in the activities of the aggressor. Surprisingly, the tendency to place oneself mentally in the position of the "good guy" was a negative predictor of Bruce's attraction measure.

The rationale linking gender to attraction to violence received a great deal of support, both in the review of earlier studies and in the data from Madison and Milwaukee. Males have consistently reported more attraction to violent media in a wide range of studies, and gender was the strongest predictor of attraction in both recent data sets. This sex difference was not universal, however. In the Madison sample, there was no difference between males and females in their attraction to classic cartoons or to reality-based action shows. Moreover, the gender difference does not provide us with any information about what it is about being male or female that accounts for the attraction difference. And particularly, most of the data do not rule out the alternative explanation that girls are uninterested in violent TV genres because female violent characters are so rare.

The analyses testing the relationship of age (grade) to interest in violence showed that age is a significant contributor to the attraction of violent television. However, the direction of this relationship varies as a function of specific genres.

The rationale linking attraction to violence with the viewer's violent disposition or behavior received support, with most previous studies finding positive relationships between dispositional violence or experimentally induced aggressiveness and interest in viewing violence. Although the causal direction is ambiguous, the Madison data provided some support for this notion as well: Parents who rated their children as violent also rated them as more interested in action cartoons. Moreover, girls who were rated as violent were reported to be more interested than their less aggressive peers in classic cartoons.

The rationale relating exposure to violence in the real world to attraction to violent television was consistent with previous research and received support in Bruce's survey. Central-city Milwaukee children were more interested in viewing violence than were their suburban counterparts, and the index of exposure to community violence was significantly related to interest in violent television. Bruce's survey provided possible explanatory data for this finding as well, since exposure to community violence was positively related to gratifications associated with learning about things related to their own lives.

The anxiety-reduction hypothesis yielded the most complex and seemingly contradictory findings. The data from Madison are most consistent with the notion that anxious children seek out violent programming that features heroes triumphing over villains in an effort to control their anxieties. Children in Madison who had been frightened by something on television were rated as being more interested than the other children in action cartoons, live-action shows, and reality-action programs—the three genres that feature clear delineations of good and evil and the reliable restoration of justice at the end. And they were not differentially interested in classic cartoons, the one genre where considerations of justice are absent, and in which anxiety is unlikely to be increased or reduced in any event.

The Milwaukee-area data paint an entirely different picture of this relationship. Contrary to the anxiety-reduction hypothesis, severe anxiety was a significant negative predictor of interest in television violence. Moreover, the less intense measure, concern about violence, was unrelated to interest in TV violence. However, consistent with the anxiety-reduction hypothesis, concern about violence was significantly correlated with feeling good when seeing the "bad guys" brought to justice.

One way of resolving the apparent contradictions between the Madison and Milwaukee studies regarding the relationship between anxiety and attraction to violence is to look more closely at the two attraction-to-violence measures. The attraction measures for the Madison survey related to interest in specific violent genres that reliably present violence in well-determined ways. The attraction measure for the Milwaukee survey was quite different. The question, "Would you watch a television show if you knew it contained a lot of violence?" could, in essence, be characterized as a measure of attraction to violence for violence's sake. In contrast to the attraction-to-genres measures used in Madison, nothing is implied about any potentially reassuring outcome or the triumph of good over evil. Thus, it is not surprising that the Milwaukee attraction-to-violence measure correlated positively with enjoyment of watching people fight and hurt each other, but negatively with feeling good when the "bad guys" get caught. In the Milwaukee sample, then, it seems logical that anxiety would be negatively related to attraction to violence per se. It is interesting that exposure to violence in the child's own life was strongly related to this violence-for-violence's-sake measure and to sheer enjoyment of watching people fight and hurt each other. This attraction measure, it will be recalled, was positively associated with empathizing with the aggressor and *negatively* associated with empathizing with the "good guy."

One conclusion that these analyses support is that it is important to specify the type of violence in posing questions about violence's attractiveness. Typical violent television series might be characterized as anxiety-reducing, justice-restoring genres that attract anxious, more empathic children, who side emotionally with the "good guy" over the "bad guy" and use the programs to control their anxieties. Violence for violence's sake should be considered separately. Children who are attracted by something described only as "very violent" are more likely to be children with a good deal of exposure to violence in their own lives, who watch it in a detached, unempathic fashion and enjoy the violence irrespective of moral considerations or outcomes to protagonists.

The preceding explanation is highly speculative, of course, and certainly warrants examination in a more systematic fashion. Research in which both of the observed relationships occur in the same data set needs to be done. In addition, interest in viewing violence should be assessed directly, by providing children with actual viewing choices (and perhaps varying the content of program descriptions, or better yet, creating programs in various versions). In addition, the tendency to feel different emotions or to differentially empathize should be measured at the time of viewing rather than assessed retrospectively or with regard to hypothetical viewing situations.

In conclusion, this chapter has brought together a wide array of data and theories relevant to the issue of children's attraction to violent television. The data and these arguments seem to point directly to the conclusion that violence is attractive to children and that it is one way to attract a large audience. According to the speculations advanced above, violence may have the advantage that it provides different attractions for different types of children. For a jaded, calloused, violence-battered child, it might provide the sheer exhilaration of watching a "good fight." For a less "macho," more sheltered, more empathic and emotionally reactive child, violent television, especially that which shows the triumph of good over evil, may provide a means of coping with anxiety.

If these speculations hold up under more systematic scrutiny, they may explain, in part, why violent programs are repeatedly successful with child audiences: In catering to both the jaded and the meek, they perhaps provide "something for everyone."

But in the final analysis, the popularity of violence must be seen in the context of other genres. The data on program ratings revealed that it is situation comedies, not violent programs, that currently attract the largest audiences of children in the United States. Researchers should therefore begin to study the reasons for the attractiveness of nonviolent genres as well. Understanding what draws children to watch and enjoy family interactions as they typically occur on television would indeed be useful. It is also important to remember that even highly violent programs are composed of a variety of other elements that may contribute to their attractiveness. As the opening quote of this chapter suggests, even the highly controversial Power Rangers spend a good portion of broadcast time portraying nonviolent, affiliative relations among teenagers. The contribution of such portrayals to the appeal of this and similar programs cannot be overlooked if we want to more fully understand the important role that children's entertainment choices play in their daily lives and their long-term development.

Notes

I would like to give my sincere thanks to Lisa Bruce for performing the analyses on her data set that are relevant to the various issues addressed in this chapter. I would also like to thank Amy Nathanson for assisting me with the data analyses on the Madison data set. I thank both Lisa and Amy for their thoughtful input into the issues discussed.

1. For these data, 1 ratings point translates to 377,000 child viewers.

2. To simplify presentation of data, the sample size associated with each correlation will not be presented. Correlations computed on the Milwaukee survey were based on N's ranging from 257 to 313. Unless otherwise indicated, all r's are significant at $p < .01$; correlations significant at $p < .001$ are designated with an asterisk (*). More detailed data regarding these correlations can be found in Bruce 1995a.

3. For the gender difference, $t(310) = 4.50$, $p < .001$.

4. For action cartoons, $F(269) = 47.74$, $p < .001$; for live-action shows, $F(1,267) = 19.40$, $p < .001$.

5. Overall $X^2(2) = 6.07$, $p < .05$.

6. For the interaction between gender and violence level and interest in classic cartoons, $F(1,260) = 5.52$, $p < .05$; for the main effect of aggressiveness on interest in action cartoons, $F(1,260) = 14.91$, $p < .001$.

7. For the central-city/suburban comparison, $t(311) = 2.25$, $p < .05$.

8. The main effects of fright reactions were associated with $F(1,260) = 9.38$, $p < .01$; $F(1,258) = 5.55$, $p < .05$; and $F(1,258) = 5.86$, $p < .05$, for action cartoons, live-action shows, and reality-action shows, respectively.

6

"A Test for the Individual Viewer": *Bonnie and Clyde*'s Violent Reception

J. HOBERMAN

The Case of *Bonnie and Clyde*

To posit sexual display and violent action as the two most universal "attractions" of Hollywood movies is merely to state the obvious. In a practical sense, success for American movies may be gauged by the degree to which they are able to mass-produce audience excitement. There have, however, been instances in which that mass excitement has itself been deemed dangerously overstimulating.

Initially characterized as "tasteless" and "grisly" (*Time*, Aug. 25, 1967); as "stomach-turning" (*Newsweek*, Aug. 21, 1967); as "reprehensible," "gross and demeaning," featuring "some of the most gruesome carnage since Verdun" (*Newsweek*, Aug. 28, 1967); as "dementia praecox of the most pointless sort" (*Films in Review*, Oct. 1967), Arthur Penn's 1967 release *Bonnie and Clyde* served, more than any commercial movie made in America before or since, to redefine the nature of acceptable on-screen violence. "A test for the individual viewer for his own threshhold," per one early reviewer, *Bonnie and Clyde* encouraged laughing "at sadism and murder [but] eventually repels you, and makes you angry or ashamed at having had your emotions manipulated" (*Newsday*, Aug. 14, 1967).

American mass culture may be considered a form of spectacular political theater that also functions as a feedback system. It is within this public space—which overlaps the arena of electoral politics—that rival scenarios and contending abstractions struggle for existence, definition, and acceptance. Thus, at once highly popular and extremely polarizing (itself an unusual accomplishment for a Hollywood movie), *Bonnie and Clyde* is significant as much for what it symbolized as for what it actually depicted.

Written by Robert Benton and David Newman, *Bonnie and Clyde* takes as its subject the quasi-historical, increasingly violent criminal exploits of a young couple and their accomplices throughout the central Southwest during the early 1930s. The story was sufficiently compelling to have inspired a number of previous movies. Nevertheless, *Bonnie and Clyde* was unprecedented both in foregrounding mayhem as a choreographed spectacle—most notoriously in the two-minute *danse macabre* that, ending the movie with a metaphor for the cinema itself, offered the startling image of the protagonists' corpses reanimated by a barrage of gunfire—and in offering a scenario that, despite its period setting, was widely cited for its contemporary relevance.

Bonnie and Clyde remains important today as much for the shift in attitude that it embodies as for its intrinsic value as film—or even for the particular magnitude of its violence. Within two years of its release, the movie had already been supplanted as the ultimate in cinematic carnage by Sam Peckinpah's *The Wild Bunch*, which featured even further distended slow motion, additional spurting blood, and more kinetic editing. "A pace-setter in the display of violence," *The Wild Bunch*'s climactic Götterdämmerung served as the "aggressive" film footage in a 1973 National Institute of Mental Health study, "Motivated Aggressiveness Perpetuated by Exposure to Aggressive Films and Reduced by Exposure to Nonaggressive Films."[1]

Nevertheless, over a quarter century after *Bonnie and Clyde*'s controversial premiere, political pundit David R. Boldt used the editorial page of the *Philadelphia Inquirer* (Aug. 1, 1993) to attack the movie as the source for Hollywood "pornoviolence." If *Bonnie and Clyde* has been "largely forgotten," Boldt wrote, it is only "because its wretched excesses have been exceeded so often." For Boldt, *Bonnie and Clyde* represents something akin to a national fall from grace: "I think we went wrong with the release of *Bonnie and Clyde* . . . the first in a wave of movies that came to the screen immediately after Hollywood's self-policing apparatus was dismantled in 1966. . . ."

Boldt remembers his own negative response to *Bonnie and Clyde* as having been sharpened by a sense of social foreboding and alienation from the rest of the audience—which, he imagined, was enjoying the movie for the very reasons he loathed it: "All I knew the first time I saw it was that *Bonnie and Clyde* was a malignantly manipulative movie—and that all the other people in the theater around me seemed to be eating it up. I can actually recall thinking to myself at the time, 'This is it. We've had it.' " As Boldt further notes, *Bonnie and Clyde* is not simply a violent display. It is a violent display given a particular perspective: "The entire film is told from the point of view of the criminals."

The implications are clear. Liberated from the constraints of the movie industry's traditional "self-policing apparatus," the movie audience may be manipulated into passive complicity with the portrayal of criminal violence. Indeed, this complicity is perhaps an integral aspect of the mass audience's enjoyment. A movie like *Bonnie and Clyde* is thus itself a sort of symbolic crime—it makes us something like accomplices to murder. Of course, it is also possible that a discussion of the violence in *Bonnie and Clyde* is a way to talk about something else.

Historical Precedents

The question of violence in American movies has typically been linked to the representation of some criminal activity—most frequently episodes of gangsterism or juvenile delinquency. In fact, it is sometimes only in the context of criminal behavior that screen violence may even be perceived as problematic. Senator Bob Dole's widely publicized June 1995 attack on the American entertainment industry singled out *Natural Born Killers*, a movie concerning a murderous outlaw couple clearly modeled on Bonnie and Clyde, as a "nightmare of depravity" while citing *True Lies*, a scarcely less bloody film in which Arnold Schwarzenegger plays an American espionage agent, as being "friendly to families."

In any case, the question of violence in American movies has largely been secondary to issues of sexual behavior. The earliest reported case of American movie censorship—in which Chicago police denied an exhibition permit to Essanay's 1908 *The James Boys in Missouri* for "criminalizing" American history—involved the representation of violent lawbreaking (de Grazia & Newman, 1982, pp. 177–78). Nevertheless, the 1927 Motion Picture Association of America (MPAA) Production Code, administered by Will B. Hays, was almost exclusively concerned with issues of sex and nudity. The treatment of illegal behavior was not even raised as a question until the revised 1930 MPAA Code, which had been formulated in response to silent gangster films, like Josef von Sternberg's 1927 *Underworld* and 1928 *The Docks of New York* (Bergman, 1971, p. 5).

Little Caesar, released by Warner Brothers in early 1931, helped stimulate a subsequent cycle of gangster talkies. Popular and controversial, these movies made so great an impact that, as film historian Carlos Clarens would later note, "a mere 10 percent of [Hollywood's] yearly output suddenly came to represent the dominant trend" (1980, p. 81). Gangster movies were blamed for inciting violence—perhaps even that of the historical Bonnie and Clyde—as well as for providing practical information as to its application. In the summer of 1931, for example, it was reported that a New Jersey twelve-year-old returned from seeing

The Secret Six and consequently shot another child through the head (Bergman, 1971, p. 4).

The presumed threat was thus the possibility that impressionable members of the audience might wish to participate in that which the movie seemed to celebrate. "Does not the exhibition of gangster pictures in the so-called high delinquency neighborhoods amount to the diffusion of poison?" the 1933 best-seller *Our Movie Made Children* asked in devoting a major portion of its penultimate chapter to the sometimes fatal impact that *Little Caesar* had had upon impressionable young slum dwellers (Forman, 1935, pp. 195, 265ff.).

Attempting to maintain respectable perimeters for screen violence, the Hays Office proscribed on-screen bleeding and stipulated that a firearm and its victim not be framed together in the same shot. Hays was, however, challenged by the most violent gangster film of the cycle, Howard Hughes's *Scarface*. The MPAA office returned *Scarface*'s script with the following directive from Hays: "Under no circumstances is this film to be made. The American public and all conscientious State Boards of Censorship find mobsters and hoodlums repugnant. Gangsterism must not be mentioned in the cinema. If you should be foolhardy enough to make Scarface, this office will make certain it is never released" (Clarens, 1980, p. 82). Hughes, unimpressed, is supposed to have told his director, Howard Hawks, to "screw the Hays Office [and] start the picture." Despite some cuts and a few local bans, Hughes—who would, a decade later, tangle with the Hays Office over the issue of Jane Russell's cleavage in *The Outlaw*—prevailed (Clarens, 1980, De Grazia & Newman, 1982, p. 36).

The first "General Principle" of the 1930 MPAA Production Code was that "no picture shall be produced which will lower the moral standards of those who see it. Hence the sympathy of the audience should never be thrown to the side of crime, wrongdoing, evil or sin." (It was further mandated, under the section "Crimes against the Law: Murder," that "brutal killings [were] not to be presented in detail" and any "use of firearms [would be] restricted to essentials.") Nevertheless, the MPAA Code was not truly enforced until 1934, when the Hays Office was given additional muscle by the Catholic Legion of Decency. Again, the association of violence with criminal behavior was crucial. In the mid-1930s, Warner Brothers revamped and elevated the gangster genre with movies like *G-Men* (1935), *Bullets or Ballots* (1936), and *Public Enemy's Wife* (1936), which glorified the role of the FBI and were, in some cases, endorsed by its director, J. Edgar Hoover (Bergman, 1971, pp. 84–88).

Thereafter, despite an occasional incident—the 1941 *Blood and Sand* remake was, for example, required to tone down a "gruesome" bullfight sequence (Leff & Simmons, 1990, p. 119)—the issue of on-screen violence lay largely dormant until several years after World War

II, when cuts were demanded in the 1949 juvenile-delinquency drama *City across the River* (Doherty, 1988, p. 119). The juvenile-delinquency cycle also included *Knock on Any Door* and *Bad Boy*, both 1949, as well as two other 1949 movies that can be seen as thematic precursors of *Bonnie and Clyde: Gun Crazy* and *They Live by Night*. A subsequent juvenile-delinquency movie, *The Blackboard Jungle*, and the Mike Hammer thriller *Kiss Me Deadly* (both 1955), initially rejected by censors, were prominently cited in the 1955 hearings held by presidential hopeful Estes Kefauver's Senate subcommittee on juvenile delinquency—as was the as yet unreleased *Rebel without a Cause* (Schumach, 1964, pp. 174–78).[2]

In 1957, Don Siegel's *Baby Face Nelson*, made for the low-budget studio Allied Artists, broke the MPAA interdiction against the representation of historical criminals. The following year, another small studio, American-International Pictures (which specialized in topical, drive-in fare) resurrected two early-1930s bandits for a teen-oriented double bill, *Machine Gun Kelly* and *The Bonnie Parker Story*. Roused to action, J. Edgar Hoover nostalgically warned that "In the face of the nation's terrifying juvenile crime wave we are threatened with a flood of movies and television productions which flaunt indecency and applaud lawlessness. Not since the days when thousands passed the bier of the infamous John Dillinger and made his home a virtual shrine have we witnessed such a brazen affront to our national conscience" (*Motion Picture Herald*, May 10, 1958). Despite this concern, however, violence in the movies would not reemerge as a significant issue for another decade—and only then in the context of a presidential assassination, an escalating, if undeclared, war, and a succession of civil disorders that would shock and convulse American society.

The Problem of Pornoviolence

David Boldt doesn't define (or credit) his apparent neologism "pornoviolence," but the term, like the movie to which he applied it, first appeared during the summer of 1967. Attempting to answer the question, "Why Are We Suddenly Obsessed with Violence?" posed by the July 1967 issue of *Esquire*, Tom Wolfe's essay, "Pornoviolence," analyzed such variegated phenomena as the sensational weekly tabloid the *National Enquirer*, an episode of the TV western *Gunsmoke*, Truman Capote's best-selling nonfiction novel *In Cold Blood*, and the sustained popularity of James Bond as exemplars of a "new pornography, the pornography of violence."

What was it that made this "pornography" new? Albeit restricting his discussion to the realm of cultural production, Wolfe was struck by the widespread, obsessive interest in the minutiae of John F. Kennedy's death: "There has been an incessant replay, with every recoverable clinical detail, of those less than five seconds in which a man got his head blown off." Imagining that the preferred "vantage point" was "almost never that of the victim [but rather] the view from Oswald's rifle," Wolfe described a pornoviolence that was essentially spectacular and purely sensational: "The camera angle, therefore the viewer, is with the gun, the fist, the rock. . . . You do not live the action through the hero's eyes. You live with the aggressor, whoever he may be" (Wolfe, 1977, pp. 161–62).

Wolfe linked this desire to align oneself with the instrument of aggression to the experience (and, in its compulsive repetition, Freud would suggest, to the attempted mastery) of a national trauma. As profoundly abrupt and disorderly as it was, the Kennedy assassination undermined the logic of the American democratic process. A history-altering crime by its very nature, the murder of the American president could not help but support the notion argued by the French revolutionary theorist Georges Sorel (1847–1922) that all great social change is inevitably marked by violence (Roth, 1980, pp. 50–51). For a sizable part of the American public, then, violence was not simply a source of excitement but an integral part of the historical process.

Among other articles, the July *Esquire* included one far less judgmental than Wolfe's. In "Now Let the Festivities Begin," regular contributors Robert Benton and David Newman surveyed those cultural artifacts that embodied " 'the fun' of violence." Casting a wider net than Wolfe's to better snare the zeitgeist, the writers cited evidence ranging from true-crime best-sellers (*The Boston Strangler* and *In Cold Blood*) and current theatrical offerings (*Marat/Sade, Dutchman, MacBird*) through musicians as varied as the Rolling Stones and Archie Shepp to images as disparate as Andy Warhol's electric chairs, Francis Bacon's flayed bodies, and Marvel comic books. What these all had in common, per Benton and Newman, was their attitude: "The rules of reaction have changed: it's not that old catharsis any longer, but that new kick."

Catharsis connotes tragedy. But unlike Aristotle (or Tom Wolfe), Benton and Newman did not take any particular moral attitude toward the artistic representation of mayhem. Rather than a new pornography of violence, they would seem to propose a wide-ranging and fashionable aesthetic of violence for violence's sake—a violence of style as well as content. Benton and Newman were not only the screenwriters for *Bonnie and Clyde*; they had originated the entire project. Although the writers scrupulously avoided plugging their long-germinating but soon-to-be-released film, the entire issue of *Esquire* may be seen as a rehearsal for its reception.

Bonnie and Clyde had its world premiere on August 4, 1967, as the gala opening attraction of the Montreal International Film Festival (itself part of the world's fair, Expo 67). Bosley Crowther, the *New York Times* critic and then dean of American daily movie reviewers, was in attendance and subsequently declared himself amazed that "so callous and callow a film should represent [the] country in these critical times." *Bonnie and Clyde* was the "indulgence of a restless and reckless taste, and an embarrassing addition to an excess of violence on the screen" (*New York Times*, Aug. 7, 1967).[3]

Crowther was already in the midst of a campaign against movie violence, up until then exemplified by *The Dirty Dozen*, a new and highly popular war film. *The Dirty Dozen* had its world premiere in New York on June 16. The movie set house records at the Loew's Capitol, a large Broadway theater, and, after opening nationally over the July 4 weekend, enjoyed the highest grossing week of any single picture in distributor MGM's history. Indeed, *The Dirty Dozen* sold an unprecedented $15 million worth of tickets during its first two months in release—a period that also brought a marked increase in American civil violence, much of it racial in nature and virtually all of it directed against the police.

On a symbolic level, the hot summer of 1967 opened on the afternoon of May 2, when eighteen representatives of the Oakland-based Black Panther Party for Defense provoked a media sensation by appearing, armed with M1 rifles and twelve-gauge shotguns, at the California state capitol building in Sacramento. Two weeks later, a Houston policeman was killed by sniper fire during disturbances at the predominantly black Texas Southern University. That same night in Washington, D.C., the controversial Student Non-Violent Coordinating Committee (SNCC) chairman Stokely Carmichael declared that "we're going to shoot the cops who are shooting our black brothers in the back in this country" (*U.S. News and World Report* May 29, 1967). A number of American cities, including Boston, Tampa, Dayton, Atlanta, Buffalo, and Cincinnati, experienced a series of race riots over the next month. (Meanwhile, on June 23 in Los Angeles, police—for the first time—used force to break up a demonstration against President Lyndon Johnson and the American war in Vietnam.)

The Dirty Dozen's extraordinary popularity thus coincided with a season of nationally televised violence. June's relatively minor disturbances set the stage for the far more extensive Newark disorders that raged from July 12 through July 17, leaving twenty-three dead and causing $10 million in damages. The following weekend's Detroit riots (which ultimately required a force of eight thousand National Guardsmen and forty-seven hundred paratroopers to put down) produced nearly twice as many casualties and doubled the estimated cost of destruction. On July 30, the same day that order was finally restored in Detroit, the *New York Times* had published the latest missive in Crowther's crusade under the perhaps dismissive headline "Another Smash at Violence."

Here, the critic took issue with those who had written to the *Times* to attack his attack on *The Dirty Dozen* (or, in one case, question his objections to the Italian western *For a Few Dollars More*, released in late June). To those who argued that violent movies manifested an accurate reflection of current American social reality and, in particular, the war in Vietnam, Crowther replied that, "By habituating the public to violence and brutality—by making these hideous exercises into morbid and sadistic jokes, as is done in *The Dirty Dozen*—these films of excessive violence only deaden their sensitivities and make slaughter seem a meaningless cliche."

Hardly clichéd, however, *The Dirty Dozen* evoked World War II in a drastically revisionist way. The film's eponymous antiheroes are a unit composed of murderers, rapists, and other violent misfits, released from the brig and commanded by a tough colonel (Lee Marvin) who has been ordered by the cynical American brass to lead them on a suicide mission behind enemy lines. On one hand, *The Dirty Dozen* is a glorification of dirty fighting that openly mocks society's ambivalent dependence on the killer instinct. An army psychologist calls the Dozen "the most twisted bunch of antisocial psychopaths," adding that he "can't think of a better way to fight a war" and thus endorsing what could be termed the movie's tough-minded realpolitik, its "dirty" secret. On the other hand, the movie is an attack on authority—of any kind. American commanding officers, no less than their German adversaries, are shown as essentially corrupt and unfeeling.[4]

Although *The Dirty Dozen* opens with a graphic representation of a hanging (the first of the "repellent subjects" that the 1930 MPAA Code stipulated be "treated within the careful limits of good taste"), extraordinary mayhem is withheld until the final mission. Then, with an undeniable slapstick quality, the Dozen trap the German generals—together with a number of innocent civilians, most of them women—in an underground bunker. They then pour gasoline through ventilator shafts and drop in live grenades. Unfolding in an atmosphere of frenzied cruelty, this astonishing sequence manages to invoke mass death by a combination of gas-chamber asphyxiation, saturation bombing, and napalm.

When *The Dirty Dozen* opened in New York, many reviewers appeared to be shocked and revolted. Despite the movie's ambiguous relation to violence, few experienced the excessively graphic *Dirty Dozen* as antiwar so much as a crude and overly enthusiastic celebration of war—and this at a time when their own country was engaged in a major military operation. Crowther was the most outspoken in labeling the film "a raw and preposterous glorification of a group of criminal soldiers who are trained to kill and who then go about this brutal business with hot sadistic zeal . . . an astonishingly wanton war movie. . . . morbid and disgusting beyond words" (*New York Times*, June 16, 1967).

By Crowther's lights, *The Dirty Dozen* was not only violent but irresponsible. The movie's mayhem constituted a form of dangerous hyperbole akin to demagoguery. In objecting to the portrayal of the Dozen themselves, Crowther might almost have been attacking those leaders, SNCC chairman Carmichael and his successor H. Rap Brown, whose inflammatory rhetoric was widely reported and condemned before and, particularly, throughout the summer's riots. "To bathe these rascals in a specious heroic light—to make their hoodlum bravado and defiance of discipline, and their nasty kind of gutter solidarity, seem exhilirating and admirable—is encouraging a spirit of hooliganism that is brazenly antisocial, to say the least."

A number of *The Dirty Dozen*'s reviews are similarly characterized by an unusual concern for the movie's effect upon its spectators. *Newsweek* (July 2, 1967) complained that the "orgy of unrestrained violence" with which *The Dirty Dozen* climaxed was designed "to stir only the atavistic passions of this audience." The *New York Post* (June 16, 1967) termed it "roughage for an audience needing entertainment increasingly hyped for the hardened" in which "kill-crazy brutality is exploitated to the utmost" and concluded that it "could be a crowd pleaser." The *Daily News* (June 16, 1967) remarked that *The Dirty Dozen* opened to "the loudest blast of applause ever heard on old Broadway," while the *New Yorker* (July 22, 1967) observed that "the moronic muggings of the title characters were hailed by colleague thugs in the audience with gales of comradely laughter."

Mass excitement may be deemed overstimulating when violence is linked to the representation of criminal activity. *The Dirty Dozen* was understood less as a comment on warfare than, at once violent and antiauthoritarian, something that might be incitement to riot—although there is no evidence of any disturbances in any theater during the course of its release.

Andrew Sarris in the *Village Voice* (June 29, 1967) was somewhat more specific and politically attuned in terming *The Dirty Dozen* "a glorification of the dropout [that was] well suited to slum fantasizing." Without specifically mentioning America's season of violence, Sarris theorized the source of the movie's appeal:

> Jean Renoir has observed that people are moved more by magic than by logic. To sit in the balcony of the Capitol while Clint Walker and Jim Brown [both relatively sympathetic members of the Dirty Dozen] are demolishing two finky noncoms is to confirm this observation. All the well-intentioned Operation Bootstrap cinema in the world cannot provide underdog audiences with the emotional release achieved almost effortlessly with one shot to the solar plexus. It's sad, but true. Blood is thicker than progressive porridge.

So it would be with the even more "political" and antiauthoritarian *Bonnie and Clyde*.

Bonnie and Clyde's Critical Reception

Considering *Bonnie and Clyde*'s violence quotient, *Variety* (Aug. 9, 1967) had recommended a "hard-sell exploitation campaign." Warner Brothers complied, using one of the most outrageous slogans of the period for the first advertisement to run in the *New York Times* (Aug. 13, 1967): "They're young . . . they're in love . . . and they kill people."[5]

Such flippancy was provocative, and the critical response when *Bonnie and Clyde* opened in New York, on August 13, 1967, was no less strong. The "blending of farce with brutal killings is as pointless as it is lacking in taste," Crowther wrote in the *New York Times*. Then, something unusual happened. "We got advertising we never could have afforded," director Arthur Penn would recall twenty-seven years later in the course of a public interview at the American Museum of the Moving Image (Nov. 12, 1994). The *Times* was flooded with letters attacking Crowther, who felt compelled to publish yet a third denunciation of *Bonnie and Clyde*, this time accusing the movie of distorting history and, like *The Dirty Dozen*, pandering to a fashionable anti-Establishment anger.[6]

Such anger may have been even more fashionable than Crowther feared. That same week, in an unprecedented second review (Aug. 28, 1967), *Newsweek* critic Joseph Morgenstern recanted his original, *Dirty Dozen*–like characterization of *Bonnie and Clyde* as "a squalid shoot-'em up for the moron trade."

Now, Warner Brothers was running print ads in which the Barrow Gang thanked New York for its support while *Variety* (Aug. 30, 1967) gleefully reported the fracas as "Crowther's 'Bonnie'-Brook." The *Times* published another half-dozen letters praising *Bonnie and Clyde* as well as an interview with Arthur Penn in which he responded to Crowther's charges, arguing that his film was, if anything, a cautionary treatment: "The trouble with the violence in most films is that it is not violent enough" (Sept. 17, 1967). Let *Films in Review* (Oct. 1967) call *Bonnie and Clyde* "evil"; the *New Yorker* ran two positive reviews. Critic Penelope Gilliat's original notice was followed two months later, in the October 21 issue, by freelancer Pauline Kael's nine-thousand-word manifesto: "The innocuousness of most of our movies is accepted with such complacence that when an American movie reaches people, when it makes them react, some of them think there must be something the matter with it—perhaps a law should be passed against it."

Kael raised the rhetorical stakes considerably by linking her defense of *Bonnie and Clyde* to issues of free speech, illegality, and even insurrection, while implicitly defending the overthrow of the MPAA Code. At the same time, she suggested that *Bonnie and Clyde* was perceived as dangerous precisely because it succeeded in popularizing a hitherto rarefied attitude toward criminal violence: "*Bonnie and Clyde* brings

FIGURE 6.1 *Variety* had recommended a "hard-sell exploitation campaign" and Warner Brothers complied, using one of the most outrageous slogans of the period for *Bonnie and Clyde:* "They're young . . . they're in love . . . and they kill people." Courtesy of Warner Bros. © 1967 Warner Bros.—Seven Arts and Tatira-Hiller Productions.

into the almost frighteningly public world of movies things that people have been feeling and saying and writing about." Presumably, these might include the cultural artifacts that Benton and Newman surveyed in "Now Let the Festivities Begin" as well as the philosophical justification for political violence found, for example, in Frantz Fanon's *The Wretched of the Earth*.

Movies, as the anxious response to *The Dirty Dozen* suggests, considerably democratized the audience. "Once something is said or done on the screens of the world, once it has entered mass art, it can never again belong to a minority, never again be the private possession of an educated, or 'knowing' group." The movie *Bonnie and Clyde*, like the historical Bonnie and Clyde, appeared to Kael to be acting out "forbidden roles" and popularizing illicit thrills. Indeed, establishing itself as a post-MPAA (and post-liberal) release, *Bonnie and Clyde* wastes little time establishing a social or psychological basis for its protagonists' criminal behavior—the better to dwell on that behavior itself. Moreover, from the onset, the capacity for criminal violence is shown alternately as a substitute for or a stimulant to sexual relations.

Bored waitress Bonnie Parker (Faye Dunaway) and brash ex-con Clyde Barrow (Warren Beatty) meet on a dusty, depressed West Dallas afternoon when she foils his attempt to steal her mother's Model T. The scene is frought with erotic suggestion. Bonnie, who observes Clyde from her bedroom window, is herself nude when first seen by him (and us). After thwarted Clyde proudly shows her his revolver, she fondles the barrel suggestively and taunts him into robbing a grocery store. Clyde does so and Bonnie is so aroused she literally throws herself at the gunman as they careen off in their newly stolen getaway car. To her disappointment, he is sexually impotent. In a scene thus frought with embarrassment and anxiety, Clyde reasserts control by appealing to Bonnie's desire for glamour and successfully enlisting her as his accomplice in crime. Clyde, as he says, may not be a "lover boy," but he is evidentally a crack shot and much is made of his teaching eager Bonnie how to handle a gun.

The movie's initial tone is saucy and lighthearted, with frequent use of the rollicking banjo piece "Foggy Mountain Breakdown" as a theme for the outlaw pair's comic mishaps. Holding up another grocery, Clyde narrowly avoids having his head split by a clerk who attacks him from behind with a meat cleaver. ("He tried to kill me," he tells Bonnie in amazement.) After attempting to rob a bank that has already failed, Bonnie and Clyde pick up a loveably stupid accomplice, C. W. Moss (Michael J. Pollard), as a driver, only to be confounded in their next job when he parks the getaway car. Here, for the first time, the comedy becomes too real. Clyde is compelled to shoot the bank teller who pursues them point-blank in the face—a shock image that deliberately re-

FIGURE 6.2 From the outset of *Bonnie and Clyde,* capacity for criminal violence is shown alternately as a substitute for or a stimulant to sexual relations. Courtesy of Warner Bros. © 1969 Warner Bros.—Seven Arts Inc.

calls the violent death of an elderly, bespectacled woman in the Odessa Steps sequence of Eisenstein's *Battleship Potemkin.*

This first killing is followed by an even more obvious film citation with a cut to Bonnie, Clyde, and C. W. at the movies watching the now-campy opening number, "We're in the Money," from a thirty-four-year-old Warner Brothers musical, *Gold Diggers of 1933.* Bonnie, who is least affected by the death of the bank officer, will later reprise the song before her mirror. In general, she and Clyde act as though they are living a movie. Their initial relationship—defined by Clyde's discovery, training, and casting of Bonnie—is suggestive of a producer grooming a prospective star. For virtually the entire period that they are fugitives from the law, the couple can be seen explicitly constructing their public images—posing for photographs, introducing themselves as celebrities, enjoying their press clips, and, in the case of Bonnie, writing doggerel verse to celebrate their exploits.

It is the newspaper publication of "The Ballad of Bonnie and Clyde," and thus public recognition of his existence, that inspires Clyde to a successful sexual performance. "Once incarnated as myths," as Richard Maltby notes in *Harmless Entertainment: Hollywood and the*

Ideology of Consensus, Bonnie and Clyde are shown to behave "just like 'normal' people: their subsequent assassination may then be presented as a tragic irony, in which they are victimized for their non-conformity by a vindictive society" (1983, p. 309). Significantly, once Bonnie and Clyde achieve what might be termed ordinary sexual satisfaction, the capacity for outrageous—and outrageously punitive—violence resides entirely with the state.

Even before the movie's climax, the audience has been conditioned to fear mayhem. Pursued by the Texas Rangers, the increasingly celebrated Barrow Gang joins forces with Clyde's older brother, Buck (Gene Hackman), and Buck's wife, Blanche (Estelle Parsons). After an initial flurry of enthusiasm, the mood darkens. The Barrows are twice trapped in rustic motor courts by small armies of lawmen and twice compelled to shoot their way out to freedom, killing several police officers in the process. *Bonnie and Clyde*'s obvious aestheticism, its pleasure in broken glass and overturned automobiles, appeared to trivialize violence. When the members of the Barrow Gang were themselves the victims of gunshots, however, the movie raised the firepower to wartime dimensions. (*Esquire*'s November 1967 issue described the penultimate gun battle as "the Siege of Dienbenphu.") This allowed for some painful verisimilitude, as when Buck is naturalistically shot in the head and Blanche, herself wounded, launches into what would be an Oscar-winning rant of denial.

Similarly, the protagonists' climactic, bloody perforation has a tremendous finality. The shooting stops, the lawmen emerge from their ambush and advance toward the car. At this point, the movie literally stops dead; Bonnie and Clyde no longer exist, the screen goes black.

Bonnie and Clyde as Arbiters of Fashion

Bonnie and Clyde divided American critics but the civil war was a brief one. Bosley Crowther retired at the end of 1967 (ultimately replaced by Vincent Canby, whose sympathetic Penn interview had signaled the senior critic's waning power); Kael went on staff at the *New Yorker* to become the most influential American movie critic of the next two decades. By that time, *Bonnie and Clyde* was certified pop art, featured on the cover of the December 8, 1967, issue of *Time* as interpreted by Robert Rauschenberg for an essay entitled "The New Cinema: Violence . . . Sex . . . Art."

Time, which had earlier panned *Bonnie and Clyde* under the headline "Low-Down Hoedown" as "a strange and purposeless mingling of fact and claptrap," blandly reversed itself to proclaim the movie "the sleeper of the decade." Whereas *Time*'s original review parroted Crowther's outrage that *Bonnie and Clyde* had represented the nation in Montreal, the newsweekly now echoed Kael's assertion that audiences left the movie in a state of stunned reverie: "There is usually a hushed, shaken silence to the crowds that trail out of the theaters."

By some accounts, the anonymous *Time* staffer who initially reviewed *Bonnie and Clyde* was subsequently relieved of such responsibilities (Clarens, 1980, p. 259). *Newsweek* (Dec. 18, 1967), meanwhile, would amusedly cite *Pravda*'s fuddy-duddy blast against the "decadent" *Bonnie and Clyde*. If the Russians missed the fun of violence, *Time*'s cover essay was ostentatiously au courant in invoking *Cahiers du Cinema* and paraphrasing Jean-Luc Godard to explain how narrative, in the movies, may only serve as a pretext, that filmmakers need not adhere to conventions, and that comedy and tragedy might be blurred: A "segment of the public wants the intellectually demanding, emotionally fulfilling kind of film exemplified by *Bonnie and Clyde*." Tastes had grown more sophisticated. Violence was no longer restricted to the moron trade. Television had taken over Hollywood's function and the "cinema" was now "the favorite art form of the young."

The generational relationship was clinched when the December 26, 1967, issue of *Time* ran a letter written by an eighteen-year-old college freshman from Peoria, maintaining that *Bonnie and Clyde* was "not a film for adults," which was precisely why it had incurred such Establishment wrath. Nor was it the violence, she wrote, that had shocked her peers: "The reason it was so silent, so horribly silent in the theater at the end of the film was because we *liked* Bonnie Parker and Clyde Barrow, we identified with them and wanted to be like them." But what exactly did *that* mean?

One can hardly imagine such a letter being written to *Time* in defense of *The Dirty Dozen*. As the authors of the discarded MPAA Code feared, the attractive protagonists of *Bonnie and Clyde* had seduced impressionable viewers into complicity with criminal violence. Appropriating the romantic saga of the Outlaw Couple, *Bonnie and Clyde* drew legitimacy from one of Hollywood's oldest stories even as it invited a new and sophisticated complicity with the perhaps illicit pleasures purveyed by the movies. *Bonnie and Clyde* signaled a willingness to suspend moral judgment and go with the flow. Its success, as Richard Maltby notes, demonstrated "the extent to which the obligatory moral certainties of the Production Code's linear narratives had been discarded in favor of a self-regarding opportunism which allowed performers to act as they pleased, as free from social conventions as they were from narrative responsibilities" (1983, p. 312).

Bonnie and Clyde promoted an appreciation of crime as a game ruined by a grown-up society's tedious insistence that acts have consequences. Some took this literally. The *New York Times* (Mar. 23, 1968) reported that five teenage boys in dress "apparently inspired by the movie *Bonnie and Clyde*" were arrested in the affluent suburb of Westport, Connecticut, and charged with breach of the peace after "creating a disturbance at a local bank" by brandishing a toy gun as an armored car pulled up across the street.

Not simply as photogenic as pop stars (in one sequence, the Barrow Gang playfully cluster around the car of a hapless undertaker and his date, mashing their faces against the windows as if imitating the Beatles in *A Hard Day's Night*), Bonnie and Clyde are simultaneously victims and aggressors. Meanwhile, as Maltby points out,

> the interplay of comedy (in which the gang is always seen to laugh) and violence (in which the gang is always seen to suffer) enforces the audience's emotional attachment to them. . . . The ingratiating nature of the central performances allows the spectator no viewpoint other than that of the characters themselves, and the narcissistic display of style as its own justification obliges the audience to make its judgments on the appearances with which Beatty and Dunaway are so obsessed. (1983, p. 313)

It should not be surprising then that, for some, *Bonnie and Clyde* was not so much overly violent as excessively glamorous: "Pretty people who kill, and the killing they do is pretty too," wrote Jimmy Breslin in *New York* (July 8, 1968), adding that if "you want to see a real killer, then you should have been around to see Lee Harvey Oswald."

Good looks, swell clothes, and impossible cool set Bonnie and Clyde apart from their dowdy environment. That Beatty and Dunaway themselves appear too old to be a couple of crazy mixed-up kids is part of the movie's pronounced figure-ground problem. These were no ordinary delinquents. Crowther had complained that *Bonnie and Clyde*'s "sleazy, moronic" protagonists were shown "as full of fun and frolic as the jazz-age cut-ups in *Thoroughly Modern Millie*" (*New York Times*, Aug. 14, 1967), and couturiers, certainly, understood that they were scarcely a pair of dust-bowl losers. If anything, Bonnie and Clyde's style suggested that of the wealthy young couple in *The Great Gatsby*, motoring heedlessly through the hinterlands, smashing up the lives of lesser "little people," and then retreating into their money.

Bonnie and Clyde were too beautiful to grow up, become domestic, join the middle class. Their vehicle was about going over the edge, hence the joke of the January 13, 1968, *New Yorker* cartoon in which a laughing pair of pear-shaped middle-aged bourgies announce themselves on an apartment intercom, "Open up. It's Bonnie and Clyde!" According to screenwriters Benton and Newman, the couple's real offenses were not robbing banks and killing policemen but, rather, crimes of lifestyle: Bonnie's insolent poetry and cigar smoking, Clyde's sexual hang-ups, the couple's "existential" relationship and self-absorbed desire for celebrity.

In their original film treatment, Benton and Newman wrote that "if Bonnie and Clyde were here today, they would be hip. . . . Their style, their sexuality, their bravado, their delicacy, their cultivated arrogance, their narcissistic insecurity, their curious ambition have relevance to the way we live now." Bonnie, in particular, was for them "a kind of strange and touching vision: a pretty girl who was both tough and vulnerable, who was both Texas and universal, who wrote poetry and shot policemen, who loved life and courted death" (*Mademoiselle*, Mar. 1968). One wonders if the writers weren't responsible for the photo gallery of "Jail Birds," comely young women currently in jail for crimes of violence, that postscripted *Esquire*'s dossier on violence.

From the perspective of thirty years, what is most striking about *Bonnie and Clyde* is the public's widespread and largely spontaneous desire to participate more fully in that which the movie seemed to be. Unlike *The Dirty Dozen, Bonnie and Clyde* inspired songs recorded by artists as disparate as Merle Haggard, Brigitte Bardot, and Mel Torme. Bonnie Parker's sister cut an album-length interview. British singer Georgie Fame's mock ragtime "Ballad of Bonnie and Clyde" was banned in Norway (as was the movie itself) and France because it used the sound of machine-gun fire as percussion. Unprepared for the movie's extraordinary success, Warner Brothers scrambled to issue a soundtrack album six months after *Bonnie and Clyde*'s original release had placed its bluegrass theme, "Foggy Mountain Breakdown," in the top ten (number one in England).

By early 1968, when Warren Beatty prevailed upon Warner Brothers to rerelease *Bonnie and Clyde* with a new, more dignified advertising campaign that stressed its artistic merits, the film had ignited several clothing fads on both sides of the Atlantic. These included a return to calf-length "midi" or "maxi" skirts, a revival of fedoras, wide ties, and (for the first time in years) berets. Nor did viewers fail to notice that Faye Dunaway wore no brassiere. Even before the March issue of *Harper's Bazaar* showcased "The Gangster Game," *Life* put Dunaway on the cover of its January 12, 1968, issue as "Bonnie: Fashion's New Darling."

Newsweek's March 4, 1968, Dunaway cover proclaimed her "a with-it girl of the '60s," the first American actress to "electrify the world's moviegoers" since Marilyn Monroe. But was it the actress or the role that so captivated the public? Or was it the sense, articulated by the Weimar social critic Siegfried Kracauer, that "an idea bursts out of the darkness and can be formulated"?

> The social world is at all times filled with countless spiritual forces or entities that one can simply call ideas [and] what these ideas have in common is that . . . they all want to become reality themselves. They appear within human society as a concrete, material should-being [*Sollen*] and have an inborn drive to realize themselves. (Kracauer, 1995, p. 143)

Women's Wear Daily announced that the hot shade for spring 1968 was "the gun-barrel gray of Bonnie's pistol" (*Newsweek*, Dec. 18, 1967). The March 1968 *Mademoiselle* gave Dunaway a "special award," explaining, in suitably Kracauersian terms, that "Every so often a new look comes into being. It may float the air unlabeled, unclaimed in origin, before it crystalizes and people say, "That's it. That's what we're talking about." Which is what happened with *Bonnie and Clyde*'s Faye Dunaway. Suddenly *she* brought a look to life, focused it by the way she walked and talked and wore her clothes. . . ." In short, the movie was an event. It meant something. It was Now.

Bonnie and Clyde as a Political Text

As Arthur Penn defended *Bonnie and Clyde* by pointing out that "violence was part of the American character" (1967), so the mayhem in his movie was not only unusually bloody and vivid but appreciated in a contemporary, as well as a period, context.[7] Like an updated version of the anarchist Bonnot Gang, who robbed banks (and invented the motorized getaway) in pre–World War I France, Bonnie and Clyde even seemed to articulate a political justification for their criminal activities. They several times express their solidarity with dispossessed farmers and other victims of the Depression and link this to their hostility toward banks. Humiliating authority is another one of their specialties.

Moreover, the movie suggests that, for the sexually dysfunctional Clyde, guns are in some way compensatory. In the libidinal economy of *Bonnie and Clyde*, violence is thus a consequence of repression—sexual or otherwise. (As Andrew Kopkind wrote in the September 28, 1967, issue of the *New York Review of Books* that "to be white and a radical in America this summer is to see horror and feel impotent," so Dunaway cited the source of her identification with Bonnie: "The biggest thing about Bonnie was her frustration. She was up against a stone wall—a girl with potential who is blocked" [*Newsweek*, Mar. 4, 1968].) Just as Bonnie and Clyde's lack of sexual fulfillment is presented as a contributory cause of the Barrow Gang's violence, so their hard-won sexual happiness must be punished by the police.

To some degree, *Bonnie and Clyde* initially appeared as a semiotic jumble. The *Nation*—which, back in January 1931, had accused Hollywood of crowning the lawless "with the Romantic halo of bravery and adventure that helps to disguise their fundamental moronism"—had the sense that *Bonnie and Clyde*'s actions would "strike the viewer with icy familiarity in our day of motorcycle gangs and flower children, Nazi insignia, cheap beads, incense, drugs, apathy and motiveless violence" (Cawelti, 1973, p. 90).

The same week that *Time* highlighted *Bonnie and Clyde* on its cover, that of the *New York Review of Books* (Dec. 8, 1967) featured a David Levine caricature depicting President Johnson as a suitably degenerate Clyde, with Secretary of State Dean Rusk as his demure and diminutive Bonnie. Critic Stanley Kauffmann made a similar connection at a lower level, noting in the *New Republic* that Gene Hackman, who played Clyde's brother, looked and sounded like "a young LBJ." Indeed, the month *Bonnie and Clyde* opened, Rap Brown had called the president "a wild, mad dog—an outlaw from Texas" (*Time*, Aug. 4, 1967).

But the equation between *Bonnie and Clyde* and America's leaders got things backward. Although fundamentally anarchic in its celebration of self-absorbed hatred of authority, *Bonnie and Clyde* was generally felt to be a film of the left. Penn made a specific link to Black Power, proudly telling *Cahiers du Cinema* that, during one of the preview screenings, the "five Negroes present . . . completely identified with Bonnie and Clyde. They were delighted. They said: 'This is the way; that's the way to go, baby. Those cats were all right' " (Cawelti, 1973, p. 19).

Penn's anecdote, his evident pride at this particular endorsement, and his subsequent observation that African Americans were at "the point of revolution" suggest that *Bonnie and Clyde*'s appeal (as well as its danger) was less mayhem per se than a new attitude toward mayhem. The movie spoke to and popularized the neo-Sorelian cult of violence that Tom Wolfe would eventually label "radical chic." Reporting in the December 21, 1967, *Village Voice*, where *Bonnie and Clyde* was "the apotheosis of the New Style," in London theater critic and playwright Charles Marowitz summed up this stance in somewhat gentler terms: "If you are a bonnie-and-clyder, you are pro-camp and anti-Ugly; pro-permissiveness and anti-authoritarian; an advocate of the easy, improvised approach to life rather than a Five Year Planner. You pledge allegiance to the Pink Floyd and the Rolling Stones and all they stand for, and walk imperturbably toward the exit-doors while the National Anthem is playing."

Marowitz maintained that "the heady ecstasy with which Bonnie and Clyde break the law is echoed in the arcane pleasure that attends pot parties in north and southwest London." In the United States, of course, the youthful outlaw culture not only encompassed taking drugs but equally included demonstrating against the government, evading the draft, and, in the most extreme case of the Black Panthers, shooting it out with the police.

No less than Arthur Penn, white protesters and student radicals were drawn to violence by the example of Black Power. The issue of *New Left Notes* (June 26, 1967) published to coincide with the Students for a Democratic Society (SDS) annual convention anticipated Bonnie as fashion's darling by emblazoning its cover with a smiling, rifle-toting "New American Woman." Appropriating a term from the Black Panthers, *New Left Notes*'s September 25 issue would be the first to characterize the authorities as "pigs." Indeed, the period of *Bonnie and Clyde*'s production is identical to the development of the Black Panther Party, whose ten-point program was written in Oakland by Huey P. Newton and Bobby Seale as the movie began filming outside Dallas in October 1966.

The Dirty Dozen reigned as a box-office hit during the season of urban riots; the righteous outlaws of *Bonnie and Clyde* seemed to anticipate the fall 1967 escalation in antiwar political rhetoric and symbolic activity. "Here I was," wrote Berkeley activist Michael Rossman of Stop the Draft Week, "trying to sing what it's like to see the vectors of the war, the breaking black thing, the incipient hippy pogrom focus on our heads, and us on the streets of Oakland and at *Bonnie and Clyde* for the third time, trying to learn what to do next while the culture decides to eat its young" (1971, p. 238). The notion of *Bonnie and Clyde* as text (the great fear of the old Production Code) is striking. For Rossman, *Bonnie and Clyde* had an oracular quality. Nor was he alone. The first line of Abbie Hoffman's proposed advertisement for the scheduled October 14 "exorcism" of the Pentagon was "Don't miss *Bonnie and Clyde*" (Hoffman, 1968, p. 41).

An international revolutionary martyr had been born on October 7, when Bolivian soldiers captured and executed Che Guevara. Two weeks later, Black Panther leader Huey P. Newton was wounded and imprisoned after a gunfight with the Oakland police. From the point of view of the counterculture, then, *Bonnie and Clyde* was right on time. (At the same time, fall 1967 saw the use of incendiary buzzwords in various advertising campaigns for automobiles, liquor, cigarettes, detergents, and deodorants—the best-known of these being the "Dodge rebellion," which cosponsored the 1967 World Series.)

SDS militant Gerald Long wrote a piece in the September 9, 1967, issue of the *Guardian* explaining that *Bonnie and Clyde*'s true subject was "the violation of bourgeois property relations." *Bonnie and Clyde* is not a liberal or sociological film—times are hard, this is the result: "Anybody with a grain of sense would be out robbing these banks." Bonnie and Clyde, C. W., et al. "are just out there doing their thing, the thing they should be doing, and the camera and the audience are digging it and zooming along with them on the flight of the banjos plunking in the background. The banjos are freedom, integrity, spirit, all the things that bourgeois bankers, sheriffs and undertakers are not."

When the two "consciousness-expanding outlaws" drive into the service station where C. W. Moss is pumping gas, Long wrote, it's as though "a Mustang convertible pulls up with Luis Turcos, Frantz Fanon, and Nguyen Van Troi inside and they hold the door open and say, 'Hop in man, we're driving on down to the Pentagon.' " Long, who would sign the Weatherman manifesto in June 1969, expressed his hope that *Bonnie and Clyde* would break attendance records: "The audience really gets angry when the anonymous Minions of Bourgeois Order blast down the Blyth Spirit of the Revolution."

Long's celebration of *Bonnie and Clyde* was topped four months later when *New Left Notes*, which had never before reviewed a commercial movie, devoted fully a quarter of its January 8, 1968, issue to a discussion of the movie. Arguing that Long gave Hollywood "more ideological credit than it deserves," Neil Buckley asserted that *Bonnie and Clyde* was revolutionary beyond the filmmakers' intentions in part because historical context had overdetermined its reception. The current incidence of violence in America precluded viewing the movie as a "tragedy of youth gone bad." Rather, *Bonnie and Clyde* was "the political equivalent of a horror movie" in its demonstration that the punishment for challenging the capitalist order is death: "The viewer leaves the film with a tingling sensation where the bullet holes might have been in his body had he too gone wrong—had he too violated property rights."

Buckley's reading of the movie deliberately blurs the distinction between the fictional scenario on the screen and the political scenario he imagines for himself and his comrades:

> We are not potential Bonnies and Clydes, we are Bonnies and Clydes, the real things, challenging America in a real and fundamental way (which Bonnie and Clyde did not do—which makes us exceedingly dangerous).
>
> In its essential element, *Bonnie and Clyde* is revolutionary because it defines possible futures for us based on the reality of conditions under which we struggle. The film does not depict a revolutionary ideology. It does much more than that; it defines a revolutionary's lot.

What defines a revolutionary's lot? For Sorel, violence had the additional value of acting as a scission to split a political movement from the larger society. Although both describe the mayhem committed against Bonnie and Clyde, neither Long nor Buckley directly addresses the Barrow Gang's own capacity for violence—even though it is precisely this violence that not only defines the outlaw band but also creates that scission dividing the movie's most appreciative viewers from those most offended.[8]

Post–*Bonnie and Clyde* Hollywood Cinema

Bonnie and Clyde grossed $22.7 million—ten times its budget and the thirteenth highest grossing American movie up to that date—and was nominated for ten Oscars at a ceremony that had to be delayed for two days to acknowledge the assassination of Martin Luther King. By then, the movie had become the symbol of media violence. Three weeks after the King assassination, the *New York Times Magazine* (Apr. 28, 1968) published a symposium entitled "Is America by Nature a Violent Society?" Two of the nine participating intellectuals cited *Bonnie and Clyde*. *Life*'s June 21, 1968, cover story, "The Psycho-biology of Violence," by Albert Rosenfeld, links the assassination of Robert Kennedy to "the climate of violence . . . where real life and fictional—as in the popular movie *Bonnie and Clyde*—are filled with images of brutality."

The same, of course, was true for *Life*. The first page of Dr. Rosenfeld's essay is illustrated with a frame enlargement of Faye Dunaway in the throws of Bonnie's death spasm: "The casual acceptance of violence, epitomized in the movie *Bonnie and Clyde*, creates a climate which some scientists believe can arouse susceptible people to violent acts." Similarly, Arthur Schlesinger Jr.'s 1968 broadside *Violence: America in the Sixties* deplored *Bonnie and Clyde* for "its blithe acceptance of the world of violence—an acceptance which almost became a celebration" (p. 53).

Within a week of Robert Kennedy's death on June 5, President Johnson's executive order established the National Commission on the Causes and Prevention of Violence. *Bonnie and Clyde* was cited repeatedly (albeit frequently sight unseen, according to testimony) during the commission hearings held in December 1968. Asked about the movie, Jack Valenti obscured his own evident ambivalence by pointing out that it had been singled out for praise by the National Catholic Office of Motion Pictures (*Violence and the Media*, 1969, p. 206).

Valenti's remarks prompted a reply from Representative Hale Boggs, Democrat from Louisiana, that echoed the complaints of the 1930s:

> We had a murder in my town committed by an 18-year-old boy who had come out of *Bonnie and Clyde* one hour before. He killed a young man who was running a drive-in grocery store. And it was just a senseless murder. Now, whether or not what he saw in *Bonnie and Clyde* had any impact on the murder, I don't know. But I know that what I say to you is a fact—that he saw this movie which glorifies violence.

Boggs, who pointed out that "those *Bonnie and Clyde* characters lived in my State," was particularly annoyed by Valenti's use of the award (for the best "mature" picture of 1967) by the National Catholic Office of Motion Pictures to defend *Bonnie and Clyde*, citing in reply the new MPAA Code: " 'Detailed and protracted acts of brutality, cruelty, physical violence, torture and abuse shall not be presented.' That's the essence of that movie" (*Violence and the Media* 1969, p. 206).

By the time Lyndon Johnson left the White House a few weeks later, in January 1969, with U.S. military personnel in Vietnam at a wartime peak of 542,400, violence was popularly understood as central to American culture and history. The introductions to the anthologies *Violence in America: A Historical and Contemporary Reader* (1969) and *American Violence: A Documentary History* (1970) are typical; the foreword to *Violence in America: Historical and Comparative Perspectives*, a report to the National Commission on the Causes and Prevention of Violence, published in June 1969, took the even more radical position that "the growth of this country has occurred around a series of violent upheavals and that each has thrust the nation forward."

That same month, *New Left Notes* ran a cover illustration of two young men, one white and one black, crouching on a rooftop above a burning city, both armed with automatic rifles and wearing crisscrossed ammunition belts ("in order to get rid of the gun it is necessary to take up the gun"), while the Museum of Modern Art concluded a lengthy retrospective series, *The American Action Movie: 1946–64*, having dropped the rubric *Violent America* for the retrospective after one film distributor refused to furnish prints for presentation in a program that was so called (Twitchell, 1989, p. 187).

Needless to say, none of the films MoMA screened had anything approaching the degree of mayhem by then available in contemporary Hollywood movies. Indeed, *Variety* opined that *The Wild Bunch*—which also appeared in June 1969—might be "the most violent US film ever made." Among other things, *The Wild Bunch* was designed to obliterate *Bonnie and Clyde*. Dub Taylor, who appeared in both *Bonnie and Clyde*, as the father of C. W. Moss, and the first scene of *The Wild Bunch*, as a temperance movement leader, remembers director Sam Peckinpah boasting that *The Wild Bunch* would be "better than *Bonnie and Clyde*" (Fine, 1991, p. 124). Similarly, another co-worker, Gordon Dawson, recalls Peckinpah announcing that "We're going to bury *Bonnie and Clyde*" (Weddle, 1994, p. 331).

The fourth-and fifth-largest hits of 1967 (behind one romantic comedy dealing with the generation gap, *The Graduate*, another on the subject of integration, *Guess Who's Coming to Dinner?*, and Walt Disney's animated feature *The Jungle Book*), *Bonnie and Clyde* and *The Dirty Dozen* offered a volatile mix of ultraviolence with blatant antiauthoritarianism. As period films, both advanced a revisionist view of the national past that, in effect, argued the centrality of excessive violence to American history. *Bonnie and Clyde* provided a contemporary form of the righteous outlaw while *The Dirty Dozen* effectively besmirched the reputation and questioned the conduct of the most justifiable of all American wars. At the same time, both movies were understood by initial audiences as articulating some hitherto unacknowledged aspect of their lives. If *The Dirty Dozen* provided an inchoate parallel to the riotous summer of 1967, *Bonnie and Clyde* was incorporated into the fall's escalation in antiwar rhetoric and activity among white protesters and student radicals.

Bonnie and Clyde was further experienced as a harbinger of fashion and, not surprisingly, engendered all manner of cinematic progeny, including the top box-office attraction of 1969 (and, for a time, the highest grossing western ever made), *Butch Cassidy and the Sundance Kid*. At the same time, *The Dirty Dozen* spawned a 1968–1970 cycle of "dirty" war movies concerning similar pariah groups sent on morally ambiguous commando missions.

The synthesis of *Bonnie and Clyde* and *The Dirty Dozen* was *The Wild Bunch*, which concerns a collection of aging western outlaws who jump from the frying pan of the closed American frontier into the fire of the Mexican Revolution. (Indeed, Kenneth Hyman, who had produced *The Dirty Dozen*, was now head of production at Warner Brothers.)

The Wild Bunch code of honor is founded on male camaraderie. Pike, the group's leader, proclaims that "when you side with a man, you stay with him." No less than *Bonnie and Clyde, The Wild Bunch* and even the insipid *Butch Cassidy and the Sundance Kid* embodied a striking inversion of values. At once cynical and romantic, both of these westerns presented the unregenerate criminal as a sympathetic figure, expressing regret at his elimination by the agents of law and order.[9]

Shadowed by a sense of inevitable catastrophe, *The Wild Bunch* is bracketed by the spectacle of civilians caught in a murderous crossfire. Repeatedly, the viewer watches disaster unfold—the botched stakeout that provides the movie's opening bloodbath, the collision on the railroad tracks, the explosion on the bridge, the final massacre. Like Arthur Penn, Peckinpah presented his project as essentially cautionary and demystifying, echoing Penn's assertion that "the trouble with the violence in most films is that it is not violent enough." Unlike Penn, however, Peckinpah acknowledged something of his own fascination with mayhem:

> The point of [*The Wild Bunch*] is to take this facade of movie violence and open it up, get people involved in it so that they are starting to go in the Hollywood television predictable reaction syndrome, and then twist it so that it's not fun anymore, just a wave of sickness in the gut. . . . It's a terrible, ugly thing. And yet there's a certain response that you get from it, an excitement because we're all violent people. (Weddle, 1994, p. 334)

Pauline Kael, who did so much to promote *Bonnie and Clyde*, had ambivalent feelings about *The Wild Bunch*, arguing that, although Peckinpah "thought that by making violence realistically bloody and gruesome he would deglamourize warfare and enable the audience to see how horrible it is," he became "so intricately involved in the problems of violence that [the movie] tore itself apart. A brilliantly directed and photographed study in confusion, it played to audiences who apparently didn't take it as an attack on violence but simply enjoyed it as a violent Western (*New Yorker* Mar. 21, 1970)."

William Wolf observed in the August 30, 1969, issue of *Cue* that "the killings in *Bonnie and Clyde* were necessary to illuminate a subject. The cop shot in the face was a horrible sight, as was the demise of the

FIGURE 6.3 William Holden in *The Wild Bunch*. Imbuing a western with a carnage of a war movie was understood, in 1969, as a form of naturalism. Courtesy of Warner Bros.

gang. But the violence was meaningful in a context of larger drama. We could hardly enjoy it." Even if one accepted Peckinpah's antiviolence intent in *The Wild Bunch*, "he sure as hell wasn't getting any such message across to the more vocal members of this audience—or to me."

> At one point, after someone is shot in the head, the audience laughed at the high-pitched voice of a little boy in the theater exclaiming: "I like this picture." It is the kind of film that makes many grown-ups behave the same way. Perhaps we have become so conditioned to violence that we delight in the audacity of a film that piles it on with such gusto.

Perhaps because, as a western, *The Wild Bunch* seemed targeted at a less sophisticated segment of the movie audience, the movie inspired some of the same anxieties as did *The Dirty Dozen*. On the other hand, possibly as a result of the controversy that had dogged *Bonnie and Clyde*'s, *The Wild Bunch*'s reception was characterized by an unusually high degree of historical consciousness. The *Daily News* was reminded of the "hue and cry" over the gangster cycle of the 1930s. Richard Schickel employed multiple oxymorons in praising *The Wild Bunch* in

Life as "the first masterpiece in the new tradition of the 'dirty western,'" pointing out that the old "clean" western was "no more firmly located in time than a dream . . . referring us endlessly to a lost Eden that we probably never inhabited, a land whose inhabitants, when they killed one another, usually did so for an understandable reason" (1970).

For Schickel, excessive violence enhanced naturalism in *The Wild Bunch*. The same point was made even more forcefully by the *Catholic Film Newsletter* (June 30, 1969). "It would be an easy matter to dismiss [*The Wild Bunch*] as simply another celluloid blood-bath," noted the anonymous representative of the National Catholic Office of Motion Pictures. Yet, earlier westerns, in which "death was shown as a bloodless, almost painless action," were in their obfuscations at least partially responsible for "the violence in our society today." Peckinpah, by contrast, deserved credit for aiming "to demythologize the conventional past and present it as it really was." *The Wild Bunch* made violence central and inescapable. Peckinpah's movie, the reviewer concluded, "could help thoughtful viewers to understand who we are and where we have come from in a way that, considering the history of the Western genre, is singularly healthy." This, of course, presupposes a reasoned response to the movie.[10]

Conclusions

That Warner Brothers's recent silver-anniversary rerelease of *The Wild Bunch* was held up for a year when the MPAA deemed the movie's restored version too violent for its original R rating suggests that public attitudes toward violent imagery are historically determined. Indeed, spectator antipathy or attraction to screen violence may, in fact, concern something other than the violence itself. The controversy around the 1991 movie *Thelma and Louise* demonstrates that an otherwise unremarkable movie scenario—two fugitives on the run from the law after committing an unpremeditated (and almost justifiable) act of murder—can be considerably transformed by shifting the identity of the protagonists, in this case from male to female. Albeit minimal (as well as imaginary), *Thelma and Louise*'s mayhem was perceived by many commentators as a form of dangerous hyperbole, its rhetoric akin to irresponsible demagoguery.

Thus, *The Dirty Dozen* disturbed reviewers by presenting criminals trained as commandos to perform a job more virtuous soldiers could not accomplish and *Bonnie and Clyde*'s popularization of a previously unusual attitude toward criminal violence—a willingness to suspend moral judgment—was regarded as all the more dangerous for being placed in the context of "a squalid shoot-'em up for the moron trade."

Criticized for expanding the parameters of "outlaw" violence, *The Dirty Dozen* and *Bonnie and Clyde* were understood and appreciated by their initial audience as articulating some aspect of contemporary life hitherto unacknowledged by the movies. Similarly, at the time of its first release, *The Wild Bunch* reflected a new permissiveness regarding the representation of sex and violence on the screen, as well as the free use of taboo language. Moreover, in elaborating on *Bonnie and Clyde*'s redefinition of group morality and by raising comradeship to the ultimate value, *The Wild Bunch* presaged all the postwar Vietnam films where the idea is to stay alive, help your buddy, and get the hell out.

In the context of 1969, Peckinpah's outrageously stylized violence, which imbued a western with the carnage and body count of a war movie, was perceived as a form of naturalism—by idealists and cynics alike. Hence the truth of producer Phil Feldman's grandiloquent pronouncement when *The Wild Bunch* had its stormy preview at a Warner Brothers junket: "The era of escapism is over; the era of reality is here. . . . The entertainment industry has a right and duty to depict reality as it is."

Notes

1. While the study's findings did not support the argument that exposure to such material contributed to "the elicitation of aggressive acts in the severely provoked individual," the authors, Dolf Zillmann and Rolland C. Johnson, concluded that filmed violence served to "sustain aggressiveness."

2. During this period as well, an old-fashioned gangster film, *Black Tuesday* (1954) and the cavalry western *Fort Yuma* (1955) were reedited for violence.

3. Other current and recent movies deemed excessively violent, at least by *Esquire*, were the psychological thrillers *Straight Jacket* and *Lady in a Cage* (both 1964), the westerns *A Fistful of Dollars* (1964; U.S. release 1967) and *Nevada Smith* (1966), *The Chase* (1966), and Andy Warhol's avant-garde talk-athon *The Chelsea Girls* (1966), as well as such imports as Roman Polanski's *Repulsion* (1965) and Elio Petri's futuristic *Tenth Victim* (1965), in which the violence "problem" is solved by the sport of legal murder. Two upcoming releases, *The Saint Valentine's Day Massacre* and *In Cold Blood*, were expected to contribute to the trend.

4. *The Dirty Dozen* was shot in the spring and summer of 1966 and completed postproduction in October. Robert Aldrich, a director who had previously experienced censorship problems with his *Kiss Me Deadly*, expressed some concern that *The Dirty Dozen* be "a 1967 picture and not a 1947 picture"—telling the *Saturday Review* (June 17, 1967) that "in the midst of a highly unpopular war, I certainly didn't want to do a film either about the hawks or the doves." While Aldrich himself seems to have been a political liberal, the presence of star Lee Marvin (in a role first offered to John Wayne) gives the movie a right-wing militarist inflection. In March 1966, Marvin, a decorated ex-Marine, had hosted *Our Time in Hell*, an ABC documentary on the Marine Corps so enthusiastically gung ho that even *Variety* (Mar 29, 1967) deemed it "an hour-long public relations plug."

5. This unusually callous sell line appeared almost simultaneously in the

national consciousness with H. Rap Brown's memorable formulation that "violence is necessary and it's as American as cherry pie."

6. A parallel, unmentioned by Crowther, could be found in a contemporaneous issue of the *New York Review of Books*, which was notorious for featuring a diagram of a Molotov cocktail on its cover.

7. As *Esquire's* violence issue repeatedly noted the murder of John F. Kennedy as the prologue to America's season of violence, so *Bonnie and Clyde* referenced the Kennedy assassination in several ways. For one thing, the production was based at the North Park Motor Inn in Dallas on the third anniversary of the Kennedy assassination and, as David Thomson reports in his Beatty biography, "people on the crew [were] impressed by the local aftershock." Then too, director Penn, who had helped coach Kennedy for his televised debates with Richard Nixon and had contrived an iconic reenactment of Lee Harvey Oswald's shooting in his previous movie *The Chase*, connected *Bonnie and Clyde*'s savage denouement to the same Zapruder footage cited by Tom Wolfe: "There's even a piece of Warren's head that comes off, like that famous photograph of Kennedy" (Comolli and Labarthe, 1973, p. 16).

8. *New Left Notes* (Feb. 19, 1968) includes a sympathetic review of Sorel's *Reflections on Violence* that, among other things, notes that "proletarian violence makes the future revolution certain." The author, Tom Rose, is identified as a graduate student at the University of Wisconsin at Milwaukee writing his dissertation on the theory and practice of violence in America. Rose subsequently edited the Random House anthology *Violence in America: A Historical and Contemporary Reader* (1969), one of the numerous books on the subject published between 1968 and 1970.

9. *The Wild Bunch* had its origins in a screenplay drawing on the same historical material that inspired *Butch Cassidy and the Sundance Kid*. Butch Cassidy was the leader, and the Sundance Kid a member, of the Wild Bunch. "The biggest gang of outlaws that ever harried the West," according to Dorothy M. Johnson's survey *Western Badmen* (1972), the Wild Bunch was active, robbing banks, trains, and payrolls from 1897 through 1901. Cassidy and Sundance subsequently relocated to South America, where they resumed their criminal careers until they were killed in a gunfight with Bolivian police.

10. Writing in the *Nation* (July 14, 1969), Robert Hatch described a less cerebral reaction to *The Wild Bunch*:

> Peckinpah has rediscovered something that I suspect was known to the Elizabethans: if you carry violence far enough, the audience will laugh. . . . The director has also picked up, possibly from *Bonnie and Clyde*, the device of showing the actual instant of annihilation in slow motion, so that scenes of hysterical activity are constantly punctuated by floating, dreamlike vignettes of death. And finally, he has decided, on what medical authority I do not know, that when hit by a bullet the human body bursts like a ripe melon. At this the audience laughed (and so did I), not with merriment, exactly, but in tribute to such virtuosity of gore.

This is far closer to the audience response noted at showings of *The Dirty Dozen* and unlike that observed at *Bonnie and Clyde*, the original movie that sought to make viewers pay for their enjoyment of violence.

When Screen Violence Is
Not Attractive

CLARK McCAULEY

Screen violence is not always attractive. In a volume focusing on the attractions of symbolic violence, it is useful to consider some of the limits of such attraction. In this chapter, I begin with research on disgust that found three documentary films of blood and violence that undergraduate students, at least, do not want to watch. After trying out some simple explanations of the unattractiveness of these films, I turn to theory and research aimed at understanding the genre of commercial film violence that should be most disgusting—horror films. This literature does not provide much help in understanding the unattractiveness of the disgusting films, but it leads to two new studies with results that suggest that viewers can enjoy the experience of negative emotions such as disgust and fear. I conclude by examining two possible theories of how negative emotions can be experienced as positive; both theories point to the importance of dramatic distance—framing violence as fiction—if screen violence is to be attractive.

Reactions to Violence in Research on Disgust

In their research on sensitivity to disgust, Haidt, Rozin, and McCauley (1994) put individual college students in front of a TV set to watch three documentary-style videotapes involving violence and gore. The first film shows a dinner party at a large table in which the centerpiece is a live monkey; the monkey is hammered unconscious on camera, its skull opened, and its still-pulsing brains served onto platters for the epicure diners. The second film shows a slaughterhouse; the camera follows steers as they are stunned, have their throats cut, and are hung up to be butchered. The third film shows head surgery conducted on a young girl; surgeons pull the child's face inside out away from her skull.

The student subjects in this research were given a control with which they could shut off the videotape whenever they did not want to watch anymore. (Students were told that this was a control condition for a hypnotism experiment, and that the investigators needed to find out what normal and awake subjects are willing to put up with.) The students did not find these films attractive. They turned them off, on the average, a little more than halfway into them. The expected gender differences were found: female students turned off the films at about the halfway mark, whereas male students typically endured about three-quarters before turning them off. And the expected correlation with sensitivity to disgust was found: students scoring higher on our pencil-and-paper disgust scale turned the three disgust tapes off sooner.

If undergraduate students are any indication, our three videotapes do not have much commercial appeal. Only about 10 percent of students watched these films all the way to the end, and even these few rated the films as somewhat disturbing and disgusting. Although we did not ask our students about their film- or TV-viewing habits, we are confident from other results with student populations that most of our subjects have paid to see a Rambo film, a Schwarzenegger film, or some equivalent of the *Texas Chainsaw Massacre*. Why isn't our violence as attractive as Hollywood's violence?

The difference cannot be that our violence is against animals and Hollywood violence is against people. Our facial-surgery film shows a startling violation of the features of a human child, and the results are about the same as for the films with violence against a monkey or a steer. Nor can the difference be that our violence is senseless whereas Hollywood violence is understandable and motivated. Killing to eat and disfiguring to cure are, if anything, more easily understood than the exaggerated violence of the good-guy-versus-bad-guy conflicts featured in Hollywood productions.

Perhaps the distinction between instrumental and impulsive violence can say something about our results. Instrumental violence is violence for some goal other than inflicting harm on another. Impulsive violence is violence for the pleasure of hurting another, a violence often associated with anger and revenge (Berkowitz, 1989). This distinction might suggest that instrumental violence is understandable and attractive, whereas impulsive violence is not understandable and unattractive. The immediate difficulty with this suggestion is that our films represent violence that is clearly more instrumental than impulsive. Indeed, the facial-surgery film shows surgeons doing violence to a child with the explicit intention of helping her.

At this point one might try turning the suggestion around. Perhaps it is impulsive violence that is attractive on-screen and instrumental violence that is not. But even cursory experience of screen violence contradicts this hypothesis as well. Hollywood violence is full of crazies, androids, extraterrestrials, and monsters from out of id or slime. These are typically frightening, attacking, killing, enslaving, devouring, or taking over the brains of innocent victims for reasons that have more to do with their inhuman goals (instrumental violence) than with any special reward from seeing their victims suffer (impulsive violence). Monsters are not usually seeking anything like revenge or experiencing anything like anger; anger is a moral emotion alien to an Alien, Predator, Godzilla, Mothra, Body Snatcher, Critter, or Dracula.

It appears, then, that the unattractiveness of our disgusting videotapes is not easily explained. Violence in our videotapes is not unattractive because it involves animals rather than humans, or because it is senseless, or because it involves instrumental rather than impulsive violence. Perhaps our violence is unappealing because it is real—documentary—rather than fictional. This obvious possibility is at most the starting point for an explanation, because it is not obvious why viewing fictional violence should be attractive when viewing real violence is not.

The comparison of our disgusting videotapes with Hollywood violence must now become more explicit and more detailed, and the comparison is best advanced by focusing on that genre of Hollywood film violence that contains the most obviously disgusting material—horror films. Horror films are full of representations that are known to elicit disgust (Haidt, Rozin, & McCauley, 1994): death and body-envelope violations, especially piercings and dismemberments with plenty of blood and guts on the screen. What does the literature have to say about the appeal of horror films? What can this literature suggest about why documentary violence should be unappealing?

The Appeal of Horror Films

Societal Fears

Stephen King (1981) suggests that horror films "often serve as an extraordinarily accurate barometer of those things which trouble the night-thoughts of a whole society" (p. 131). In *The Monster Show: A Cultural History of Horror* (1993), David J. Skal traces the societal fears that have been exploited in horror films. For example, Skal characterizes horror films of the 1950s as "responding uneasily to new and almost incomprehensible developments in science and the anxious challenges they posed to the familiar structures of society, religion, psychology, and perception" (p. 114). Films such as *Godzilla* and *Them*, both released in 1954, featured animals (a reptile and ants, respectively) transformed into large, destructive monsters by radiation accidents.

The underlying themes of horror films have changed with the times, and today Skal (1993) sees an underlying fear of the AIDS virus in the renewed interest in vampires. He believes that "the vampire serves a coping function, symbolically representing a dreaded plague death while at the same time triumphantly transcending it" (pp. 346–47).

Of course, horror films can also play upon fears that are chronic in the human condition. Beyond secular trends in fear, King (1981) suggests that horror films have the ability to "[point] even further inward, looking for those deep-seated personal fears—those pressure points—we all must cope with" (p. 131). Examples of such fears are fears of death and aging: "the most obvious psychological pressure point is the fact of our own mortality" (p. 68). Even types of horror that appear to lack a meaningful subtext, "slasher" films, such as *Friday the 13th*, can at least appeal to our fear of death.

Probably most horror films work on both the specific fears of a society and the universal fears of human beings. If these films are so good at finding exactly what scares us, why are they so appealing?

Catharsis

King (1981) suggests that "we make up horrors to help us cope with the real ones" (p. 13); he characterizes horror films as "barber's leeches of the psyche, drawing not bad blood but anxiety" (p. 198), "the tough mind's way of coping with terrible problems" (p. 316), and "an invitation to indulge in deviant, antisocial behavior by proxy" (p. 31). Here King is drawing upon Aristotle's conception of *catharsis*, which, as Mills (1993) points out, includes ideas of clarification and purification as well as purgation. The usual literary interpretation of catharsis emphasizes the idea of purgation, as King does (see also Carroll, 1990). As purgatives, horror films can draw out negative emotions, such as fear, rage, and disgust, to render the mind more healthy and to protect the social order by providing a safe outlet for "unsafe" emotions.

This conception of catharsis leads to three hypotheses. The first is an individual-differences hypothesis: a drama eliciting a particular emotion will be more appealing to viewers who come to the drama with more of that emotion. If there is no emotion to be purged, there should be no attraction to the drama.

The second catharsis hypothesis is that viewers will leave a successful drama with less of the elicited emotion than they came with. This is the controversial heart of catharsis theory. It is by no means obvious why dramatic instigation of anger, for instance, should decrease rather than increase the viewer's anger (cf. Mills, 1993, p. 256). The purgation hypothesis is problematic especially in light of evidence that anger is decreased by affective experience inconsistent with anger—for instance, the experience produced by exposure to humor or erotica (Baron & Ball, 1974; Baron, 1974; Ramirez, Bryant, & Zillmann, 1982).

The third catharsis hypothesis is that the greater the reduction in viewer emotion, the more appealing the drama should be. Of course, a drama may be attractive for reasons other than catharsis, but, if catharsis is a major source of attraction to drama, then any drama that fails to produce catharsis should be relatively unappealing.

A little-noted complexity of catharsis theory is that it seems to predict that drama should purge positive emotions as well as negative. That is, dramatic instigation of sympathy, or love, or triumph, should leave viewers with less of these emotions than they came in with. This prediction seems never to have been taken seriously.

With regard to negative emotions, the catharsis hypothesis has been most investigated in research aimed at assessing the effects of TV violence on viewer aggression. This literature does offer some support for the first catharsis hypothesis, the predicted link between viewer emotion and dramatic appeal. Males are more aggressive than females, and males like violent TV shows more than females do. Similarly, among males, those who are more aggressive watch more violent TV shows (Freedman, 1984).

But research on TV violence has not shown the purgation of emotion that is the central hypothesis of catharsis theory. In general, viewer aggression is reported to be increased rather than deceased by exposure to film violence (Zillmann, 1979). It is worth noting, however, that this research may not have adequately tested the catharsis prediction. The great majority of experiments on the effects of TV violence have made the dramatic experience unnatural at least to the extent of having one subject at a time exposed to either violent or nonviolent TV programming. Aristotle may never have imagined catharsis occurring with a drama staged for an audience of one.

The measure of viewer aggression used in most experiments on TV violence can also be faulted. Giving (supposed) shocks to a (supposed) other subject in a (supposed) learning experiment, for instance, does not cleanly distinguish instrumental from impulsive aggression; it may be that only impulsive aggression is purged by dramatic instigation of anger (cf. Berkowitz, 1989). Finally, TV-violence research has commonly exposed subjects to excerpts of violent films rather than showing entire films; it may be that the instigation of viewer emotion depends upon knowing more about the protagonists than is conveyed in a few minutes of fighting ripped out of context. Purgation of anger and hostility cannot be expected if dramatic violence does not succeed in instigating these emotions in the experimental subjects.

Thus, although it is correct to say that research on the effects of TV violence has found little evidence of catharsis effects, it must also be said that this research was not animated by much concern for clean tests of catharsis theory. Occasional reports of catharsis effects (e.g., Feshbach & Singer, 1971) may turn out to be only the tip of a phenomenon that deserves more careful attention.

In the research on horror films, there is some evidence that can be cited for the catharsis hypothesis. Tamborini and Stiff (1987) interviewed young people (70 percent were 18–21 years of age) who were leaving a theater after viewing a popular horror film, *Halloween II*. The interview assessed general liking for horror films and reasons for liking such films. The reasons that had the highest correlation with liking for horror films were "because they are exciting" and "because they are scary" (both $r=.67$). Although catharsis means more than just emotional stimulation, these reasons are consistent with catharsis at least in suggesting that people go to horror films in order to experience in safety emotions that are usually associated with danger.

Similarly, Tamborini, Stiff, and Zillmann (1987) found in male subjects a strong relationship ($r=.73$) between liking pornographic films and preference for graphic horror featuring a female victim. The authors' interpretation was that men who feel hostility toward women may find gratification not only in pornographic depictions of women but also in graphic horror films with female victims. This interpretation is also consistent with catharsis theory insofar as attraction to both horror films and pornographic films may depend upon the match between viewer emotion and the expression of that emotion on-screen.

Finally, it has often been noted that males report more interest in and liking for horror films than females do (Tamborini & Stiff, 1987; Tamborini, Stiff, & Zillmann, 1987; Zillmann & Weaver, 1995). Popular belief holds that male adolescents are the main consumers of the horror genre (King, 1981), although Clover (1992) points out the difficulties in trying to identify the main audience for horror when most of the revenue for horror films these days comes from videocassette rentals. Greater male than female preference for horror films is of course consistent with catharsis theory if males feel more anger and hostility than females. As noted above in considering research on TV violence, males are certainly more physically aggressive and more violent than females.

Curiosity/Fascination Theory

Carroll (1990) suggests that horror films do not so much purge negative emotions as appeal to our curiosity: "horror attracts because anomalies command attention and elicit curiosity" (p. 195). Horror movies present society's norms only to violate them. This violation of norms, which King (1981, see above) also recognized, holds a fascination for people to the extent that they rarely see these violations in everyday experience. Curiosity/fascination theory suggests that a horror film is immediately and directly enjoyed as it satisfies our curiosity, whereas catharsis theory, as already noted, suggests that the film is enjoyed only for the relief from negative emotions that it leaves in its wake.

This distinction is perhaps not so clear as it first appears, however.

According to Carroll (1990), "the condition that permits this transgression of the norm is that, when . . . the narrative achieves closure, the norm has been reconstituted . . . so the norm emerges stronger than before" (p. 201). Now curiosity/fascination theory begins to sound like a form of catharsis theory: norm violation can be experienced safely in the film precisely because the film does not in the end challenge the norm. It seems possible that those more desirous of challenging the norm would find horror films more attractive, just as those with more hostility or fear or disgust may find horror more attractive.

Consistent with this version of curiosity/fascination theory, Tamborini, Stiff, and Zillmann (1987) found that the deceit subscale of the personality trait of Machiavellianism was a strong predictor ($r=.39$) of preference for films with graphic horror. The deceit scale measures approval of the use of dishonesty to achieve goals. Tamborini et al. suggest that willingness to use deceit may be associated with liking for horror because both imply "a desire to violate the norms of socially acceptable behavior, or to see them violated by others" (p. 548). Those who like horror are likely to favor another kind of norm violation—deceit.

Sensation Seeking

Another individual-differences variable that has been related to liking for horror films is the personality trait identified by Zuckerman's (1979) Sensation Seeking Scale. This scale includes four subscales that measure tendencies toward disinhibition, boredom susceptibility, experience seeking, and thrill and adventure seeking. High sensation seekers are characterized as searching for intense stimulation, such as can be found performing thrilling activities, like skydiving. It is possible that horror films provide the kind of intense stimulation and arousal that will appeal particularly to high sensation seekers (Rickey, 1982).

As reviewed by Tamborini et al. (1987), there is considerable evidence linking scores on Zuckerman's Sensation-Seeking Scale with liking for horror films. Sparks (1984) found Sensation-Seeking scores positively correlated with his own scale of Enjoyment of Frightening Films ($r=.22$ for males, .28 for females). Tamborini and Stiff (1987) found liking for horror films positively correlated ($r=.21$) with a combination of Zuckerman's disinhibition, experience-seeking, and thrill-and-adventure-seeking subscales. Edwards (1984) found interest in horror movies strongly correlated ($r=.51$) with the total Sensation-Seeking Scale. Finally, Tamborini et al. themselves found the disinhibition, experience-seeking, and boredom-susceptibility subscales correlated with preference for films with graphic horror (rs of .29, .17, .18 for male and female subjects combined; rs of .29, .28, .29 for male subjects separately; correlation of total Sensation-Seeking Scale not presented).

There is little doubt, on the basis of this evidence, that high sensation seekers like horror movies more than low sensation seekers do. The relationship is not always strong, but it is consistent.

Sex-Role Reinforcement: The Snuggle Theory

Zillmann, Weaver, Mundorf, and Aust (1986) have suggested that one source of attraction to horror films is that these films provide the occasion for men and women to practice and fortify traditional gender roles. While watching horror films, men can prove their fearlessness and competence by remaining stoic in the face of blood and dismemberment, and women can show their sensitivity and need for protection by expressing fear. This suggestion, often called the snuggle theory of horror, entails that "enjoyment of horror derives in part from successfully behaving, under emotionally taxing circumstances, in accordance with societal precepts" (Zillmann & Gibson, 1995, p. 12).

To test this theory, Zillmann et al. (1986) showed a clip from *Friday the 13th, Part III* to undergraduate subjects who watched the film with an opposite-sex undergraduate who was a confederate of the experimenters. During the film, the confederate behaved in a manner that expressed either indifference, distress, or mastery. After the film, the subjects completed a questionnaire that assesed their affective reactions to the film. Zillmann et al. found that male subjects enjoyed the film more when they were with a woman expressing distress than when they were with a woman expressing mastery, whereas female subjects enjoyed the film more with a man showing mastery than with a man showing distress. The typical difference between males and females was also found: across conditions, males enjoyed the film more than females did.

These results support the snuggle theory in showing that both males and females like the horror film more when they can reinforce their gender roles in the watching of it. More generally, these results point to the importance of social context in affecting response to drama. As suggested earlier in connection with catharsis theory, watching a film alone may be a very different experience from watching as part of a group.

Mood Management

Zillmann's (1988) theory of mood management suggests that people choose their entertainment to create the mood they wish to experience, or to cure the mood they are in. Although Zillmann has not specifically applied his theory to liking for horror films, he has marshaled considerable evidence that different kinds of entertainment have consistently different effects on arousal and hedonic experience, and that individuals can and do take advantage of these effects in choosing among forms of entertainment.

Mood-management theory predicts that boredom should lead to a desire for arousing entertainment, including horror films. The evidence linking sensation seeking (including susceptibility to boredom) with liking for horror films is generally consistent with this prediction. Also consistent with mood-management theory are the reasons for liking horror movies that Tamborini and Stiff (1987) found to be best correlated with liking for horror: because it's exciting and because it's scary. Mood-management theory cannot work unless individuals can anticipate the effects of the entertainment they choose, and those who like horror most are evidently those who most like its arousal value.

The paradox of horror's appeal is not, however, resolved in mood-management theory. A little bit of fear or disgust may be better than boredom, but it is not clear why a massive dose of fear or disgust should be appealing. A potential answer to this quandary is suggested by the relief hypothesis.

The Relief Hypothesis

Rickey (1982) suggests that it is particularly the successful resolution of a horror film that is enjoyable. King (1981) calls this "the magic moment of reintegration and safety at the end . . . that makes the danse macabre so rewarding and magical" (p. 14). If horror movies are society's worst fears realized on-screen, it makes sense that seeing these fears resolved would be relieving, and thus enjoyable. On this account, horror films offer a kind of negative reinforcement; the removal of an unpleasant stimulus proves to be rewarding (Skinner, 1969). When the movie ends, the "monster" having been defeated, the relief is rewarding.

One difficulty with the relief hypothesis is the definition of "successful ending." Many horror films end with the threat unresolved. For example, films in the *Friday the 13th* horror series often end with a suggestion that the killer is not dead, such as a camera shot of the empty space where his dead body should be. Perhaps any ending is satisfactory because, regardless of whether the characters are still in danger, the audience is no longer threatened (Tamborini and Stiff, 1987). This idea is doubtful, because it is highly improbable that the audience truly believes itself to be threatened.

Although Samuel Coleridge (1951) suggested that it is possible to experience fiction with a "willing suspension of disbelief," it is unlikely that anyone attending to drama or literature comes to believe that the fictional is real. Carroll (1990) notes that "in order to respond appropriately to something like a horror film . . . we must believe we are confronted with a fictional spectacle" (pp. 67–68). If the audience were to believe itself in real danger, the experience of a horror movie would not be enjoyable at all; rather, viewers would be "calling out the army" (p. 67).

Despite some uncertainty about what makes a successful ending, de

Wied, Zillmann, and Ordman (1994) have used relief theory to explain the appeal of tragedy. These investigators had undergraduate subjects view a shortened version of the film *Steel Magnolias*. The film was interrupted three times to ask subjects about physical and emotional reactions of sympathy and sadness. After the film, subjects were asked about how much they enjoyed it. The major result was that subjects who were the most sad during the film were the subjects who rated the film most enjoyable ($r=.55$). High empathizers were more sad during the film and reported more enjoyment after the film. De Wied et al. interpret these results in terms of relief theory: the subjects most disturbed by the tragedy are most relieved by the end of the film, and some of the arousal value of the sadness during the film is transferred to the positive emotional experience of the ending.

De Wied et al. believe that the ending of *Steel Magnolias* is successful in offering some meaning for human suffering, but they recognize that not all tragedies have so satisfying a conclusion: "The greatest remaining challenge . . . concerns the explanation of the enjoyment of tragedy that is simply devoid of concluding events that could be construed as inducers of positive affect or as something that gives human suffering redeeming value" (1994, p. 103).

Horror Theory Interrogated

It is time to return to our three disgusting films—the epicures and the monkey, the slaughterhouse, and the facial surgery. Why are these films so much less attractive than Hollywood horror? This question can now be raised in the light of the preceding review of theory and research on the attractions of horror.

The first point to note is that the violence in the three films is not exceptional in comparison with the violence of horror films. The focus on death and dismemberment in our films is a common theme in horror films, and presumably this focus can disturb all who are conscious of their own mortality. So it is not the nature of the violence that makes the films unappealing.

As noted earlier, the catharsis hypothesis has been more popular in literary than in psychological analyses of horror. But in any case, catharsis theory does not suggest why the three disgusting films are unappealing. The fact that more disgust-sensitive individuals turn off the films faster implies that these films are indeed eliciting disgust. If horror films appeal by eliciting and purging negative emotions, such as fear and disgust, then the three disgust films should likewise appeal.

The curiosity-fascination theory of horror's appeal is likewise unhelpful. The content of the three films is certainly anomalous, at least in the sense that few of our subjects had ever seen in everyday life anything like what they saw on-screen. Subjects should have been fascinated to see something so unusual and curious to see the end of these films. All three films were norm breaking in the descriptive sense of making public on-screen what is usually private, and the monkey epicures, at least, were breaking a moral norm, against eating a live animal. Despite all this foundation for curiosity and fascination, the disgust films were not generally appealing.

High sensation seekers, in particular, should have been attracted to an opportunity to escape boredom in an unusual and arousing experience. Although the 10 percent of our subjects who did not turn off the films may have been the high sensation seekers (we did not have sensation-seeking scores for our subjects), it is difficult to see how an individual-differences theory can explain why the average reaction to our films fell short of the broad appeal of horror films.

According to Zillmann's snuggle theory, our subjects should have been attracted to the three disgust films to the extent that the social setting gave subjects the opportunity to practice their gender roles. Our subjects, male and female undergraduates, did have some opportunity of this kind. Although only one subject at a time watched the films, each subject was observed and directed through the study by two research assistants—one male and one female undergraduate. Thus each subject watched the films in the presence of one same-sex and one opposite-sex undergraduate, in front of whom the subject should have been able to practice either mastery (male subjects) or distress (female subjects). This opportunity for gender-role reinforcement was evidently not enough to make the disgust films attractive.

Mood-management theory can be applied to the situation of our disgust subjects, but two uncertainties make the application tentative. First, we do not know how many of our subjects were bored. Second, our subjects were facing unusual and unknown content, whereas people choosing to see a horror film know enough to expect excitement and scariness. Still, to the extent that horror is an antidote to boredom, our films should have had the value of reducing boredom; apparently this value was not enough to make them attractive. Indeed, from the point of view of mood management, our subjects turned off the disgusting films because they anticipated feeling better with them off.

The last theory reviewed, relief theory, is also difficult to apply to our disgust study. Our subjects probably did feel some sense of relief when they turned off the disgust films, and this negative reinforcement may well have been multiplied by the transfer of unresolved arousal elicited by the violence they had just seen. Why didn't subjects wait for the pleasure of still greater relief by letting the films go on to their conclusions? Perhaps our subjects turned off the films because they could not anticipate the kind of satisfying resolution of the violence that they expect in at least some horror films.

It is worth noting that some viewers of horror films also "turn off" the film, at least briefly, by self-distraction and looking away from the screen. Tamborini, Stiff, and Heidel (1990) report that this kind of avoidance during a film is associated with not liking the film ($r = -.43$ with index of how appealing, pleasing, and interesting subjects found a film). Thus, although subjects were probably turning off the disgust films in search of relief, this relief was probably associated with disliking the films rather than with liking them.

The conclusion of this section must be that theories and research about the appeal of horror have not been very helpful in understanding why the three disgust films were not appealing. Notably, none of these theories offers any insight into why viewing fictional violence should be attractive when viewing real violence is not. In general, our documentary films did offer what the literature suggests will make horror films attractive: vivid death and dismemberment that should elicit and purge fear and disgust, appeal to curiosity and sensation seeking, give viewers the opportunity to practice their gender roles, increase arousal and reduce boredom, and set up a powerful sense of relief when the film is over. Nevertheless, subjects turned off the disgust films.

The question remains, when is horrific violence attractive and when is it not? Together with my student and colleague Jenny Stein, I undertook two studies aimed at learning more about this question.

Two Studies and Some Surprising Results

Film Sound

One striking difference between our films and commercial horror films is the quality of the sound track. Our films had the kind of sound typical of inexpensive documentary productions: no music, no special effects, and dialogue or voice-over without the vibrancy and diction that trained actors produce with the help of a good sound lab. It seemed possible that unappealing sound tracks made our films unappealing.

The importance of the sound track to a horror film's appeal is an issue that has not often been addressed. Clover (1992) has noted that "some viewers claim that they are more disturbed by the 'music' of horror movies than the images," but that "sound in cinema in general has been undertheorized, and horror sound scarcely theorized at all" (p. 204). In her review of musical sound tracks, Cohen (1990) suggests that "music serves a narrative role" (p. 113) by providing extra information about characters' emotions and that "associations generated by music influence the interpretation of the subject" (p. 114). Similarly, Pudovkin (1985) argues that "just as the image is an objective perception of events, so the music expresses the subjective appreciation of this objectivity" (p. 91). Belton (1985) agrees: "The sound track corresponds not, like the image track, directly to 'objective reality' but rather to a secondary representation of it" (p. 66). Cavalcanti (1985) puts this popular observation most succinctly: "While the picture is the medium of statement, the sound is the medium of suggestion" (p. 109).

There seems little doubt that film sound can be important in determining the emotional impact of a film, but the impact of sound is likely to be complex. Cohen (1990) highlights the paradox of film sound tracks: "Music makes the film more real but the very presence of the music contradicts reality" (p. 118). The same can be said of film sound effects, which long ago left fidelity behind in favor of surrealism. Gunshots, auto wrecks, and footfalls in the hallway are represented in film sound as ideal types, more vivid than the reality they signal.

If film sound is a cue for unreality, perhaps our documentary films were unappealing because they were too obviously what they were: records of reality. Of course the sound quality was not the only cue that our films were documentaries rather than fictional drama, but sound quality might be important in this regard. This possibility suggested an experiment to assess the impact of a commercial sound track by showing subjects a film clip from *Friday the 13th, Part III*.

The experiment compared the reactions of subjects who were exposed to the intact film clip (both video and audio) with the reactions of subjects exposed to the same video but with the audio turned off. If the film sound track is an important cue for unreality, and if assurance of unreality is important for enjoying film horror, then subjects watching the video without audio should be more disgusted, disturbed, and distressed by the screen violence than subjects watching the same video with audio.

Enjoyment during a Horror Film and the Relief Hypothesis

Above it was noted that the relief hypothesis was not easily applied to understanding why subjects did not like the three disgusting films. The theory suggests that viewers who are most distressed during a horror film should be those who most enjoy the film after it is over. This was indeed the pattern of results reported by de Wied et al. (1994) for the appeal of a tragic film: those most distressed and empathic during the film were those who rated it afterward as most enjoyable. But subjects watching our disgust films turned them off, a behavior suggesting that they were not enjoying them (Tamborini et al., 1987).

What if subjects like being sad or scared, even as they are feeling sad or scared? Perhaps those most distressed by dramatic tragedy are also those who most enjoy it, not just in relief after the film, but even as they are watching it. And perhaps those who are most disturbed by horror (short of turning it off) are also those who most enjoy watching it, not just in relief after the film, but even as they are watching it.

These possibilities led to a study in which subjects watched the same clip from *Friday the 13th, Part III* and gave two ratings of their enjoyment of the film. One rating was during a brief pause in the middle of the film clip, the other after the film was over. If subjects enjoy being scared and disgusted, then the first rating should be as high as the second. If relief theory is correct, enjoyment of the film should be rated higher when the attacker is subdued and the film is over.

Three Measures of Affective Reaction to Horror

For both studies, the film clip used was a segment of *Friday the 13th, Part III* previously employed by Zillmann et al. (1986). This 14-minute clip offers a relatively complete episode of violence in which a young woman is repeatedly attacked by a masked killer; the woman finally escapes her attacker, leaving him covered in blood with an ax stuck in his skull. For both studies, the affective-reaction measures (0–10 scales, "not at all" to "extremely") were again taken from Zillmann et al., except that some of their positive adjectives were dropped to make room for three negative adjectives: "disgusting," "disturbing," and "distressing."

Combining subjects from the two studies, 63 female and 2 male undergraduates from Bryn Mawr and Haverford Colleges completed affective ratings of the film clip. Factor analysis of these ratings produced three dimensions that were represented by three indexes: involving (mean of involving, exciting, and not-boring scales), disturbing (mean of disturbing, disgusting, and depressing scales), and amusing (mean of amusing, not-believable, and entertaining scales). (A similar three-dimensional structure has been found in follow-up research by Susan Burggraf with students at Bowdoin College.)

These results have some interest in their own right. Tentatively, the involving index may be interpreted as assessing general arousal or excitation, whereas the disturbing and amusing indices seem to assess, respectively, negative and positive affective tone. The amusing index implies some distancing and unreality (not-believable) in addition to positive tone; it cannot be interpreted as equivalent to the more global rating of "enjoyment" that was included only in the second study. The scale that is most commonly associated with horror, "frightening," was not included in any of the indices because it correlated with both the involving and disturbing indices.

The three indices were essentially uncorrelated, indicating that arousal can vary independently of affective tone and that positive and negative affect can vary independently. The same kind of result is found in the literature on subjective quality of life (Bradburn, 1969; Warr, Barter, & Brownbridge, 1983; McCauley & Bremer, 1991), where positive and negative affect have been found to vary independently as a function of good and bad things happening to an individual during a given period of time. Overall subjective quality of life is usually assessed as some kind of balance or average of positive and negative affect. Thus, the simplest interpretation of the independence of positive and negative affective reactions to a horror film is that some aspects of the film produce amusement, some aspects produce disturbance, and overall enjoyment of the film should be related to the balance or average of these two indices.

This simple interpretation is denied, however, by the results of the second study. Subjects' ratings of enjoyment during and after the film clip were highly correlated (rs of .71 and .63) with the involving index, but not significantly correlated with either the disturbing or amusing index. The clear implication is that what subjects enjoyed about the film had little to do with the balance of positive and negative affect; rather, enjoyment was associated with finding the film involving, exciting, and not boring.

This pattern of results offers support for previous research that has found liking for horror associated with sensation seeking, including susceptibility to boredom and inclination for the thrill of new experiences. The results are also broadly consistent with mood-management theory; viewers expect horror films to be exciting and scary (Tamborini & Stiff, 1987), and our subjects are telling us they find involvement and excitement enjoyable regardless of whether viewing makes them feel good or bad.

The Impact of Film Sound

Using the involving, disturbing, and amusing indices just described, the first study compared subjects who got both video and audio tracks with subjects who got only the video. Contrary to prediction, the subjects receiving only the video were not higher on the disturbing index than subjects who got both video and audio. The two groups did not differ on the disturbing index, and there was if anything a trend toward more disturbance for subjects who got both video and audio. Nor did the two groups of subjects differ on the amusing index. On the involving index, however, the video-with-audio subjects were significantly higher than the video-only subjects. The impact of the sound track—music, special effects, a dialogue little more than exclamations—was to increase involvement. If the sound track did provide cues for unreality, these cues were either unimportant or redundant in limiting how disturbing the film was to our subjects.

Enjoyment during and after the Film

Subjects rated their enjoyment of the film significantly higher during the film than after. This result challenges relief theory, which assumes that negative emotions during a horror film are not enjoyable and predicts that the enjoyment of the film after it is over depends upon the positive emotion associated with the end of the film. Not only are subjects saying that they enjoy the film before any kind of resolution has occurred, they say that they actually like it more while involved in it than they do looking back on it. Putting this result together with the association of enjoyment with the involving index but not with the disturbing or amusing index, the implication is that many viewers enjoy their involvement in the film in a way that does not depend upon either the positive or negative affective tone of the involvement.

Summary of Results

The results of two small studies of female undergraduates can at most point the way to further inquiries. With all due caution, then, the results seem to suggest two tentative conclusions. The first is that enjoyment of horror depends not upon the balance of positive and negative emotions elicited but rather upon excitement and involvement that can be associated with either positive or negative emotions. The second is that the enjoyment of horror is in the watching, not in the relief associated with the end of watching. These conclusions do not resolve the paradox of the appeal of horror, but make the paradox more acute. Scores on the disturbing index show that viewers do feel disturbed, disgusted, and depressed by horrific violence, but they enjoy their involvement in the film anyway. How can the paradox be resolved?

A Tentative Resolution

It is worth examining the possibility that human beings are capable of enjoying being frightened, disgusted, and saddened (Brosnan, 1976). The radical quality of this possibility becomes clear when it is held up against the alternatives that have been advanced, early and late, in order to avoid it. Catharsis is one such alternative; the catharsis hypothesis suggests that what is enjoyable in drama is not the experience of fright, disgust, or sadness but the purging of these emotions. The relief hypothesis is another evasion of the same sort; like catharsis it holds that the experience of negative emotions is noxious but holds out the reward value of relief from these emotions as the source of attraction to dramatic instigation of such emotions. These alternatives are a priori unlikely to the extent that human beings are notably weak in undertaking immediate losses for long-term gains (Rachlin, 1995). Now, tentatively, the evidence of two small studies makes these alternatives look even less likely.

If we face the possibility that human beings sometimes can enjoy what are usually accounted negative emotions, there seem to be basically two ways of understanding how the negative becomes positive. One way is to assume that the dramatic distance of fiction can moderate negative emotional reactions such that they provide an enjoyable arousal jag at small cost in negative hedonic tone. The other way is to assume that emotions instigated by fiction and drama are qualitatively different emotions from their everyday counterparts, and that the dramatically instigated emotions are always enjoyable.

The first theory amounts to saying that dramatically instigated emotions are simply weaker versions of everyday emotions. Assume that, for many individuals and under many circumstances, an increase in arousal is enjoyable. Assume that the cues for unreality in any dramatic or fictional representation can reduce the negative quality of emotions such as fear, disgust, and pity more than these cues reduce the arousal value of these emotions. Then dramatically instigated emotions offer good value of arousal increase for small cost in negative affect, and the net experience during the drama is positive. Viewers feel negative emotions that are moderately arousing but only slightly negative—and they enjoy the drama.

This understanding of the dramatic instigation of negative emotions has been urged by Apter (1992). Apter's theory encompasses the attractions of drama but goes beyond the appeal of drama and fiction to a general theory of "psychological reversals" in which dangers of many kinds become attractive when the arousal associated with danger can be experienced within the safety of a protective frame. Skydiving and mountain climbing are dangerous and arousing but self-confidence provides the protective frame that makes these activities exciting rather than anxiety provoking. Identification with others who take risks can provide arousal within the protective frame of "spectator." Dramatic productions, along with fantasy and recollection of past experience, are similarly enjoyable for providing access to arousal with the reassurance of present safety.

A second theory of how the negative becomes positive is that the emotions experienced in drama are qualitatively different from everyday experience of the same emotions. Indeed, this theory would assert that we err in calling dramatic emotions by the same names as everyday emotions; the dramatic emotions are a parallel but different reality.

This theory has ancient precedent in the *Natyasastra* of Bharata, a Sanskrit treatise on drama dating from 200–300 A.D. (Masson & Patwardhan, 1970). The *Natyasastra* focuses on the nature of the *rasa*, defined as "aesthetic or imaginative experience" (p. 1). The emotions that a character in a drama experiences are in turn experienced by an observer, but in a different manner. "The spectator can go further, and in a sense deeper. For when 'love' is awakened in him, it is not like the love that the original character felt . . . the [state of mind] is transformed into an extraworldly state" (p. 23). The emotion of the character is adopted by the observer and transformed to fit the observer, yet it is not an earthly state of mind; it exists "outside both time and space altogether" (p. 32). In the *Natyasastra*, the distinction between real and savored emotion is emphasized by having two names for each of the major emotions: one name for the everyday experience of the emotion and a different name for its dramatic counterpart.

Although the *Natyasastra* does not deal with horror, it offers an interesting account of the appeal of tragedy. "Sensitive readers become more and more deeply attracted towards this aesthetic of grief whereas they tend to shun the real experience" (Masson & Patwardhan, 1970, p. 31). "Anything that takes us away from preoccupations with ourselves is considered useful" (p. 34). In short, this account of the appeal of tragedy emphasizes the extent to which dramatically induced grief transcends the personal and individual problems of viewers. One result of this transcendence might be to make individual pains and problems seem smaller and less important. Just this kind of result has been reported by Zillmann, Rockwell, Schweitzer, and Sundar (1993), who were surprised to find that subjects tolerated more discomfort after exposure to film tragedy.

This interpretation resonates with one version of catharsis theory. As Mills (1993) has noted, catharsis may better be interpreted as purification than as purgation. The experience of fear and pity in response to dramatic tragedy can be attractive because the emotions are purified of self-interest and of the necessity to act—and to pay the costs of acting—in a complex and ambiguous world.

Applied to horror films, the perspective of the *Natyasastra* suggests that the experience of fear and disgust in reaction to a horror film is qualitatively different from everyday fear and disgust. Purified of self-interest, fear and disgust can be enjoyed as marks and qualifications of humanity, just as Mills's (1993) subjects valued their experience of empathy in responding to a film tragedy. But the key to enjoying these dramatically instigated emotions is the framing of the film as drama and unreal. In Apter's (1992) terms, the cues for unreality provide the protective frame in which dramatic rather than everyday emotions can be experienced.

It is time to return one last time to the three disgusting films. The answer to the question with which we began may after all be as simple as the difference between fact and fiction: these three films were disgusting rather than enjoyable because they were loaded with cues for reality and were lacking the frame of dramatic fiction. They were unappealing because they were documentaries, too brief and unrevealing about the people in them to support identification with any of these people. Thus Apter (1992) and the *Natyasastra* can suggest why documentary violence is unattractive, whereas the literature on the attractions of horror films leads all too easily to the prediction that our documentary violence should also be attractive.

Of course documentaries and news reports of violence, even real dismemberment by the side of the highway, can be enjoyable to some people. There are reports of whole families bringing picnic lunches to watch a hanging. But enjoying real violence may require some other form of distancing or protective framing to take the place of dramatic distance. As Apter (1992) would argue, the context of drama is only one of the frames in which negative emotion can offer a positive experience.

Note

My thanks to the Harry Frank Guggenheim Foundation for supporting the two studies reported in this chapter. Thanks also to Jenny Stein, who carried out these studies and wrote them up in a report from which I borrowed shamelessly for this chapter. And thanks to Dolf Zillmann, whose kindness in sharing with me many of his recent papers, both published and unpublished, should not implicate him in any errors of mine in the use of these papers. Finally, my special thanks to Joel Wallman, whose comments on a draft of this chapter were most helpful.

8

The Presence of Violence in Religion

MAURICE M. BLOCH

This chapter concerns the place of violence in religion and more particularly in religious rituals. Although much of the discussion will refer to
peoples living outside the industrial world, in societies that would often
be qualified as simple, peasant, or even primitive, the conclusions apply
to religious practices in general.

To talk of violence in religion may at first seem surprising, especially
to North American or European audiences, which often have a somewhat sentimental view of religion and a totally negative view of violence,
in the abstract at least. That being so, the question for them seems to
be how the two things can be mixed together. In fact, violence and
religion are intimately linked all over the world. For example, a moment's reflection about the familiar Semitic religions—Judaism, Christianity, and Islam—reveals the great role that violence has always played
for them. The Old Testament is full of the celebrations of wars and
killings, of maledictions and blood-curdling threats. The same is true of
the Koran and the New Testament, in which we are told, for example,
how, in the Acts of the Apostles, a couple who had not disclosed the
full profit they had made on a property transaction to Saint Peter and
to an early Christian congregation were immediately struck dead by God
in an episode that seems to make matters worse by adding an element
of grim humor. The presence of violence, or the evocation of it, is also
very clear in rituals, such as the Muslim celebration of Abraham's sacrifice or the Christian evocation of the crucifixion. I refer in passing to
such manifestations from the world religions so that the reader does not

FIGURE 8.1 Statute of Christ, Gaucin, Spain.

forget that we are not dealing simply with religions that are very remote from the Western world.

The relation of religion to violence is and has always been close, but it is also multifaceted. It is important to distinguish the violence that religion may cause, for example, religious wars and intolerance; the way religion may accompany violence, such as the prominent place of religion as an accompaniment to military activities; and the violence that forms part of the practice of religion itself, whether it be literal violence, such as actual blood sacrifices in ancient Jewish, Muslim, and some Hindu practices, or symbolic or metaphoric violence, such as the "drowning" of Christian baptism, which is intended as a prerequisite to a second birth. It is violence as a part of the spectacle of religious ritual that particularly concerns me here.

In reality, however, it is often impossible to separate the different ways in which religion and violence are interrelated. For example, the relation that exists between the spectacle of violence in religious ritual and actual aggressive and military violence occurring outside a truly religious context will be discussed below. This relationship has been the concern of a number of historians of religion and theologians as well as anthropologists and philosophers. However, before discussing such theories and proposing others, it is necessary to consider examples of the phenomena in order to be sure of what we are talking about.

Two Examples of Religious and Ritual Violence

The types of religious rituals, which involve the most obvious cases of religious and ritual violence, are often grouped by anthropologists and other students of religion under the two rather vague labels "initiations" and "sacrifices." It is useful to reconsider what types of phenomena they are.

Initiations are rituals that introduce people into a transcendental community, often by making them undergo some form of ordeal. Christian baptism is an example of such a ritual, introducing the child into the community of the church through the symbolism of being "born again." The same is roughly true of Jewish and Islamic circumcision.

"Sacrifice" is a term given to rituals such as the ancient Jewish practice of killing a lamb in the temple of God to establish, or reestablish, a proper relation between the divine and human beings. Below I take examples of such rituals from outside of what have been called the "world religions" in order to focus our discussion of the place of violence in religion and ritual.

Initiation

The Merina of Madagascar are a group of people who number more than a million and who, although they have been Christian for more than a century, practice an initiation ritual involving the circumcision of young boys at the age of two or three.[1] This ritual much antedates Christianity. The reason that the Merina give for this practice is that it conveys the blessing of the ancestors on the children concerned as well as on all the community, in much the same way in which Jewish circumcision was the mark and the continuing creation of the covenant between man and God.

What the Merina mean by blessing is the establishment of a creative contact between the ancestors and those who are blessed. This transforms them gradually from mere living beings, similar to plants and animals, who live and die without establishing lasting social institutions and who are merely motivated by their own gratifications, into moral beings. These are beings who belong to groups that, like clans or nations, continue to exist even though the constituting members of the group die and who are motivated by absolute rules of what is right and wrong, at least as far as these rules relate to the continuation of the group. The perfect example of such superior beings that blessing creates are the ancestors, who are dead and who should therefore have abandoned individual desires.[2]

According to the Merina, being blessed, through a ritual like that of circumcision, not only puts you in contact with the ancestors but also makes you a little like them. Not too much, however, since one also wants, for oneself and one's children, to be alive, for a while at least. Blessing is, therefore, a matter of striking the right balance between making the blessed like the dead and still maintaining their vitality, a balance that changes throughout life, since when one is young one should be only a little like the ancestors, and therefore much in need of blessing, while when old one is very much like the ancestors and, therefore, almost dead.

In practical terms the act of blessing is brought about by elders spraying or blowing water on their descendants. This water has in some way been associated with the ancestors, and so the beginning of the circumcision ritual is often marked by elders going to fetch water that has been placed on the ancestors' graves and with which they will bless their descendants. Such water is a complicated symbol in that it represents life and vitality, as water so often does, but, because it is channeled through the ancestors and the elders, it is a vitality controlled by the moral authority of the dead. The purpose of the circumcision ritual is to make the children similar to such water: strong, fertile, vital, but in a way that is contained by morality and harnessed for the continuation of the group.

The circumcision ritual is the occasion for a great party with singing and dancing that lasts at least one whole night. An essential preliminary is the killing of a cow or a bull after a mock hunt and the fetching of a number of plants, such as bananas and sugarcanes. These particular plants and animals are seen by the Merina as full of life and fertility. It is this element that it is hoped will be transferred to the boy, yet, like the bull, the plants are ritually "killed" (that is, speared and cut up) during the proceedings with a great show of violence. Such dramatic violence occurs again during the night, when more water of blessing is fetched. The gourd in which it is put is threatened all the way by men carrying a spear, which is finally thrust into it as though it were a hunted animal.

What all these threatened and speared things represent is untamed vitality, not properly controlled by the social and moral order that the ancestors and the elders incarnate. The killings are the triumph of order, continuity and morality over such vitality, which then can be consumed by the ancestral element for its own higher purposes. Much the same violence, with similar purpose, will happen to the child.

While all the revelry is going on, the little boy is danced inside the house, itself a symbol that is seen in contradiction to the tomb—the source of blessing, where the ancestors united lie. The house is a place for mere everyday life, a place for women, who, in Merina representations, are more vital than men but more distant from the ancestors. Then, as dawn breaks in the east, the child is to be transformed. He is taken to the threshold of the house where the operation is carried out. This is compared to a killing and, immediately afterward at the same spot, the water of blessing is poured over him.

After this has been done, the child is taken outside. The outside in the drama of the ritual is the place of the ancestors, as opposed to the inside, which is the place of the living. But outside there are also the men, who, with shouts of joy, greet the boy as a man, as a warrior, as a destroyer of others, and as an aggressive male. From having been a victim, the circumcised child has become a soldier who will make others his victims. The moment of circumcision is thus a moment of birth and death. The boy's old, vital, feminine, uncontrolled self is killed as the prepuce is cut and, at the same time, he is born as a member of the ancestrally sanctioned group of men. The circumcision is a killing that leads to a higher form of life, the life of the dead, which itself leads to an earthly and aggressive new life.

The ritual, however, does not stop there. After having been taken out with such panache, the child is brought back to secular life, again symbolized by the house and the women, who remain inside during the operation. The boy reenters it, but this time as an aggressor, through the window. It is as though once having been made one with the ancestors he can then leave them and regain the world of women and of ordinary life as a consumer, as an aggressive master, legitimate in his future conquests, because of his contact with death and the transcendental moral beings who were his forebears. Through having been symbolically killed, he has become a blessed being with a right to consume the vitality of others, especially women, for his own higher purposes. The spectacle of violence that such a ritual offers involves both metaphorical violence directed toward such substitutes as water or bananas and actual violence directed toward the child, but it goes even beyond that, in suggesting and legitimating nonritual violence toward women and enemies. Before discussing in a more theoretical manner these elements, however, we need to look at sacrifice.

Sacrifice

As an example of sacrifice I take the wonderful description given by the anthropologist Godfrey Lienhardt (1961) of the religious practices of a group of people called the Dinka. The Dinka live in the Nilotic part of the Sudan in Africa. As was the case for the initiation ritual of the Merina, much of what will be said about Dinka sacrifice could apply equally well to many other people around the globe who practice rituals that have been labeled as sacrifice, whether these be people who practice world religions, such as Islam, or the less widespread traditional religions, which world religions arrogantly call pagan but which in fact are very similar to them, if one ignores, as do most of their practitioners, the specialized interpretations of theologians.

The Dinka carry out animal sacrifices on many occasions—at annual rituals to hasten the coming of rain, before initiating military raids, to remove the effects of sin—but above all, to bring about recovery from disease. Disease, however, is something that should be understood not as it is by the medical profession but in much broader terms, as a state of fundamental dislocation that manifests itself in symptoms, such as physical or mental illness, the failure of crops, the death of cattle, quarrels between relatives, barrenness, or a little of all these things.

The ritual is carried out at the recommendation of a diviner, who will suggest the possible cause for such a negative state of affairs and sometimes name a supernatural being who may have caused it. But the Dinka are very vague about the nature of supernatural beings and Lienhardt glosses their term for them by the word "Divinity," which can be either plural or singular. The diviner will explain the reason why a sacrifice will appease the offended supernatural being. However, all this theory is rather unimportant to the people concerned; for them it is the doing of the ritual that matters.

The ritual is focused on the killing of cattle. To understand this action it is necessary to know just how important cattle are to the Dinka. Cattle are not only their most valued resource; they are the focus of their most elaborated artistic imagination and admiration. However, although cattle represent a central value for all Dinka, they are particularly associated with the young, especially young males, who identify closely with the strength, virility, and beauty of certain animals. This admiration is focused on their majestic horns, which Dinka often imitate with their arms raised high as they sing the praises of particular beasts. However, humans are more than cattle, or rather they become more than cattle as they become more respected. This is especially so of the priestly group called the Masters of the Fishing Spear. This extra element that humans have and that cattle notably lack is especially focused on the ability of speech. Not just any speech, but the semiprophetic speech that the Masters of the Fishing Spear employ in rituals. Such speech is always truthful and therefore prophetic when referring to the future. It is that which humans can achieve and which links them to the divine. It establishes a contact with that which does not change, whither, or perish. Successful mature humans, who can accede to such speech, are therefore dual creatures. They have the animal but transient strength of cattle and the supernatural ability of a time-transcending capacity that links them to the Divine in its many forms.

It is these two elements that are, so to speak, placed in a gladiatorial contest in the rite of sacrifice. In the middle stands the animal to be slaughtered, tethered for long hours in the sun, which gradually weakens it, as its head and therefore its horns droop. Nearby is a Master of the Fishing Spear, who for many hours harangues the beast, goes over the events that led to the sacrifice, recounts family histories and much else besides, all spoken in the language of truth characteristic of the priest and Divinity. As speech grows and accumulates during the day, the beast weakens. The final victory of the speech of the Masters occurs when it is finally killed.

This can be understood as a spectacle with onlookers as audience, but to put the matter as simply as this would be misleading. Among the audience there are, first of all, those for whom the ritual is being carried out, and who are in a number of ways associated with the animal. Symbolically, as the Master of the Fishing Spear makes clear, it is they who are being weakened and then killed. The same is true, though to a lesser extent, of the other members of the "audience." This fact is marked in a peculiarly graphic way. Lienhardt noted how the muscles of those who merely watch start to twitch as the proceedings go on, and the Dinka told him that this was in unison with the weakening flesh of the cattle. In them, too, the victory of speech over flesh, or of the transcendental and divine over strength and vitality, is also taking place.

However, this is not all there is to it. It would not make sense to end with the killing of the beast and the symbolic killing of the participants. After all, the purpose of many sacrifices is to cure diseases, and one could not end with a diminishing of strength and a death.

And so matters are reversed by the very killing itself. Once dead, the animal is no longer identified with those for whom the sacrifice is being performed. The beast becomes merely meat to be cut up, butchered, cooked, and eaten. This is a great event, as meat is never eaten outside sacrifices and, because of various dietary deficiencies, its consumption creates a great feeling of well-being, elation and strength. For the participants, the vitality that was apparently lost in the first part of the proceedings is regained, in an even greater amount than was lost.

This is not merely putting the symbolic process in reverse, since the strength that was lost was native strength and it was in favor of the transcendental element that it was given up, while the strength that is obtained is derived from the outside from a mere conquered, killed, and butchered animal, there to feed humans to superior beings who have been in contact with divine speech.

It is this aspect that connects, in this case as in so many others, the ritual violence of sacrifice with more secular violence. The feeling of strength, of well-being, of vitality regained, is that which leads to curing, to the renewal of the rains, and so on. But in some cases this regaining of strength does not end there but takes a military form. For the Dinka, ideally the elation of the sacrificial meal should become the beginning of military raids against traditional enemies, the starting up again of old and murderous feuds.

Similarities between Initiation and Sacrifice

Merina initiation and Dinka sacrifice are very different types of events, but, at least as regards violence, a similar pattern emerges. Furthermore this pattern can be discerned in most, if not all, religious rituals. This has been argued more fully in my book *Prey into Hunter* (1992), but these two examples will suffice for explaining what is involved.

There are two types of violence displayed both symbolically and actually in the ritual, although the first type occurs more strictly within the ritual, while the other spills out beyond it. The first violence is a violence against the vital element of those most directly concerned in both cases; the circumcised child in Merina circumcision, the sick person in Dinka sacrifice. This first violence leads to a symbolic killing that is deflected onto substitutes: in the case of Merina circumcision onto plants and cattle, and in the case of Dinka sacrifice onto the sacrificial animal itself. In both cases these killed living things stand for the human beings concerned. Furthermore, in the case of the initiation ritual, what is done is analogical in a different way, in that, although an actual bodily mutilation is actually carried out on the principal actor, this mutilation merely evokes killing and is talked of in these terms.

This element of "killing" is present in all rituals that can be labeled initiations or sacrifices. In initiation in other parts of the world, the initiates are often secluded in a hidden place where they are said to be dead. As noted above, even in an apparently mild ritual, such as Christian baptism, all the commentaries make clear the imagery of drowning. In sacrifice the element of killing, usually of an animal, is there, almost by definition, though sometimes, as in some form of Buddhist and Hindu sacrifice or in the Christian symbolism of Easter, where Christ is identified with the paschal lamb, this killing is only alluded to and not actually carried out. In all cases of sacrifice the element of substitution is also necessarily present, often especially clearly in the myths that accompany the ritual, as in the case of the ram substituted for Isaac in the biblical sacrifice of Abraham or the substitution of a doe for Iphigenia in the famous Greek myths concerning the beginning of the Trojan War.

The second violence is different. It is in a way a rebounding violence, a resurgence of strength after the weakening and dying of the first part of the ritual. In the case of the circumcision ceremony, it occurs as the child reenters the house of women that he left at the time of the operation. This is the return of a conqueror, a leader of men, a future warrior and scourge of his enemies, all things that are said explicitly in some versions of the ritual. In Dinka sacrifice, the second violence begins with the consumption of the meat of the animal but continues in the effervescence of the feast that often leads to the initiation of a raid on outsiders.

The second violence is thus not simply a matter of recovery of the vitality that was lost, since if that was so it would be difficult to understand how the rituals had brought about anything that was new. The vitality that was present before the ritual, in the child that will be circumcised, for example, is indeed forever lost and killed in the first part and through the first violence. It is lost in order to purify, to bring out the transcendental element, that which is shared with the ancestors in the Merina case, and with the Divine in the Dinka case. This loss, however, transforms the participants into nonmundane actors who must regain vitality. This they do through the second violence, which conquers outside beings and in some sense consumes them: the plants and the cattle in the Merina case, the sacrificed beast in the Dinka case.

In both cases, this outward conquering movement, initiated by the second violence, expands ever further toward the outside. What had begun as a rite of blessing or of curing becomes a rite of conquest, and more than that, the beginning of totally nonritual aggressive and violent activities, such as raids and warfare. In the world religions the recovery from death at the end of sacrificial rituals may seem far from actual violence, but its aggressive potential is shown to be clearly there when, for example, Christian sacrificial rituals are seen, as often happened, as suitable strengthening preliminaries for war or massacres, or when, as in modern Iran, the celebration of the martyrdom of Hussain can become the idiom for violent xenophobia.

Violence is therefore a central element to rituals such as the ones discussed above, but why? And why is there such a close relationship between religion and the spectacle of mutilation, weakening, or killing?

Earlier Theories

In the history of ideas, whether in philosophy, theology, or anthropology, there have been many attempts to explain the presence of the spectacle of violence. Two recent theories about this relationship, however, have been particularly influential. One comes from the pen of a French writer, the other from that of a German. Both draw inspiration heavily from psychoanalytic theories about "original" or "primal" scenarios that, we are told, gave rise to rituals such as sacrifice. However, since we know nothing of this sort about human beings in these very vaguely specified "early" times, these origin stories remain as fanciful and unprovable as those imagined by Freud himself.

The French writer, a scholar who has mainly taught in the United States, is Ren Girard. His most influential book is suggestively entitled *Violence and the Sacred* (1972), though he has elaborated his theses in a number of subsequent publications that basically argue for the uniqueness of Christianity (1978), a claim for uniqueness that, I believe, is untenable, as the references to Christianity in this chapter make clear, but that cannot be challenged fully here. In the original book Girard analyzes the presence of violence in rituals, especially in animal sacrifice but also in initiation. He mentions the Dinka case described above. His explanation of such practices is that human nature and society are intrinsically violent and that in acting out the murderous tendencies of the darker side of our nature in violent rituals we somehow canalize and ultimately neutralize our antisocial tendencies by directing them onto a scapegoat that is the sacrificial victim.

The German writer, Walter Burkert, is a classical scholar who also is particularly interested in animal sacrifice, especially Greek animal sacrifices, since the ancient Greeks felt it was necessary to kill an animal to the gods before undertaking almost any significant enterprise (Burkert, 1983). His explanation is that sacrifice is a form of acting out a primeval hunt, which was once the basis of society, and so the reenacting of the hunt in ritual binds men together and organizes them as it tames their response to death and sexuality.

The work of these scholars is thought-provoking. They have had the virtue of drawing the attention of a wider public to this important topic, and their analyses of particular rituals are often suggestive. They stress many points that have been overlooked. For example, Burkert is right to draw our attention to the symbolism of hunting present in both Merina and Dinka rituals. Girard is right, if less original, to stress the importance of the parallelism and metaphorical element at the heart of sacrifice, which is part of his elaborate theory of what he calls "mimetic desire." Yet I find myself dissatisfied by their general theories for a number of reasons.

Girard and Burkert seem to assume that we know what human nature is outside any particular social or cultural context and that it entails an innate tendency to violence, which the history of natural selection has bred into us. In fact, we know no such thing, and it is impossible to imagine human beings outside a specific historical context, that is, what they would be like "in a state of nature." Such a being would not really be human at all, and so the observation of a "general tendency" to aggression cannot simply be derived from the observation that it occurs frequently. Careful cross-cultural psychological work might be helpful in this matter, but neither writer refers to any, though Burkert, and to a lesser extent Girard, discuss ethological evidence concerning other species, which is irrelevantly used by them and some of the writers they follow as though it could provide evidence about humans.

It is tempting to assume that we all have a need to express a certain amount of violence, in the same way as we need certain vitamins, as is assumed in the Freudian psychoanalytic theories, which both Girard and Burkert use in different ways. But no satisfactory evidence for such a claim has ever been produced and it is very difficult to see how that could be possible. The fact that human societies vary greatly in time and space, in their attitudes to violence, and in the degree of violence that they manifest makes any blanket explanation in terms of a general human characteristic necessarily unconvincing (Howell, 1989).

Again the debt to Freud present in both these writers leads them, like him, to invent a "primal scenario," occurring in the Neolithic or the Paleolithic[3] era, for which the violence of sacrifice would be a solution. However, we know nothing about these "origin periods." Furthermore, and most disturbingly for anthropologists, as has often been pointed out (Rosaldo, 1986), these imaginings by nineteenth-and twentieth-century scholars, based on no evidence whatsoever, reveal all too clearly the anachronistic ideology of their own time and culture, projected onto what must have been totally different societies.

Girard and Burkert seem little interested in why the people who perform violent rituals say they do them or what they believe. Admittedly, Girard treats myths as though they were native explanations of the phenomena (which no modern anthropologist would accept), but even this is only to tell us that these myths/explanations are mere masks for the truth. He knows better. But the ancient Greeks killed animals before battles in order to win and to bring the gods on their side. The Dinka sacrifice in order to cure or to bring about rain. The Merina circumcision ritual is meant to bring about blessing. These overt purposes simply do not interest these writers, but surely any explanation worthy of the name should tell us how the killing of cattle or the circumcising of children can be believed to bring about such results. We need not end our attempt at understanding at people's own explanations, but to take no account of them seems cavalier in the extreme.

A general explanation of sacrifice as due to an unconscious desire for male unity simply does not explain why the gods are involved or why the killing of cattle would convince them to help the Greek armies. A theory that circumcision rituals canalize violence does not explain why the Merina use banana plants in their ritual.

Girard and Burkert assume that when participants in a ritual express violence they are acting on an internal motivation that leads, or led, them to choose to act in this way. In reality, however, people act in rituals in particular ways because they have been taught to do so and because everybody else around them is doing so. Their individual motivations, whatever personal urges they might feel, are, in the short term at least, largely irrelevant for understanding what they do; they are not reinventing the rituals as they go along. In fact, in cases such as the ones discussed above, it is not that particular psychological states make them perform the ritual but rather that performing the ritual brings about particular psychological states, as with aggression at the end of Dinka sacrifice (though even in such a case we cannot be sure that the outward manifestations of such emotions necessarily indicate a deeper psychological condition).

The difficulties with the explanations brought forward by Girard and Burkert are common problems in what have been called functionalist explanations, that is, explanations that account for a social phenomenon, such as a ritual, in terms of the satisfactions (functions) its practice is believed by the author to bring about for the participants. Functionalist explanations work much better to explain phenomena that are continually being invented anew and from scratch, something that is almost never the case in religion. Since this book is concerned with several different domains of violent imagery it is worth considering why explanations that might be appropriate for violent films or television programs will not do for religious rituals.

Why the Attraction of Violence in Rituals and in Films Cannot Be Explained in the Same Way

The fact that participants in a religious ritual neither are nor see themselves as either the "authors" or the "consumers" of the work of authorship of others means that explaining the attraction of violence in rituals presents special problems. As noted above, the emotions that people feel during such a ritual cannot account for what happens. As a result the significance of the violent spectacle involved in a religious ritual is very different from the significance of the violence represented in a commercial film. In the case of violent films, if many people get a thrill from seeing them, they will presumably go to see such films often. Then, the filmmakers will realize that such films draw crowds and, in order to be successful, they will make this type of film. In such cases the pleasure of the viewers becomes at least part of the explanation for the occurrence of these films. This is not the case with religious rituals. Whether the members of a religious community do or don't derive satisfaction from participating in a ritual that contains violent imagery, such as an initiation ceremony, will not change directly or indirectly what is done.

Those who invent the ritual through time—and often this means an anonymous multitude of people over many generations, even centuries—and who act unaware of the long-term creative implications of their activity are not reacting to audience response. Most people, especially in the nonmodern world, do not choose a religion as they choose a commercial product, that is, in terms of the satisfaction they derive from it.

There is another fundamental difference between watching a violent film or television program or playing with war toys and participating in a ritual involving violent acts. In the former cases, as Jeffrey Goldstein points out (chapter 3 in this volume), it is relatively easy to draw a distinction between being violent and enjoying playing at violence. Similarly, watching a violent film is not the same thing as being violent, though it can be argued that it may lead to real violence. Rituals are different. As we have seen, in ritual it is not easy to draw the line between actor and spectator, and certainly this distinction as it appears in theatrical representations is not applicable. The Dinka onlookers to the titanic struggle between divine speech and bovine strength might seem at first mere spectators, but as they watch, their very bodies are affected by the weakening of the flesh of the animal and, even more clearly, they become principal actors in the second act of violence, through eating the animal and then perhaps in participating in the raids that follow. This kind of oscillation between being a spectator and an actor is one of the most fundamental characteristics of rituals. For example, the same change in the nature of participation occurs in a Christian church service, when the previously passive congregation is suddenly transformed into the principal actors during communion. As a result, distinguishing between the attraction of watching or being told about or playing at violence and actually being violent, which is so important when thinking about films, war toys, or fairy stories, is very difficult to maintain when we are dealing with ritual.

Finally, there is an even more fundamental difference. What happens in a film, a television program, or even a folktale is clearly separated from the life of those who read or watch such narratives. The events occur in a world in which they have never been and which they do not expect to join. The awareness of this distance is probably what makes such spectacles pleasurable. As Clark McCauley points out (this volume), when, in a film, the barrier between the show and everyday experience stops being clearly marked, what might have been exciting becomes disgusting. Religious ritual may well evoke a world just as fantastic as that of any film, and it may, by various communicative devices, "parenthesize" the symbolic from the nonsymbolic; but in the end, and as part of the very ritual (Sperber, 1974; Bloch, 1985), these parentheses are dramatically removed so that the "other world" is made continuous with "this world." Indeed, because of this key connection between representation and participation, the principals are, as a result of the ritual, made permanently part of what, at first, had seemed merely evoked allegory. Thus initiation rituals take as their raw material the actual children of the community, not imaginary characters, and transform them. A baptized child will, for the remainder of her life, be a member of the church. This lasting change may well have been brought about by making the participants take roles in the drama of ritual where they enter another world of ancestors or of gods with whom they come into contact, but, at the end of the theatrical performance, the initiated children are believed to be changed permanently; their lives will never be the same. This means that any explanation of religious rituals—and this applies to the significance of violent episodes in them—must take into account not only representations evoked in the rituals but also the continuity of such representations with the nonritual world.

An Alternative Explanation

It is precisely by noting the continuity between what happens in ritual and outside it that we begin to formulate our attempt at understanding. Our starting point must be the starting point of ritual: mundane life and the attempt to change it. That aspect of mundane life that is stressed as of prime concern in all important religious ritual is its temporality, especially the processes of change as they affect the human body, its growth and maturing, its weakening through disease, death. Rituals relate this to an order that is more permanent, more absolute in its values, more long lasting. This other world is created by the ritual, but rituals also bridge the gap between the mundane and the transcendental, sometimes by ensuring the continuance of the presence of the social and religious in the mundane by orderly transmission of the lasting order, sometimes by restoring the incomprehensible upsets within the framework of the permanent. Thus the Merina circumcision ritual is intended to bring the child in contact with the lasting moral order of its society, represented by the ancestors, to bring him into their transcendental society or, as the Merina say, to bless him. Dinka sacrifice is intended to nullify the upset of disease or of drought by restoring the relation of impermanent man with the steady permanence of the divine beings whose presence on earth can be reached through contact with the true speech of the Masters of the Fishing Spear.

This explains the presence of the first violence. The rituals that are discussed above, as well as most religious rituals the world over, begin by an attempt to leave the world of the everyday. This leave-taking, most often, as in the cases illustrated here, is visualized in the most obvious way possible, by a symbolic death, since what is being negated is the transience of human life, and to go beyond life one must pass through death. This is death brought about by the ritual and therefore a kind of killing. A kind of killing that requires for its dramatic purposes a great show of leaving vitality behind in order to be with transcendental beings, be they gods, spirits, or ancestors. A similar pattern can be seen, for example, in the Christian ritual of Easter, which begins by the worshipers "dying" as they accompany Christ in his passion and in this way reaching a God who exists beyond "this life."

The very success, at least the dramatic success, of such a representation makes it clear that the matter cannot end there. One cannot leave the Merina child with the ancestors; he would be dead.[4] One cannot cure the Dinka patient by associating him or her too closely with the cattle, since that would be to kill them. And so a return must be organized: a return to vitality. Inevitably this return is triumphant, a consumption, a conquest from "above" of what was left "below." This is the second violence, and as I noted, it is a violence that because of its outward direction can spill over into actual violence. Then the spectacle merges back into the mundane but in a potentially bloody and dangerous way.

This explanation of the presence of violent imagery may sound too intellectual. It seems to ignore the very real emotions of those concerned. This, however, is not so; the spectacle of evocation of one's own death and strengthening, or that of a person near to one, is inevitably potentially very arousing. In rituals, such as the ones I have been talking about, a whole chaos of feeling may be elicited, but this cannot explain the presence of the ritual. The explanations that the participants give are not in terms of catharsis, as are those of both Girard and Burkert, but in terms of specific, though vague, ends.

The explanation I have given is nothing more than the translation of what the participants say, though phrased in more general terms, and I have attempted to show how this requires a double evocation of violence. This is so because religious ritual is an attempt by the participants to force the processes of life, as they are experienced outside ritual, into a framework, that of the transcendental, into which they simply will not fit. This is surely the case, as much for the Merina, who through their circumcision ritual make the children members of the society of the ancestors, and for the Dinka, who remove disease by aligning themselves with a time-transcending divinity, as it is for the Christians who, after having participated in Christ's death, are "resurrected" with him, or for Jews and Muslims who, by strictly following his legislation, become undying children, not of men but of God.

Notes

1. This ritual is described and analyzed in detail in *From Blessing to Violence* (Bloch, 1986).

2. The "should" is very important here, because the Merina also believe that the ancestors may sometimes experience again human desires and as a result make a nuisance of themselves.

3. They seem to forget that the humans of the Paleolithic were almost certainly of another species from *Homo sapiens sapiens*.

4. Indeed, Merina myth considers the fantasy of such a possibility with unsurprising horror. Unlike what Girard believes, myths neither indicate the origins of rituals nor are a kind of charter for them; rather, they seem to be a phantasmagoric speculation on the limitations of the transcendental.

9

The Psychology of the Appeal of Portrayals of Violence

DOLF ZILLMANN

Man's greatest good fortune is to chase and defeat his enemy, seize his total possessions, leave his married women weeping and wailing, ride his gelding, use the bodies of his women as a nightshirt and support, gazing upon and kissing their rosy breast, sucking their lips which are as sweet as the berries of their breasts.

—Genghis Khan on superlative bliss (Rashid ad-Din, 1960)

The Khan's famous utterance actually may have lost some of its sting in the translation—probably by design, in order to make it more palatable for sensitive Westerners. Such likely cleansing seems duly corrected, however, by contemporary fiction. Events that accord with the barbarian's formula for the grandest of bliss have become mainstream entertainment in the so-called free world. They are laid open and featured in the raw, with pains taken to depict the cruelest of cruelties and the goriest of gore, along with the most profane linguistic concoctions imaginable. Granted that most modern storytelling still clings to protagonists who have retained some moral inhibitions and even pursue the common good to a degree, the blockbuster success stories tend to present barbarous villains who, like ancient emperors, see no wrong in vanquishing those who get in their way, as well as in taking possession of whatever those others cherish, including their lovers and loved ones. Villains who kill at the drop of a hat and who, after indulging themselves sexually, snuff the life out of their gratifiers, have become commonplace. In terms of displaying unmitigated selfishness, the heroes are not far behind. Fighting for a cause that has some merit, usually the sole criterion for their hero status, apparently grants them a license to kill without restraint, even to enjoy it in sadistic fashion. It also seems to entitle them to sexual ravaging, especially of the villains' playmates.

Presumably because of its capacity to present violence in compelling images, cinematic storytelling has embraced barbarian heroes and villains who slash, shoot, and machine-gun their way to the things they want, all that without accepting societal impositions or moral curtailments that restrain normal mortals. Any encounter between such heroes and villains holds promise of stupendous slaughter. There can be little doubt that slaughter of this kind has taken center stage in the movies (Hoberman, this volume). Highly destructive violent encounters are featured with ever increasing frequency (Gerbner, 1988; Sapolsky & Molitor, 1995; "The killing screens," 1994). Sadistic maiming and killing are on the rise (Zillmann & Weaver, 1993). So is the number of cripples and corpses produced by each encounter.

Is the audience dismayed? To be sure, many lament the fact that the movies "have gotten too violent." The concerned citizens' lip service does not prevent many of them, however, from rushing to see the latest superviolent film. Taking the box-office success of cinematic productions as the ultimate behavioral measure of the appeal of such entertainment, there can be no doubt that fictional superviolence is an enormous attraction. Moreover, there can be no doubt that this phenomenal appeal is not limited to audiences in the Western world, but universal. The attraction of superviolent entertainment is evident cross-culturally. Superviolence proved a success wherever people are free to consume such fare (Carey, 1994; Gerbner, 1988; Medved, 1992; Weinraub, 1993).

In light of such powerful universal appeal, could it be that there is something archaic in all of us that attracts us to these exhibitions of brutality and terror, and that even lets us enjoy what we witness? Could it be that we are all attracted to, and in awe of, heroes who display basal fighting skills—rather than ingenuity, say, in engineering, which much of modern civilization is based upon? Do we really admire the fighter who, surrounded by villains with submachine guns, can kick-box his way out of danger? And do we really deify, along with so many movie superheroes, the weaponry of death? In the stories told us, do we still listen to the makings of warriors and the heroics through which they gain adulthood and respectability, just like in the legends of hunter-gatherer times (Gibson, 1994; Henderson, 1979)? After inspection of the dominant themes in contemporary entertainment it would seem to be so, indeed.

It is easy to understand Genghis Khan's revelations. By violent means he attained the gratifications he enumerated; and as the enforcer of whatever laws there may have existed, he had no reason to fear bliss-diminishing repercussions. The situation is radically different, of course, for the consumer of fiction. In absorbing fiction, others are seen to gain access, by violent maneuvers, to gratifications that remain "a fantasy" for the witness. How could this possibly be gratifying for the spectator? How could it enrich the "poor wretch," to use a Freudian characterization of the person in the passive role of witnessing the gratification of others?

Should spectators not respond with envy and ultimately with resentment inspired by it, as they would when witnessing persons in their immediate social environment attain rewards by bullying others? Should they not recognize the fact that those in fiction get away with violations of rules of social conduct, violations for which they themselves would be held accountable and made to suffer social reproach? And consequently, should they not be disturbed when seeing brutal, violent, coercive others attain good fortune at the expense of their victims' suffering? How could anybody witnessing such brute-force accomplishments be fascinated by the display and even take pleasure from it?

It may be considered puzzling, then, why we take such a keen interest in drama that dwells on the portrayal of barbarous violence. It is equally puzzling why we enjoy sharing the consumption experience with friends, and why we feel compelled to expose children, as we seem always to have done, to violent stories capable of frightening them severely (Cantor, 1994, this volume; Tatar, this volume). Violence is also known to permeate most popular sports and presumed to add spice to athletic competition generally (Goldstein, 1983; Guttmann, 1978, 1984, this volume).

Moreover, our apparent fascination with mayhem outside fiction is bewildering. What was there about public executions that made crowds flock around gallows and guillotines? Why are the news media so very partial to reporting bad news, mostly violence and the devastation left in its wake (Goldberg, this volume; Haskins, 1984; Stone & Grusin, 1984; Stone, Hartung, & Jensen, 1987)? And what is it that has made so-called reality programs, displaying such things as women's execution by their estranged husbands, bizarre suicides, and gruesome disembowelments by alligator attack as they actually happened a winning formula (Battaglio, 1991; Goode & Hetter, 1994; Freeman, 1993; Marin & Katel, 1994; Oliver, 1994)?

Given that our attraction to portrayals of violence and its aftermath is obtrusive in filling movie and television screens and books and papers, in both fiction and nonfiction, it is astounding how little attention psychologists have paid to this phenomenon. Both the construction of theories that might explain the extraordinary appeal of the portrayals in question and the empirical exploration of this appeal have been neglected. In untiring fashion, social psychologists and others have investigated the antisocial consequences of exposure to fictional violence (Geen, 1994; Huesmann & Eron, 1986; Linz & Donnerstein, 1989). But they have essentially bypassed the issue of the appeal of fictional and nonfictional violence as a salient element of entertainment.

This does not mean, however, that explanatory efforts as to why people are drawn to depictions of mayhem are lacking. There is an abundance of suggestions, in fact, mostly in connection with the apparent appeal of horror. Some of these suggestions may seem absurd; others are not easily dismissed. In fact, some cannot be faulted by rigorous procedures. We shall discuss the more intriguing speculations of this kind and try to determine their merit. We shall do likewise with the explanatory models of early psychologists, models that permeate the discussion of violent drama and its enjoyment. Thereafter we shall turn to proposals of contemporary psychology and integrate them as far as possible to offer specific, validated explanations for the various forms of the appeal of portrayals of violence.

Sweeping Claims and Pseudo Explanations

Many film critics believe they know what it is that makes screen violence so attractive. Commenting on Peckinpah's trend-setting piece *The Wild Bunch*, Ansen (1995), for instance, simply declares that the celebrated director managed to make us see the beauty of a massacre, among other atrocities. As spectators, he states, "we're alternately horrified by the butchery and exhilarated by the orgiastic energy his balletic spectacles stir up" (p. 71). Slaughter, then, is said to be beautiful, at least when presented within cinematic conventions that critics deem appropriate. Granted that poorly presented violence might be unattractive, the argument ascribes aesthetic appeal to all aptly presented displays of violence. Under the assumption that cinematic storytelling is handled competently most of the time, if not almost always, it thus ascribes attractiveness to the display of violence in the vast majority of cases.

Such ascription, unfortunately, fails to shed light on why portrayals of violence are attractive. Rather than explaining that attraction, it merely restates what is to be explained. If the appeal of portrayals of violence is presumed due to the beauty of these portrayals, the question becomes why there is beauty in witnessing violence, if there is.

Conceptually, equating aesthetic appeal in roundabout fashion with appeal in general (Heller, 1987; Moeran, 1986) seems a moot exercise. Only to the extent that aesthetic appeal could be empirically isolated, and its contribution to appeal at large demonstrated, would it be meaningful to involve the beauty concept in efforts to explain the appeal of portrayals of violence. As it stands, however, claims of aesthetic merit seem afterthoughts and rationalizations for the enjoyment of something thought not to call for euphoria. For instance, as we see a bullet-riddled, blood-squirting body hit the ground, in extreme slow motion or otherwise aestheticized, we can invoke the beauty of the presentation and thus be absolved from condemning ourselves for poor taste, just like male adolescents do when blaming their enjoyment of horror on special effects (Zillmann & Weaver, 1995).

Most alternative attempts at explaining the appeal of displays of violence have in one way or another embraced the catharsis doctrine, usually attributed to Aristotle. In what amounts to an exceedingly liberal extension of the doctrine, exposure to portrayals of violence is thought capable of diminishing fears and phobias as well as antisocial inclinations, especially violent impulses. Proposals continue to enumerate conditions from which the consumption of violent entertainment is said to provide relief. This is done despite mounting evidence that challenges the idea that exposure to the material in question can foster purgation of emotions that are deemed undesirable, pathogenic, or life threatening (Baron & Richardson, 1994; Geen & Quanty, 1977; Zillmann, 1979).

Among the most frequently cited conditions said to demand relief by consumption of violent fiction and, to a lesser degree, violent nonfiction are an ancient and hereditary fear of the dark (Douglas, 1966), a similarly archaic and hereditary fear of the nonhuman (Thomas, 1972), a fear of the mentally and physically deviant (Denne, 1972), a fear of fading prosperity, political instability, social upheaval, and anarchy (Harrington, 1972), and a fear of monstrous transformation (Evans, 1984) and bodily deterioration (Alloway, 1972), with apprehensions about death defining the ultimate fear (Buruma, 1984; Dickstein, 1984; King, 1981). For men, apprehensions about diminishing sexual capacity and related social dominance are also invoked, especially in view of apparently increasing sexual assertiveness in women (Tudor, 1989). Apprehensions about the breaking of sexual taboos are enlisted as well. With considerable imagination, such taboos are spotted in more or less all evil and demonic actions (Derry, 1987; Wood, 1984).

Finally, there are numerous misgivings about technological advancement and the burden of rationality associated with it. Rosenbaum (1979), for instance, holds the confining logic of science accountable for a seemingly growing appetite for the mysterious and supernatural. A revival of the deep-rooted fear of demonic forces, accomplished by much exposure to cinematic and literary terror, is viewed as essential for the embrace of benevolent supernatural forces capable of warding off and overcoming the evil powers. Along these religious or sacrilegious lines, Father Greeley of Chicago sought to explain the attraction of vampire movies by asserting that it is "a hunger for the marvelous" (Ramsland, 1989). The marvelously evil and macabre is, of course, thought to inspire a longing for opposing powers that are even more marvelous.

Rockett (1988) cites Huxley (1971) on the radical inadequacy and isolation of human existence to argue the blessings attainable through interfusion of self and other. "Ideally," Huxley states, "one would rec-ognize and feel this interfusion with the company of Good and the Just, with saints, angels, and the Deity. Alternatively, one might hope to feel at least a oneness with all of humanity. However, one can also transcend normal existence through feeling the interfusion of one's existence with the Evil and Unjust, with vampires, demons, and Satan" (pp. 6–7). It is transcendence of this kind that exposure to brutality and terror, cine-matic or otherwise, is supposed to foster. Moeran (1986) echoes such elaborations by contending that the spectacle of "violence is a kind of *communitas*" that creates oneness in that the "conquering of time be-comes the conquering of space between self and other" (p. 116).

Such rather mystical accounts of the appeal and power of witnessed violence are complemented, however, by more sober, down-to-earth sug-gestions. Dickstein (1984), for instance, writes that "civilized man, as he grows out of childhood and adolescence, is taught to subdue his fears and superstitions and to accept the notion that society will protect him. We are told that if we behave with rational self-restraint others will do likewise. But in some level we never really believe this" (p. 70). Literary and cinematic terror, he contends, makes this nagging social distrust explicit and invites the contemplation and "vicarious" practicing of cop-ing responses. In this regard, the more fantastic and the less fantastic claims converge. In both cases it is claimed that displays of violence "help people deal with real fears of things within and without them-selves, even enabling them to rehearse their own deaths, preparing for the inevitable." Moreover, these displays are said to "help audiences to confront personal guilt indirectly, so that they might expiate real or imagined sins through the controlled trauma of the film experience" (Rockett, 1988, p. 3).

There can be no doubt, then, that dramatic exposition that dwells on violence is thought capable of freeing the consumer from conjectured fears and phobias, distrusts, and ill emotions. How such miraculous cleansing can occur is not entirely clear. Those who specialize in the analysis of fiction's benefits usually rely on notions such as identification and vicarious experience. We shall address such mechanisms later. At present, we attempt to systematize the various ways in which the ca-tharsis doctrine has been invoked to explain the apparent appeal of por-trayals of violence.

The application of the concept of cathartic relief implies, of course, that conditions exist that allow relief to manifest itself. Catharsis simply presupposes conditions for relief or betterment of some sort. The pre-sumption of fears, deficiencies, or impulses is thus paramount. Unfor-tunately, it is this presumption that, as we will see, gets in the way of providing testable, verifiable proposals.

Only if the presumption of deep-rooted relief-demanding conditions is made can cathartic relief be invoked to explain the appeal of displays of violence. It can be assumed that the encounter of relief-providing stimuli, incidental as it may be, functions as negative reinforcement (Nevin, 1973; Skinner, 1969). Repeated encounters can then be expected to foster and strengthen the motivation to seek out the stimuli that have the capacity in question. Displays of violence might constitute such stimuli. In simple terms, should the presumed array of essential anxieties exist, and should exposure to brutality and terror relieve them, the desire for further exposure, construed as the appeal of violent materials, can be expected to grow from incidental initial encounters.

The problems with such a reinforcement explanation of the appeal of literary and cinematic terror are twofold. First, the existence of the presumed anxieties and ill emotions from which relief is sought is by no means established; and second, the presumed power of violent expositions to provide relief from these anxieties and ill emotions is very much in doubt.

For instance, the presumption that there exists a fear of the nonhuman, in and of itself, is not without merit. Intra-and interspecies xenophobia is well established (Gray, 1971; Marks, 1987; Panksepp, Sacks, Crepeau, & Abbott, 1991). Apprehensions about creatures never before encountered can be considered part and parcel of xenophobia. Reacting with curiosity and caution to encounters with unfamiliar nonhuman species would seem superbly adaptive, in fact (Beer, 1984). What must be questioned, however, is the suggestion that such apprehensions *motivate exposure to displays of violence for the purpose of relief.* The same applies to fear of the dark. Such fear is hardly in question. It is the contention that this fear motivates us, even in daylight, to seek exposure to unspeakably violent action that is.

Other fears, such as concerns about anarchy or future wars, similarly may exist—off and on and to various degrees. The suggestion that these concerns are ever-acute and drive us to see violence in order to feel more secure or closer to other humans or assorted deities amounts to a gigantic leap of faith, however, and provokes contempt.

In principle, apprehensions about all ills of society can be enumerated and claimed to foster an appetite for fictional and nonfictional expositions of violence. We are told, for instance, that the atomic bomb created a new climate of fear, and that because people now are more death conscious than ever before, they seek exposure to displays of violence and death to work out their fears (Fulton & Owen, 1987–1988). Surely, the bomb occasionally gives us cause to contemplate carnage, although one might doubt that the carnage in earlier wars and during prehistoric times warranted lesser apprehensions among those immediately threatened. But to connect the bomb with everlasting, ever-present fear of death that motivates exposure to portrayals of violence seems irresponsibly speculative—recklessly speculative at the very least. Then again, in making a case for the freedom of speculation, far-fetched or not, it must be acknowledged that the contentions in question are sufficiently broad and vague to escape falsification. Who could decisively fault, for instance, the claim that a fear of overpopulation is behind our interest in seeing as much slaughter of humanity as we can muster? Sweeping claims of this sort are thus bound to continue to be as popular in the discussion of literary and cinematic terror as they have been in the past.

Regarding the cathartic provision of relief, the situation is somewhat different. Although most of the proclaimed eminent fears are deemed inaccessible, which renders their being relieved undemonstrable, the experience of relief in emotional terms, transitory as it may be, can be ascertained empirically. But as already stated, the evidence concerning cathartic effects of exposure to expositions of violence, fictional as well as nonfictional, is entirely nonsupportive (Geen & Quanty, 1977). Consumption of violent material has not been found to provide relief from ill emotions and motivations. If anything, these states are intensified and the likelihood of antisocial behavior is facilitated (Berkowitz, 1993; Huesmann & Eron, 1986). With regard to fear of violent victimization specifically, fictional and nonfictional violence are likely to exacerbate this fear (Gerbner, Gross, Morgan, & Signorielli, 1994; Tamborini, Zillmann, & Bryant, 1984; Zillmann & Wakshlag, 1985). In fact, Gerbner and Gross (1976) contend that the ubiquity of portrayals of violence creates fears of bodily mutilation and death in the citizenry, and that these created fears are pronounced enough to foster an acute need for, and a ready acceptance of, established authority and militant protection in particular. "Fear is a universal emotion and easy to exploit," they write, and "symbolic violence may be the cheapest way to cultivate it effectively" (p. 193). So confident are these scholars of the "heightened sense of risk and insecurity" that is promoted by the displays of violence that they characterize the violence-saturated media as "the established religion of the industrial order, relating to governance as the church did in earlier times" (p. 194).

The speculation that fears might have appetitive properties that lend portrayals of violence their apparently extraordinary appeal also could not be supported by experimental research. When apprehensions about violent victimization were manipulated, violent drama actually lost much of its attraction, especially for women (Wakshlag, Vial, & Tamborini, 1983). This effect on the selection of entertainment drama was particularly strong when respondents believed that the drama would not feature a just resolution to the violent injustices perpetrated during the course of the play (Goldstein, chapter 3 in this volume).

Such findings are consistent with the suggestion that it is not violence per se that attracts; much of the appeal of violent drama derives from the projection of the successful control of threats and dangers. It appears to be the promise of safety in a just and orderly world, manifest in the good forces' ultimate triumph over the evil ones, that is "music to the ears of the fearful" and that defines an essential element of the appeal of violent drama (Zillmann, 1980, 1988). This, it should be noted, contrasts sharply with the proposal that slaughter most foul is what constitutes the big draw.

However, as indicated already, those who are committed to holding undemonstrable basal fears accountable for the apparent fascination with the destructive powers of evil, as presented in various dramatic genres, will find demonstrations of effects of actually measured fears on the appeal of a limited number of highly violent dramatic pieces most unconvincing, if not pitiful and offensive. Science-minded scholars, in turn, will find the discussed sweeping claims and grand speculations unacceptable. The kinder ones among them will treat these speculations as hypotheses ranging from reckless to intriguing. They will point to the unverifiability (due to the impossibility of falsification) of most of them and insist on the purely hypothetical status of the claims. The less kind ones, on the other hand, are likely to dismiss most of the claims as ill-conceived, contrived speculation, if not as confounded rubbish.

On Archetypes, Identification, and Transcendence

Nothing has influenced the popular contentions about the appeal of portrayals of violence more than two concepts from analytical psychology: Jung's (1951/1970, 1951/1959) archetypes and Freud's (1900/1968, 1919/1963, 1923/1964a, 1921/1964b) identification. These two concepts permeate the literature, and with untiring fascination and conviction they are used to project vital benefits of a postulated state of transcendence thought to be achievable by the confrontation with terror, especially fictional terror (Iaccino, 1994; Rockett, 1988).

Jung distinguishes two domains of the unconscious: the personal and the collective. The personal unconscious is said to be "made up essentially of contents which have at one time been conscious but which have disappeared from consciousness through having been forgotten or repressed" (1951/1959, p. 42). In other words, these contents are personal memories retrievable with different degrees of difficulty. In contrast, "the contents of the collective unconscious have never been in consciousness, and therefore have never been individually acquired, but owe their existence exclusively to heredity" (1951/1959, p. 42). These primordial contents are equated with instincts (Marx & Hillix, 1963) and are termed *archetypes*. Jung focuses on the stimulus quality in these instinctual patterns when he defines his archetypes as "the unconscious images of the instincts themselves" (1951/1959, p. 44).

With regard to violence and the observation thereof, the *shadow* archetype is pivotal. This archetype is thought to integrate our prehuman and, hence, premoral impulses; in other words, our animal instincts

(Marx & Hillix, 1963). The shadow is conceptualized as our dark side. It is said to have obsessive and possessive properties; and as it is pre-moral, it is thought to constitute a continual threat to the ego and its moral striving.

Jung contends that the shadow's force is most destructive when it goes unrecognized. Considering coercive, violent impulsions, this is quite obvious. Recognition of such urges seems a precondition for any curtailment by moral means. But Jung also included primordial fears deriving, among other things, from prehistoric cosmic catastrophes—colliding planets, comets plunging to earth, and all (Velikovsky, 1956). Encounter of such themes in myths was thought to help cope with basal anxieties of this sort.

Jung argues that "no one can become conscious of the shadow without considerable moral effort" (1951/1970, p. 8). He accepts, however, a technique referred to as *active imagination* as a means through which the shadow also can be revealed. This technique is described as "a sequence of fantasies produced by deliberate concentration" (1951/1959, p. 49). But nondeliberate fantasies—"fantasies which 'want' to become conscious" (p. 49)—are listed as successful as well. They are described as fantasies from trancelike and dreamlike states.

It is this proposal of trancelike access to the shadow that has inspired uncounted claims that the consumption of fiction in literary or cinematic form analogously offers a state of involvement that enables consumers to come to terms with their animal instincts and to be better persons for it. Although it is never made clear how the mere witness of fictional violence is supposed to elicit morally relevant cognitions capable of subduing animalistic fears and behavioral impulsions, the notion that fictional violence helps us to control antisocial emotions and even to lose our fear of death is deemed plausible by most analysts. Dickstein (1984), for instance, contends that "horror films are a safe, routinized way of playing with death, like going to a roller coaster or parachute jump at an amusement park" (p. 69). Rockett (1988), as might be recalled, similarly suggests that such films allow audiences to confront guilt feelings, work them out, and attain absolution of sorts. He and others (Meth, 1987) also claim that death anxieties are curbed by the rehearsal of dying that violent fiction affords its consumers.

Skeptics are left wondering how indiscriminate slaughter on the screen or elsewhere could evoke moral contemplations that subdue the shadow and thus enhance the fiction consumers' humanity. They might take comfort from the research evidence cited earlier that suggests that exposure to fictional as well as nonfictional violent deaths only intensifies apprehensions about dying. Most analytically inclined scholars are bound to bypass all empirical demonstrations, however, and continue to interpret the appeal of violence in terms of Jung's unquestionable doctrine of archetypal mediation.

In their explanatory efforts, these scholars usually combine Jungian archetypal suggestions with Freudian concepts (Iaccino, 1994; Rockett, 1988). Freudian proposals can be quite different, however. From his treatise about the uncanny (1919/1963) it is apparent that Freud did not consider most pertinent anxieties phylogenetically determined. Instead, he thought them to be spawned in early ontogenesis. He emphasized the "awful anxieties of childhood" (p. 59), and unlike Jung, derived these fears from, or otherwise connected them with, sexual development. For instance, he considered anxieties about loss of eyesight or loss of limb to be expressions of a "castration complex." Anxieties concerning loneliness, silence, and darkness are analogously thought to be expressions of the more basal fantasy of returning to the mother's womb.

In principal terms, Freud thought that the appeal of the exhibition of something uncanny materializes "when *repressed* infantile complexes are revived, or when primitive beliefs thought to have been *overcome* seem supported after all" (1919/1963, p. 80). At the heart of his argument is that things may be disturbingly unfamiliar because they have been so very familiar—if only prenatally or during a short postnatal period.

Although Freud's habit of connecting seemingly all attractions and pleasures with something sexual has inspired uncounted writers to behave likewise, those pondering the appeal of portrayals of violence included, it is the sex-transcending concept of identification that proved more influential than any other single concept (Freud, 1923/1964a, 1921/1964b). Much of its original meaning has been lost in popular applications, however, and interpretations vary accordingly (Zillmann, 1994). What has survived is the idea that people identify with fictional heroes (Gabbard, 1987; Rimmon-Kenan, 1976; Skura, 1981), but also with the cruelest of fictional villains (Biro, 1982; King, 1981), in order to attain "vicariously" the gratifications that these agonists experience. Through such identification, it is said, people transcend their limited personal experience (Friedberg, 1990; Rockett, 1988). Transcendence through identification has become commonplace psychology (Mendelsohn, 1966), and it has remained the gospel in most literary and cinematic analyses (Friedberg; Kaplan, 1990).

Freud developed the concept of identification in connection with the Oedipus complex. To him, identification characterizes the earliest emotional bond between a child and another person. He focused on the male child, who develops an ideal conception of his father, and then seeks to attain this ideal by adopting all aspects of the father's behavior (1921/1964b). It is the adoption of mother-directed libido, of course, that eventually creates the Oedipal dilemma. Notwithstanding such complications, Freud apparently believed that identification serves to attain valued, wanted traits, and that it fosters behavioral emulation and the adoption of traits. He insisted, however, that identification is more than overt imitation (1900/1968), and that the desire "to be like" an external agent results in the assimilation of this agent. The fact that the specifics of the proposed more-than-imitation assimilation have never been adequately articulated opened the door to interpretations ranging from pretended or actual emulation to transitory or permanent ego-confusion. Freud explicitly acknowledged that identification could reach a point where "one becomes confused about one's own self as one puts the other's self in the place of one's own, such as in cases of self-duplication, self-partition, and self-exchange" (1919/1963, p. 62).

According to Freud, then, the specified ego-confusion allows experiential sharing. The identifier is thought to have access to the pleasures experienced by whoever and whatever it targeted for identification. Most important, such identification does not seem to require any particular effort on the identifier's part. The engagement of all cognitive operations required seems deliberate only with regard to the choice of identification targets. The mere witnessing of persons or their personas is considered sufficient to initiate the processes in question.

In discussing these matters, Freud (1905–1906/1987) points to the powers of the playwright and actor. These agents are seen as providers of a *scheinwelt* that enables the spectator, characterized as "a poor soul to whom nothing of importance seems to happen, who some time ago had to moderate or abandon his ambition to take center stage in matters of significance, and who longs to feel and to act and to arrange things according to his desires" (pp. 656–57), to attain the fulfillment of his thwarted wishes. The spectator, says Freud, "wants to be a hero, if only for a limited time, and playwrights and actors make it possible for him through *identification* with a hero" (p. 657). Accordingly, the fictional exposition may be seen as a forum that offers a cast of heroes and others with desirable characteristics from among whom the spectators, depending on their hedonistic inclinations, can choose parties for identification. Spectators are free, in fact, to enter into and abandon identifications. But it is generally held that there shall be identification with only one party at a time.

Freud's winning formula thus suggests that we have our pick of the lot of heroes and villains. We enter into their emotional life, and we exit it as we please. We share euphoric experiences, but we also suffer through dysphoric ones. We enter into heroes as they fight and conquer. Should they suffer and be vanquished, we can always desert them and identify with persons whose prospects seem brighter. This ability to withdraw is deemed crucial, as it insures that identification-induced suffering cannot get out of hand. However, some analysts consider identification with victims particularly beneficial. It is seen to provide the opportunity for expiation. Rockett (1988), for instance, contends that, through identification with a victimized party, the audience "vicariously accepts its punishment . . . as their own" (p. 3).

The formula, then, is truly all-encompassing. If applied *post facto*, which it always is, it cannot fail in making emotional reactions to fiction (and nonfiction) appear plausible. Reactions to displays of violence specifically may be considered enjoyable and wholesome if they are deemed mediated by identification with a successful aggressor. If deemed mediated by identification with a victim of violence, they may be considered expiatory and cathartic and, ultimately, also enjoyable and wholesome. Presumably it is this belief in wholesomeness through identification with others, fictional others in particular, that inspires most analysts with a Freudian bent to proclaim that fictional portrayals of violence are instrumental in holding down societal violence (Buruma, 1984). Notwithstanding these claims of the wholesomeness of violent displays, however, the discussion should have made it clear that it is not the observation of violence as such that is deemed attractive and enjoyable. The attainment of pleasure from violent spectacles is tied to the identification with aggressors and victims as they act out their respective parts in the spectacles.

Evolutionary Conceptions

Jung has not been alone in trying to trace our apparent fascination with exhibitions of violence back to prehistoric times. Rather than simply declaring this fascination due to instincts controlled by inherited residual imagery that surfaces in myths, however, the alternative speculations have been based on knowledge of specific behaviors of various nonhuman species, early hominids, and the tribal people of so-called primitive societies.

Beer (1984), for instance, contends that something akin to morbid curiosity and the pondering of death may already exist in some nonhuman species. He relies on reports of elephants that, upon encountering dead and partly decomposed members of their species, spend hours examining the corpses (Bere, 1966; Douglas-Hamilton & Douglas-Hamilton, 1975). The fact that elephants tend to carry around the remains of others—especially cows carrying their stillborn calves—and even bury these remains is likened to a "necromantic rite" (Beer, 1984, p. 59). Gorilla and baboon mothers, along with those of numerous other mammalian species, similarly cling to and defend the corpses of their dead offspring (DeVore, 1965; Hinde, 1970; Lawick-Goodall, 1968; Marler & Hamilton, 1968).

Beer also cites instances of what seems to be death-defying curiosity. Thompson's gazelles and wildebeests, for instance, "have been observed to approach and scrutinize lurking predators, such as hyenas, cheetahs, and lions, sometimes at deadly cost" (1984, p. 62). Such fate tempting (Zahavi, 1975) has been observed in monkeys as well. It has been reported (Simonds, 1974) that bonnet macaques, sitting by the roadside, dare onrushing vehicles "until the last moment when they jump aside or merely casually swing their tails out of the way" (Beer, p. 63).

Do such behaviors constitute an acceptable basis for the development of morbid curiosity and the enjoyment of risk and danger in humans, as Beer contends? Hardly. Rather than constituting prehuman death rites and expressions of death defiance, the cited observations are easily explained as imperfections in maternal instinct and as the result of habituation. Specifically, the instances in which mothers defend their deceased progeny can be construed as cases in which rigid instinctive behavior patterns prove temporarily nonadaptive. This instinct-gone-awry reflects, if anything, the animals' inability to comprehend death. The instances of apparent death defiance similarly do not reflect daring and, implicitly, excitement seeking. On the contrary, they can be explained as the result of habituation, that is, of getting used to dangerous conditions to the point where adaptive anxieties and resulting caution deteriorate. It is common knowledge that prey, such as gazelles, graze in dangerous proximity to predators, such as lions, once a kill is made (Zillmann, 1979). The fact that, on occasion, preyed-on animals get close to feeding or resting predators thus is neither surprising nor indicative of prehuman zest for danger and violence.

Similarly inconclusive are speculations about hominid behavior. As long ago as two million years, hominids ate meat, and they obtained their meat by scavenging rather than hunting (Blumenschine, 1987; Lewin, 1984; O'Connell, Hawkes, & Blurton Jones, 1988; Shipman, 1986). For millennia, then, hominids are presumed to have lacked hunting skills sufficient to kill prey with regularity. Along with nonhuman primates, such as baboons and chimpanzees, they had to wait their turn for the scraps left on carcasses after the predators had their fill. The early hominids apparently learned to crack bones for the marrow, suggesting that they may have been last in line.

The idea is that for millennia blood and gore were linked to the gratifications of food intake, to well-being, and to survival, that those with the keenest interest in the kill by others had a feeding advantage translatable into greater reproductive success, and that this selective linkage left a trace in the paleomammalian brain (MacLean, 1964), a trace that manifests itself in a continuing interest in blood and gore and kills made by others.

Such speculation may strike us as exceedingly contrived and untenable. We must acknowledge, however, as we have done earlier in connection with other phylogenetic speculations, that the contention is unfalsifiable. We can treat it as a pseudo explanation that, for all practical purposes, merely restates the observation that today's humans are attracted to displays of violence.

Our ancestors eventually acquired hunting skills, mostly as a result of advancing tool usage, and converted themselves from scavenger to predator. Although hunting, in evolutionary terms, is a comparatively recent achievement (Bartholomew & Birdsell, 1953; Clark, 1959; Howell, 1968) and as such highly variable culturally, it tends to be treated as an essential of human nature. Whether glorified or treated with dismay, hunting—and the killing that it implies—is thought to characterize human existence (Dart, 1953). The hunt not only secured food but also brought recognition and status to the food-providing hunter or hunter groups. So did the extended form of hunting: intraspecific killing in theft-inspired warfare between groups (Zillmann, 1979). The ability to hunt, kill, and plunder efficiently, then, proved empowering. It tended to empower men and to render women gatherers. Irrespective of such considerations, however, for participants and spectators alike, communal hunting and the killing that it involves were undoubtedly extremely exciting, and the successful procurement of food was invariably linked to immense gratification (Bloch, this volume). Intraspecific fighting, no doubt, had similar, if not more desirable, consequences. Successful fighting and killing yielded social dominance and the much celebrated spoils of war (Zillmann, 1984).

It is this vision of the danger of hunting and fighting, the excitement of overcoming fear and of confronting life-threatening conditions, as well as the gratification from the successful kill and its fringe benefits, that is pivotal to yet other speculations about the appeal of violence. Elias and Dunning (1970) expressed the issue succinctly when they talked about "the quest for excitement in unexciting societies" (p. 31). Unlike in the doom-projecting speculations discussed earlier, the premise is that modern society protects us too well. It fails us, at least much of the time, in providing the threats and dangers that permeate life in primitive society. The underlying assumption is that we are built to cope with a dangerous environment, and that, when deprived of such an environment, we seek out substitute challenges and dangers—such as in cliff climbing or skydiving.

Zuckerman (1979, 1995) has been most explicit in making this assumption. He has shown that stark individual differences exist in what he considers to be a biologically determined need for stimulation. It should be clear, however, that the demonstration of differences in daredevil appetite does in no way validate the assumption that such appetite derives from earlier times in which humans were more or less continually confronted with life-threatening dangers, and that this kind of confrontation defines the ideal match for our biological constitution. It also would appear that the suggestion of substitute thrill-seeking applies to activities that entail the possibility of actual harm to the performer rather than to the spectator who is satisfied witnessing violence from a safe distance.

The main conclusion to be drawn here is that speculations about the origin of the apparent interest in displays of violence might best be dealt with as interesting and entertaining ideas, intriguing and plausible at best and contrived and incredible at worst.

Archaic Aggressive Response Tendencies

There is one contention concerning the origin of attention to displays of violence that corresponds better than others with a multitude of relevant facts at hand. It is the proposal that humans share fundamental aggressive response tendencies with at least all other mammalian species, that these tendencies are organized in the older structures of the brain, and that they exert their influence despite the fact that much of the overt behavior that they control lacks utility (Cannon, 1929, Delgado, 1968, 1969; MacLean, 1958, 1968; Zillmann, 1984, 1996a). It is posited, essentially, that self-preservation dictated for early humans, as for other species, that the environment had to be continually screened for danger, and that upon the encounter of danger, the organism had to prepare for fight or flight. Such responding had survival value in prehistoric times, but it is of limited utility in contemporary society. In fact, the emotions linked to the fight-flight response are often counterproductive under the conditions of modern life (Zillmann, 1979, 1996a). Today's humans rarely can act on their fears and their anger by destroying the agents or circumstances that instigate these emotions. Feeling threatened by air pollution or global warming, for example, is unlikely to be remedied by any physical assault or by literally running away from it. The apprehension, as an archaic response to endangerment, will nonetheless stir emotions and result in maladaptive stress (Zillmann & Zillmann, 1996). The proposal thus entails the assumption that the structures of the brain that control the emotions, largely the limbic system, have not appreciably changed over the last fifty thousand years or so.

It is this lack of evolutionary adjustment by the brain, then, that can be held accountable for a continuing, not entirely appropriate sensitivity to danger. We now trace different manifestations of this particular sensitivity.

PROTECTIVE VIGILANCE AND CURIOSITY

On the premise that monitoring the environment for danger, for potentially threatening violent events in particular, proved adaptive over millennia, and that a deep-rooted inclination for such monitoring persists, it can be projected that violent incidents still draw strong attention. In fact, the inclination to take sharp notice of physically threatening occurrences is still adaptive, as our environment on occasion produces assaults in the form of muggings, stabbings, and shootings. Mostly, however, such threats are directed at comparatively few others but are related to the populace at large by the news and entertainment media, which, by trial and error, detected our economically exploitable curiosity for violence some time ago.

The sharing of information about danger used to be adaptive and on occasion still is. Knowing about a killer on the loose can foster adaptive communal action. It would seem to be the rare exception, however, that media reports of violent danger have such utility. It is more likely that unrepresentative, danger-exaggerating incidents make the news and that, rather than having adaptive quality, reports of such incidents will create maladaptive anxieties. Gibson and Zillmann (1994) demonstrated this for the violent crime of carjacking. Reports of sensational, brutal carjackings were found to foster greatly exaggerated perceptions of the danger posed by that crime.

Protective vigilance is not limited to screening for immediate dangers. It extends to the circumstances of victimization, conceivably to provide additional information about a particular danger. It might prove useful, for instance, to know how a serial killer stalks his victims. The knowledge could be utilized in taking appropriate precautions. The interest loses its utility, however, when it focuses on the macabre—such as whether or not a murderer was necrophagously inclined. Nonetheless, interest of this sort, usually referred to as morbid curiosity, can be regarded as an extension of agonistic curiosity.

We now take the unorthodox position that the satisfaction of violent curiosity, even in its extreme form of morbid curiosity, generally does not result in pleasurable reactions. Excluding sadists, who might take pleasure from seeing, say, the dismemberment of a person, solely curiosity-driven exposure to displays of destructive violence yields distress and fearful apprehensions (Denny, 1991; Gray, 1971; Marks, 1969, 1987; Rachman, 1990). The satisfaction of violent curiosity is not pleasurable in itself. More than that, agonistic curiosity is a trap that violates hedonistic principles. It is an impulsion to witness particular events that operates despite the fact that witnessing these events proves distressing.

The apparent eagerness to share distressing information about violence with others once again may have been useful in communal settings and on occasion still may be useful. More likely, however, such sharing of information amounts to gossiping in which persons can express their dismay and thereby, perhaps, attain some degree of relief (Pennebaker, Hughes, & O'Heeron, 1987; Pennebaker & Susman, 1988).

Ultimately, aggressive curiosity extends to fiction in the broadest sense of the term. It is human ingenuity, the extraordinary ability to imagine, to combine, and to construct, that produced the world's myths and tales, laden with dangers posed by imagined demonic forces that transcend human experience and with deities and other supreme beings whose capabilities exceeded whatever the storytellers could have seen and heard. Aggressive anxieties invited exaggerated perceptions, and the bragging of those who returned alive from highly dangerous confrontations added to the exaggerations (Zillmann & Gibson, 1995). The results are fire-spitting dragons and uncounted animal admixtures with phenomenal fighting abilities, along with menacing giants, evil gnomes, and devious witches. Not to be forgotten, there also are superhuman humans who, with their superior killing skills, could save and free the panic-stricken commoners.

This is by no means to argue that aggressive curiosity is the main reason, or even the only one, for the attraction of violent fiction. Obviously, if the premise that violent fiction is enjoyable is accepted, as it should be, aggressive curiosity cannot be viewed as a critical contributor to its appeal. But such curiosity contributes to an *interest* in violent fiction, including an *interest* in fiction that features the extraordinary, imaginative combat between superpotent forces. Displays of destructive violence that apply to humans, however, even when presented in imaginary settings, are bound to distress rather than bring bliss.

We eventually turn to the analysis of the enjoyment of portrayals of violence specifically. Before we do so, we explore social factors capable of explaining the fascination with fictional and nonfictional terror, especially the fascination of adolescents with cinematic horror.

Empathic Distress and Its Mastery

Cinematic horror has been said to function as a contemporary forum for the rites of passage of adolescents (Zillmann & Gibson, 1995). Analogous to these rites in hunter-gatherer societies (Gennep, 1960), the confrontation with terrifying events is seen, essentially, as a test of teens' courage, to show that they are unperturbed by danger. The fact that such tests used to be arranged by communal elders and now tend to be self-administered is considered immaterial. So is the fact that the confrontation with actual danger is reduced to reflections off a screen. It is obviously assumed that cinematic terror is capable of terrifying. To the extent that it is, it does provide the conditions for a test of courage (Armbruster & Kuebler, 1984; Orwaldi, 1984). More surprising, and greatly disconcerting for most investigators, is the fact that stark gender differences apply to the passage rites under consideration—gender differences that seem to derive from hunter-gatherer times and that persist despite their lack of utility in contemporary society.

There can be no doubt that in the vast majority of cultures, children have been trained in a highly gender-specific fashion (Barry, Bacon, & Child, 1957). Boys have been taught to be assertive and self-reliant, girls to be supportive and nurturing. In cultures where agonistic skills were essential, such as for hunting and warfare, this gender segregation was particularly strong. Considerable pressures were brought to bear on compliance with designated gender roles. In particular, the expression of fear by boys was disallowed and duly punished. Girls, in contrast, were free to express their anxieties, even encouraged to do so.

In contemporary societies, boys are still expected to inhibit any display of fear, and girls are still expected to exhibit distress and apprehensions (Brody, 1985; Saarni, 1989, 1989; Shennum & Bugental, 1982). However, the enforcement of societal precepts concerning the display of fear has changed drastically. In formal rites of passage, boys could be sent into hostile territory or subjected to physical torment and then be ridiculed and whipped for crying. Additionally, their parents, brothers, and sisters could be shamed into seclusion (Zillmann & Gibson, 1995). Following the abandonment of such practices, alternative conventions and institutions emerged to serve the societal regulation of the expression of fear and fearlessness. The horror tale initiated a transition to the informal control of compliance with expected displays of emotion. Boys expressing distress and fear in response to such tales were no longer whipped by elders or similarly punished by parents, although these former agents of control may intentionally or inadvertently have made their displeasure and stern disapproval known. Be this as it may, cinematic horror is to be considered the latest manifestation of terrifying tale-telling, where the telling occurs under conditions that give minimal, if any, control to chaperons.

This does not mean, however, that the gender-specific reinforcement that promotes fearlessness in boys and squeamishness in girls has been removed. Rather, the contingencies that used to be enforced by elders and parents are now enforced by peers, without apparent loss of effect. Boys, as before, must prove to their peers, and ultimately to themselves, that they are unperturbed, calm, and collected in the face of terror; and girls must similarly demonstrate their sensitivity by being appropriately disturbed, dismayed, and disgusted. Such demonstration seems important enough to adolescents to make them seek out cinematic horror and to subject themselves to emotional torment. In fact, if the societally prescribed display rules for fear and fearlessness could readily be mastered by all, cinematic horror could not constitute a challenge or test that some master and others fail. The eighteen-year old founder of a German horror-video club appreciated these circumstances. He focused on men's bragging about their mastery of fear and disgust, stating that a horror film is most enjoyed when it gives a boy a chance to claim: "Everybody threw up. But not me!" ("Alle haben gekotzt," 1984).

At least for boys and male adolescents, then, there is the suggestion of incentives that are accessible by consuming horror tales, especially in specific social settings. Exposure to terrifying violence in solitude is atypical (Grings & Dawson, 1978). It is before peers that the exhibition of "fearlessness" bears fruit in elevating the exhibitors' social status in terms of respect by same-gender peers and attractiveness to opposite-gender peers. Self-esteem is likely to increase along with such achievements. Girls and young women, on the other hand, are likely to benefit the most if they adhere to their societally prescribed role of exhibiting squeamishness and distress, whether actually felt or pretended, and of signaling a need for being comforted and "protected." Female adolescents can make themselves attractive, even romantically desirable, by showing their distress and helplessness—rather than by a show of self-confidence and independence.

Somewhat surprisingly, female adolescents often comprehend the game they are to play. Farber (1987) conducted interviews of adolescents waiting to see a horror movie to learn what attracted them to this genre. A fourteen-year-old explained her attraction as follows: "They're fun to watch. You go with your friends and try to get scared and everything. And you can just be rowdy. You can get all rowdy with boys and jump into their lap, and they can comfort you. They say, 'Don't worry, I can protect you' " (p. 109). An eighteen-year-old showed similar comprehension: "I like everyone yelling and screaming. I like going with my boyfriend and pulling him close in the scary parts" (p. 109). In contrast, male interviewees were surprisingly uninsightful, claiming an interest in special effects and considering horror grand comedy. Interviews conducted by Brosius and Schmitt (1990) proved more revealing. Students were eager to volunteer stories of classmates who were grossed out and acutely distressed by particularly violent, scary scenes. Such eagerness discloses, of course, the pleasures that those of superior maturity (i.e., of proven callousness) can obtain at the expense of their overly sensitive, failing peers. Also, accomplished desensitization would seem best expressed by laughing at what makes others cringe. The overt amusement might then be *misattributed* to cinematic horror, leading to the assessment that horror is amusing. Lastly, the fact that male adolescents are known to invest considerable efforts into getting female adolescents to accompany them to terrifying movies would seem to suggest that they have a notion that their "scared" companions might snuggle up to them during the scary scenes. In advancing prescriptions for superior lovemaking, such male intuition was first articulated by the Roman poet Ovid (1957). He recommended taking the ladies to scary entertainments, like bloody gladiatorial combat, as an effective seduction formula.

The social gratifications that the consumption of cinematic superviolence offers are predicted by the gender-socialization theory of affect—of fear and its expression in particular (Zillmann & Weaver, 1996). Zillmann, Weaver, Mundorf, and Aust (1986), for instance, have demonstrated that young men enjoy horror more in the company of squeamish others than in the company of self-assured, fearless others. Young women, in contrast, were less distressed in the company of young men who radiated a potential for protection by not blinking an eye in the face of terror than by young men who gave indication of being distressed. Moreover, men proved to be more attracted to squeamish female companions than to secure, "uppity" ones, whereas women were romantically drawn to callous, aggressively more potent male companions than to apparently fearful ones.

In addition to curiosity that can trap us into exposure to displays of violence, then, such displays can be attractive for reasons other than that the reaction to these displays may be gratifying in and of itself. *Specific social conditions under which exposure to the displays in question occurs are apparently capable of exerting a degree of influence that can make intrinsically distressing displays enjoyable, even amusing.* This is not to suggest, however, that the enjoyment of violent drama critically depends on the social conditions of reception. Obviously there is more to storytelling and the pleasures it can generate. We now turn to factors that control such pleasures. We concentrate on the conditions within drama, and more generally on essentially the same circumstances in life at large, that make the witnessing of destructive violence a matter of joy.

Enjoyment of Displays of Violence

Why do some displays of destructive violence make onlookers respond euphorically and with jubilation, whereas other such displays make them cringe with displeasure? The former condition is especially puzzling. How can the portrayal of the brutal infliction of suffering, of torture, mutilation, and death, foster exultation in spectators? How can it do so in fiction? And perhaps more surprisingly, how can it do so in a nonfictional context?

Empathy and Emotional Involvement

As indicated earlier, the concept of identification in explaining emotional involvement with fictional and nonfictional characters has been severely challenged (Carroll, 1990; Tan, 1994; Zillmann, 1980, 1991b, 1994). The heart of the criticism is that if onlookers are free to selectively identify with parties who attain gratifications in order to maximize their own "vicarious gratifications," all reactions should be pleasant—and yet they clearly are not. More important, however, the contention that people identify with others clashes with a wealth of research in connection with the study of empathy and emotional responding generally (Berger, 1962; Hoffman, 1977, 1978; Hygge, 1976; Stotland, 1969; Vaughan & Lanzetta, 1980; Wilson, Cantor, Gordon, & Zillmann, 1986; Zillmann & Cantor, 1977). This research has led to the conception of the respondent to drama and to drama-like events, such as athletic competition, as a *mere witness whose emotional reactions are controlled by the same factors that control these reactions in actual social exchanges* (Tan, 1994; Zillmann, 1994; Zillmann & Paulus, 1993).

The behavior of children most clearly reveals the mere-witness perspective. Imagine a Punch-and-Judy show in which Punch, happily conversing with children in the audience, is threatened by a crocodile sneaking up on him. Anyone who has ever watched children in such a situation will agree that the kids are unlikely to share their hero's calmness—which they should if they were identifying with him. Instead, they surely will be distressed and scream, "Watch out!" and, "Look behind you!" giving evidence to their efforts at averting harm to Punch. Such apparent desire to intervene reveals that the children respond as observers, as third parties, *who succumb to the theatrical illusion that social reality is unfolding before them.* They treat Punch as if he were a "real-life" friend, and they respond to him the way they would to an actual friend in a similar situation.

Adults have learned that intervention is pointless and childish and usually inhibit it. At times it breaks through, however. During horror films, involved spectators yell such things as "Get him!" and "Kill him!" And as a rule, adolescent audiences applaud when their heroes manage to put hordes of villains to death.

Alfred Hitchcock (1959) discusses the same witness mechanism. A couple engaged in lively conversation approaches an open manhole on a sidewalk. An identifying audience should partake in the conversation and not be apprehensive about imminent mishaps. If we take Hitchcock's word for it, however, the audience will cringe in suspense, fearing that the couple, although only a flicker on a screen, might stumble, fall, and knock their teeth out. Clearly, if we were to witness, in reality, an acquaintance or a stranger in the same dilemma, we undoubtedly would also cringe; and if we could intervene to prevent an accident, we probably would. But in this case nobody would contend that we did so because we identified with the witnessed person. Why, then, should we with fictional characters?

Once we accept the witness perspective, we can proceed to explain the spectator's reactions in accordance with the available research (Zillmann, 1991a): Fictional characters toward whom an audience holds particular dispositions will draw emotional involvement and responses similar to nonfictional persons toward whom the same dispositions are held. We will see, however, that different emotional dispositions prompt vastly different reactions. In both fiction and social reality, a principal consideration is the formation of these dispositions. In a fictional context, the formation is usually treated as character development. We now turn to this issue.

Moral Monitoring

As we are exposed to characters, fictional or otherwise, we continually stand in judgment of their action. This perhaps perplexing premise is essential to understanding emotional involvement with drama and emotional responses to the behavior of characters, even to anticipated events that would affect their behavior. Specifically, the conduct of a person—toward whom a respondent is initially indifferent—is judged as virtuous or selfish, as acceptable or intolerable, as laudatory or condemnable, as good or evil, or as right or wrong. Such moral judgment is continually applied to friends, foes, and strangers in fiction and outside of fiction (Jose & Brewer, 1984; Wilson et al., 1986; Zillmann & Bryant, 1975).

The result of such monitoring is threefold: (1) A favorable, positive disposition develops for characters whose actions are deemed good and right. Eventually they are regarded and treated as friends. (2) An unfavorable, negative disposition develops for characters whose actions are deemed evil and wrong. Eventually they are regarded and treated as enemies. (3) A neutral, indifferent disposition is maintained for characters whose actions are deemed (a) neither good or right nor evil or wrong or (b) equally good or right and evil or wrong.

Hopes and Fears as Anticipatory Emotions

Moral judgment is further involved in determining which outcomes directed at and experienced by the characters are just and equitable. The moral sanction or condemnation of the behavior of characters fosters not only favorable or unfavorable dispositions toward them but also specific moral expectations that yield pleasure when confirmed and displeasure when disconfirmed. Moreover, the mere expectation of confirmation is pleasurable, and the mere expectation of disconfirmation is unpleasurable. Specifically, a favorable disposition toward friendlike characters is thought to instigate hopes for benefaction and fears of aversive outcomes. Liked characters, in other words, are deemed deserving of good fortunes and undeserving of bad ones. In contrast, an unfavorable disposition toward enemy-like characters is thought to instigate hopes for aversive, punitive outcomes and fears of benefaction. Disliked characters, then, are deemed deserving of bad fortunes and undeserving of good ones. In drama and drama-like contexts, nothing seems to be more distressing than witnessing a good and thus liked character suffer or about to suffer grave harm, the latter defining the condition of gripping suspense (Zillmann, 1991b, 1996b). Similarly distressing is witnessing the grand benefaction of an utterly evil and undeserving character. For good reason, such benefaction may exist transitionally, but it is exceedingly rare as the final resolution of drama.

The point is that all these anticipatory emotions are mediated by moral judgment. The existence of acute hopes and fears concerning the fate of protagonists and antagonists implies that those who experience these affective states have prejudged outcomes in terms of what the characters deserve, that is, in moral terms. Again, these expectations have been confirmed by pertinent investigations (Jose & Brewer, 1984; Wilson et al., 1986; Zillmann & Cantor, 1977).

Dispositions Overrule Empathy

Empathy is expected to yield affective reactions in an observer that are similar to those displayed by an observed party or presumed to be experienced by that party (Zillmann, 1991a). The intensity of empathic emotion is less than the intensity of affect experienced by the observed character. However, for empathy to have occurred, affect in character and observer must be concordant (Berger, 1962), that is, of the same type. A character's pain is expected to make the observer cringe and experience distress, and a character's benefaction and euphoria is expected to foster a joyous reaction in the observer. We can only speak of empathy if a model's pleasure of whatever particular kind prompts a pleasurable reaction in the witness; and likewise, if a model's displeasure of whatever particular kind prompts an unpleasurable reaction in the witness.

Except for a few reflexive response tendencies, empathic responses are under dispositional control. Specifically, negative affective dispositions virtually override empathic inclinations. Presumably because of their potent moral component, negative dispositions allow us to disband moral concerns about resenting and hating and about hoping for misfortunes and stern punishment. Most important, justified hatred and the call for punishment allows us to uninhibitedly enjoy the punitive action when it materializes. *Negative affective dispositions, then, set us free to thoroughly enjoy punitive violence.* As we have morally condemned a villain for raping and maiming, for instance, we are free to hate such a person, can joyously anticipate his execution, and openly applaud it when we finally witness it. In fiction, we can enjoy his being bullet riddled; and outside fiction, we can rejoice at the drop of the guillotine.

In terms of empathy theory, negative affective dispositions not only disband empathic concerns but invert affective reactions because of their powerful moral component. This response tendency is known as *counterempathy*.

In fiction and elsewhere, the analysis of emotional involvement in terms of empathic mechanics necessitates the concept of counterempathy. Only with such a mechanism of inverse empathy is it possible to explain why one person's (the model's) joy is another's (the observer's) pain and why one person's pain is another's joy. It obviously is so in responding to fiction and nonfiction, such as in sports but also at the workplace.

The existence of the empathic and counterempathic response tendencies has been amply documented (Berger, 1962; Hygge, 1976; Stotland, 1969; Zillmann & Cantor, 1977). An investigation by Wilson et al. (1986) is of particular interest in showing that counterempathy hinges on a system of moral judgment. When such a system is not developed, as in mentally challenged children, responses to utterly undeserved benefaction or punishment are empathic rather than, as morally appropriate, counterempathic.

A wealth of research evidence accumulated in connection with disposition theory (Zillmann, 1980, 1983a, 1991b; Zillmann & Cantor, 1976; Zillmann & Paulus, 1993) further supports the contention that negative affective dispositions contribute greatly to the enjoyment of the humiliation, disparagement, defeat, and destruction of resented parties.

The discussed chain of events leading to enjoyable empathic or counterempathic affect in response to witnessing others' fortunes is detailed in figure 9.1. For the enjoyment of displays of violence, the lower-half sequence of events is of particular interest. Stages 2 and 7 indicate the involvement of moral considerations in the formation of affective dispositions. Stages 3 and 4 show the resulting affective dispositions and their influence on anticipatory affects. Stages 5 and 6 specify affective reactions to pertinent outcomes, such as gratification or aversion, and to their expressive consequences, such as elation or distress. Feedback loop *c* indicates the influence of formed dispositions on moral judgment, such as amity fostering tolerance and enmity strictness. Loop *b* suggests a similar influence of witnessed outcomes through their impact on dispositions. For instance, punitive treatments deemed overly severe are likely to foster sympathy and promote liking, and gratifications deemed too generous might dismay and promote disliking. Feedback loop *a*, finally, indicates that the process described in stages 1 through 7 is recursive and can be chained to arbitrary length. The righteous enjoyment of witnessed displays of violence is specified in the lower half of the chart. Transgressive violence is morally condemned (stage 2), fosters a disposition of resentment and hatred (stage 3), leads to acute hopes for corrective, punitive action (stage 4), and prompts counterempathy (stages 5–6) that inspires elation in response to violence that inflicts suffering and death upon parties deemed deserving of such treatment.

Justice through Violence

The proposal that moral precepts allow us to rejoice upon witnessing the administration of retaliatory violence should not be narrowly interpreted. It has been indicated already that persons inject their vital interests in sanctioning punitive measures. Those who are apprehensive about the possibility of becoming a victim of violent crime, for instance, are likely to condone and demand more severe punishment for violent offenses than those who are less perturbed about crime in society; and the former are less likely than the latter to expose themselves to displays of arbitrary, gratuitous violence, while being more likely to seek out dis-

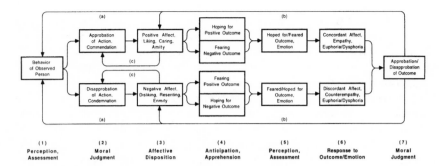

FIGURE 9.1 A model of affect from witnessing the actions and experiences of others.

plays of punitive violence (Zillmann & Wakshlag, 1985). The desire to live in a safe world, then, especially when this hoped-for safety is believed to be threatened, can greatly influence the acceptance of violence that helps to secure public safety. Moreover, such violence is readily deemed justified by those whose fears it pacifies.

In fiction, the vast majority of tales speak of persons whose transgressive conduct threatens social harmony and who are promptly rendered innocuous by virtuous persons who restore the lost harmony and who, in this sense, bring justice to the situation (Henderson, 1979; Zillmann, 1991b). Because those who help to restore social harmony tend to be deemed purveyors of justice, their usually excessively violent action, as it apparently serves "the common good," can be morally sanctioned. The means are justified by the ends, even when the brutality of these means obtrusively exceeds the brutality of the actions to be punished. In the moral mediation of reactions to displays of violence there is little deliberate pondering of ethical principles. Perpetrators rarely have recourse to mitigation and easily lose their right to live. For example, story consumers who have come to resent a lawyer for cheating an old, feebleminded lady out of her life's savings are unlikely to shed a tear when learning that he became a paraplegic in a car crash. Even when seeing him burn and die in a crash they can applaud his misfortune as *poetic justice*. The world, they seem to think, is better off without such people.

Counter to likely impressions, such apparent mismatch between transgression and sanctioned "punishment" is not limited to fiction. Clearly, in fiction there always has been, there is, and there always will be a market for stories that project the decimation of villains of any kind by heroes with superior fighting skills and destructive powers (Zillmann, 1980, 1988, 1991b; Zillmann & Wakshlag, 1985). It is, after all, these heroes' devastatingly thorough housecleaning, best achieved by the death of anyone who might constitute a threat to society (such as terrorists, murderers, rapists, drug pushers, or military-secret sellers), that insures public safety and that, hence, is music to the ears of concerned citizens. It would be erroneous, however, to think that in dealing with actual social conditions our morality would drastically change. Granted some exceptions, citizens have been jubilant when seeing royalty, having lived extravagantly at the people's expense, getting their heads chopped off, when seeing horse thieves dangle from the gallows, and when seeing a lethal injection snuff the life of a serial killer. The fact that citizens are free to applaud such punitive actions would seem to indicate that, at the very least, they are not perturbed by moral misgivings that would prevent their euphoric reactions. Their euphoria, then, shows that they are able to morally condone the punitive violence, considering it right and proper.

It is commonplace to say that for punishment to be just, it must fit the crime. However, nobody can reliably determine the magnitude of suffering that a particular transgression has caused and the magnitude that a particular corrective punishment would cause. The relationship between transgression and punishment is largely arbitrary and a matter of convention. Transgression calls for punishment only in the sense that the transgressor shall be deprived of coercively attained advantages and, perhaps more important, shall suffer for the suffering inflicted upon victims. If the retaliatory suffering comes in the form of violence, such violence can be applauded to the extent that it is deemed just (or at least not unjust).

This conceptualization (Zillmann, 1979) is capable of explaining the vast cultural and subcultural differences in the moral sanction of punitive actions. It can explain, for instance, why in some cultures a wife's sexual infidelity will prompt her husband to retaliate against the presumed real transgressor, her lover, possibly by killing him, whereas in other cultures the husband is limited to, and perhaps satisfied with, voicing his disapproval. Moreover, it explains why the fictional or nonfictional report of the killing of a lover who disregarded marital arrangements draws enthusiastic applause in the former culture and is met by bewilderment in the latter. Similarly, be it in response to cinematic fiction or to a broadcast news report, only those embracing Islamic law can rejoice when witnessing the hacking off of an adolescent's hand and foot in retaliation for stealing a trivial amount of money. Western reactions based on presumptions of moral superiority are sadly misplaced, however. Observing the audience of any contemporary action film, especially the apparent euphoria of young men upon seeing the bad guys being riddled with bullets and collapsing in deadly convulsions, should convince the doubtful that Western audiences fully exercise their moral right of rejoicing in response to exhibitions of *righteous violence*, that is, in response to the display of violence whose perpetration serves, however remotely, the common good.

Our discussion of the conditions under which portrayals of even the most gruesome, destructive violence foster euphoric reactions, in large measure because the violence is morally sanctioned if not prescribed, implies that conceptions of "appropriate" retribution are not only variable across cultures but are capable of shifting over time. For instance, what was deemed appropriate punishment for horse thievery a century ago is no longer acceptable. Changing chivalry conventions alone make formerly enjoyable violent treatments unenjoyable, and whatever could not be enjoyed formerly now may be. Some time ago, for instance, cinematic etiquette would not allow true heroes to slap a woman or shoot a villain in the back. Nowadays the audience is invited to applaud heroes for punching dishonest ladies in the stomach and for killing a drug lord execution style. However, as we still adhere to concepts of "fair retaliation," *any gruesome retributive killing has to appear just, and this appearance has to be prepared by witnessing the party to be punished perform increasingly despicable heinous crimes.* This is to say that escalations in the portrayal of righteous, enjoyable violence necessitate escalations in the portrayal of morally enraging, evil, and distressing violence. The specification of depictions of enjoyable retributive violence, then, appears to be a function of the depiction of deplorable violence. In other words, the specification of enjoyable displays of violence is unstable and shifting. It constitutes a moving target.

On Thrill Maximization

The recent escalation in both the explicitness and frequency of displays of transgressive and retaliatory violence (Gerbner, 1988; Sapolsky & Molitor, 1996; "The killing screens," 1994) insures the maximization of enjoyment of drama, that is, the experience of intensely positive affect upon favorable resolutions of conflict. This is for two related reasons: the overcoming of diminishing response intensity (habituation) and the response facilitation by excitation from distressing experiences.

There can be no doubt that excitatory reactions to displays of violence, in drama as well as outside of it, habituate with repeated exposure to such displays (Geen, 1994; Grings & Dawson, 1978; Linz & Donnerstein, 1989; Zillmann, 1979). Persons who initially respond to depictions of violence with great emotional intensity will experience a fading of this intensity. In the extreme, persons with massive exposure to depictions of violence will not respond affectively at all. The consequence of such habituation is that these persons, as they find nothing exciting in the displays in question, will be blasé about the drama that features these displays.

The process is analogous to that in those who seek pleasures from skydiving, for instance. Research has shown that novice jumpers, as they prepare for a jump, experience intense excitedness that they appraise as anxiety, but that upon safe landing this anxiety, having lost its cognitive basis, converts to intensely felt euphoria (Epstein, 1967; Fenz & Epstein, 1967; Klausner, 1967, 1968). In experienced jumpers, the excitatory reaction linked with anxiety is greatly diminished, and as a result anxiety is less intensely felt. To the dismay of these veterans, the successfully completed jump also has lost its emotional intensity, however. As their anxiety is lost, so is the apparently contingent euphoric reaction upon reaching safety.

The excitation-transfer paradigm (Zillmann, 1978, 1979, 1983b, 1984, 1996a) explains this dependency as follows:

1. The cognitive adaptation to changing environmental stimulation is nearly instantaneous.

2. In contrast, the excitatory adaptation to stimulus changes is sluggish and persists for some time after the termination of response instigation. The sluggishness is the result of slow, humoral mediation. Specifically, the excitatory component of the emotions under consideration is controlled by the release of catecholamines into the bloodstream, which results in elevated activity of the sympathetic nervous system until regulation causes the complete neutralization of the mediating chemical agents. In practical terms, this means that persons experience heightened blood pressure, accelerated heart rate, and related peripheral reactions, and that they feel excited and aroused.

3. Based on this time discrepancy in adapting cognitively and excitationally to stimulus changes, transfer theory posits that residues of excitation from an earlier instigation will intensify the emotion in response to subsequent instigation. Such transfer facilitation of the subsequent emotion is expected for all emotions characterized by sympathetic dominance in the autonomic nervous system.

Returning to skydiving, residual excitation from the novices' high anxiety persists after the safe landing. Cognitively speaking, anxiety has become groundless, and the mastery of the jump with all its glory benefits can be enjoyed instantly. The excitedness from their anxiety reaction lingers, however, and now can fuel the euphoric reaction. Veterans obviously cannot benefit from such excitation transfer, and their enjoyment reactions will be emotionally flat as a result. They are forced to move on to new challenges, to new and greater dangers capable of bringing back the arousing apprehensions that are necessary to experience the thrill of having survived the chances taken—or put more positively, the thrill of having mastered the self-imposed challenge.

The enjoyment of violence-laden fiction is similarly fueled by affective reactions that, in and of themselves, have little to do with joy. Suspenseful dramas, for instance, evoke mostly negative emotions. By featuring liked and cared-about protagonists in perilous situations, they instigate empathic distress for extended periods. (The chain of events is shown in the upper part of figure 9.1.) However, these protagonists do not succumb to the impending misfortunes. They master the situations. At the very least, they successfully escape from apparent doom. These moments of triumph over opponents or, minimally, of acute relief from getting off unscathed are expected to foster pleasurable reactions in spectators, and these reactions, in turn, are expected to be intensified by residual excitation from empathic distress (Zillmann, 1980, 1991b, 1996b). Intense enjoyment of suspenseful expositions thus necessitates negative affective responding. Only respondents who duly suffered through the suspense treatment will intensely enjoy satisfying resolutions. For the emotionally uninvolved, the drama will be nondistressing, but also rather unenjoyable. Enjoyment, then, can be fueled by prior distress, that is, by residual excitation from affective responding that is hedonically opposite.

The discussed facilitation of the enjoyment of suspenseful drama by excitatory residues from empathic distress has been experimentally demonstrated (Sparks, 1991; Zillmann, 1980; Zillmann, Hay, & Bryant, 1975). Even as the torment of tragedy comes to a halfway satisfying resolution, greater empathic suffering has been observed to convert to greater ultimate enjoyment (de Wied, Zillmann, & Ordman, 1994).

There can be little doubt, then, that righteous violence, however brutal but justified by the ends, will prompt gloriously intense euphoric reactions the more it is preceded by patently unjust and similarly brutal violence. In other words, *displays of monstrous gratuitous slaughter and the distress they evoke are a necessary prelude to the portrayal of righteous maiming and killing that is to spark euphoric reactions.* Without such prelude, violence cannot be righteous and, hence, is rendered unenjoyable—at least for nonsadists, who should constitute the vast majority of the drama-consuming public.

Excitation transfer also sheds light on the enjoyment of forms of entertainment that tend to be treated as merely tangential to drama proper. On occasion, children's fare, the fairy tale in particular, is singled out as different and unique. But clearly, most of such fare, in line with other forms of storytelling, features the clash of evil versus good forces, usually ending in the triumph of the latter over the former. The fact that these forces are often endowed with supernatural abilities, similar to those in horror tales, is immaterial to affective responding. Vital is that respondents experience distress that can fuel enjoyment upon satisfying turns of fortunes. Efforts to sanitize fairy tales, in order to spare children the distress reactions, have invariably led to bland, unenjoyable stories and a call for the return of the monsters (Jones, 1990). However, fairy tales are quite capable of eliciting lingering apprehensions (Cantor, this volume). In fact, such elicitation may have been by design to foster obedience with not-to-be-done directives (Tatar, this volume). These apprehensions need not detract from the enjoyment of the tale, however. Tales that end tragically in the punishment of likable wrongdoers still can be greatly enjoyed, as children find comfort in the arms of the tale-telling caretaker. The caretaker, by radiating security, constitutes a happy ending of sorts, a happy ending that can be intensely enjoyed. In this connection it has been suggested that the transfer-intensified experience of being comforted may further the child's feelings of dependence on the caretaker (Zillmann & Gibson, 1995).

Reality television (Battaglio, 1991; Oliver, 1994) might be considered another special case. It is not. The more it dwells on the brutalization of the innocent and thus distresses, the more the audience will enjoy learning about the potentially even more brutal restoration of justice. The enjoyment of the drama of reality television is governed by the same principles that govern the enjoyment of fiction. The only appreciable difference may be a greater intensity of affective responding, due to the witnesses' inability to discount the events before them as "mere fiction" (Geen, 1975; Geen & Rakosky, 1973; McCauley, this volume).

Finally there are sports, which are different to some extent. Athletic competition obviously does not produce fatalities, at least not with regularity or by design any longer (Guttmann, this volume). It involves and tolerates violence, however, and physical injury is commonplace in some sports. It has been suggested that vigorous, potentially injurious behavior is a direct, if primitive, means to convince spectators of the combative disposition of competing athletes (Bryant & Zillmann, 1983; Zillmann, Bryant, & Sapolsky, 1989). To the extent, then, that athletic competition involves animosity that can erupt in hostile and injurious action, it creates tensions and distress capable of intensifying the enjoyment of play, especially when the play yields hoped-for outcomes. Exactly this has been shown to be the case (Bryant, Brown, Comisky, & Zillmann, 1982; Bryant, Comisky, & Zillmann, 1981; Comisky, Bryant, & Zillmann, 1977).

Epilogue

This excursion into the psychology of the appeal of portrayals of violence should have made it clear that there is no single quality of violence, nor a single circumstance in the exposure to its depiction, that could adequately explain the apparent attraction of the portrayals in question. Rather, there seem to exist a multitude of conditions that are poorly interrelated and, hence, difficult to integrate into a universal theory. We may have to be satisfied, at this point of exploration, with psychological theories that successfully cope with a good portion of the appeal of portrayals of violence. We must, moreover, content ourselves with acknowledging and enumerating the conditions that contribute to the appeal of these portrayals, conditions that remain isolated theoretically.

Comparatively speaking, the enjoyment of fictional and nonfictional portrayals of violence is better predictable from integrated theory than are other facets of appeal, such as exposure seeking. The consequences of affective dispositions toward parties who inflict harm through violence or who suffer such infliction by others, along with moral and plain selfish partialities, are reasonably well understood. However, the consequences of numerous traits of respondents are not. There appears to be a need for clarification of the enjoyment-modifying influence of personality characteristics.

The influence of the social circumstances of exposure to portrayals of violence, while established to some degree, is also poorly integrated in theoretical terms. Much remains to be done before we can claim to understand the various aspects of the seemingly contradictory attraction to stimuli that foster distress, even disgust.

The premise that portrayals of violence are inherently appealing is simply untenable. Dependent upon dispositional and related conditions, these portrayals are capable of evoking both grief and elation at extreme levels. The expectation of the latter emotion, at least upon the ultimate resolution of conflict, is what should attract. But this hedonistic maxim is liberally violated. People expect to be dismayed, shocked, or disgusted, yet still seek exposure to the portrayals. Curiosity of whatever type is readily invoked as an explanation. Social circumstances, like wanting to be informed (if only to be in a position to gossip with friends), offer some insight but hardly give a satisfactory, complete answer. Speculations about evolutionary origins, on the other hand, are ambitious but likely to remain speculations that enjoy some plausibility at best.

Future research will undoubtedly achieve a better understanding of the conditions that control the appeal of portrayals of violence, even offer better integrated theory than presently possible. Regardless of the degree of superior enlightenment, however, the socially more relevant question must be what our fascination with barbarous violence in entertainment efforts does to us and ultimately to society. The question, What are we doing to ourselves? has emerged in this connection (Plagens, Miller, Foote, & Yoffee, 1991). The research consensus projects nothing but ill effects from the thrills of violent entertainment (Geen, 1994; Huesmann & Eron, 1986; Linz & Donnerstein, 1989). On the other hand, our love affair with the First Amendment in absolute terms is unlikely to allow any curtailment of the freedom of artistic, nonartistic, and patently exploitative expression. Moreover, the primarily aesthetic outrage of a few elitists is unlikely to grow into a grassroots movement that could gain the power to impose moderation. Does this mean that we shall have to accept an ever increasing utilization of violence and terror for entertainment purposes? Considering excitatory habituation and the need for excitation transfer from distress and similarly negative affective reactions, it would appear to be so, indeed.

10

Why We Watch

JEFFREY GOLDSTEIN

We have heard the thoughts, experiences, and experiments of a disparate group of experts regarding the extent, nature, and attractions of violent imagery. By sampling from their insights perhaps we can arrive at the state of the art. What do we know about the appeals of violent imagery, and what gaps remain to be filled? Is it possible to devise nonviolent entertainment that is as appealing as its violent counterparts?

Violent Imagery in Perspective

Violent imagery is not a single entity. Maurice Bloch believes it would be a mistake to regard all displays of violence as stemming from the same source or serving the same purposes. Ritual violence, he believes, requires a different explanation than violent entertainment. In rituals the line between participant and spectator is not clear. Furthermore, the barrier between daily life and ritual, Bloch claims, is not as clearly demarcated as the separation between reality and imagery in film, television, literature, and sport. Vicki Goldberg suggests a continuum, with personal experience of violence and death at one extreme and violence as entertainment at the other. In between are ritual violence and violence as news. Meaningful distinctions can also be made among genres of violent entertainment—for example, whether it is animated or whether it purports to be documentary or historically accurate. The type or genre of violent imagery may be an important element in its attractiveness, but genre is given short shrift in many discussions of violent imagery, such as the recent reports on televised violence by Cole (1995) and the National Television Violence Study Council (1996). Finally, it is important to bear in mind that what is regarded as violent imagery changes from time to time and across media.

How Attractive Is It?

While there seems always to have been an audience for violent enactments and portrayals, it is worth remembering that violent entertainment is not as popular as other forms of entertainment, such as comedy. Most popular entertainments are devoid of violent images. A particular violent film or video game with a violent theme may be a best-seller, but the sales of such items are greatly exceeded by the sales of nonviolent fare. Film, television, and video comedies are far more popular than those featuring violence. In Joanne Cantor's research (chapter 5), *Mighty Morphin Power Rangers* was said by 26 percent of parents to be among their children's favorite TV programs, but a sitcom, *Full House*, was the favorite program of 33 percent of the children. War toys and video games with fighting themes account for a small portion of the market. Toy guns account for between 1 and 2 percent of the toy market while best-selling video games include strategy games like Tetris and nonviolent games featuring Sonic the Hedgehog and Super Mario Brothers (Toy Manufacturers of America, *Toy Industry Fact Book, 1995–1996*).

While a great many people seem attracted to—or at least not wholly repelled by—violent imagery, there may be a small audience that demands violent images in its entertainment. For some boys and men, the violence is the thing. But for many, it may be not the violence per se but other satisfactions that are its main attractants. For the majority of consumers of violent imagery, the violence is a means to ends, an acceptable device valued more for what it does than for what it is. Players who like video games with action/adventure or martial-arts themes, for example, are not necessarily attracted by the violence. These games have other features that appeal to players—their engaging fantasy, challenge, and stimulation, scorekeeping, feedback, graphics, and sound effects (Malone, 1981).

The Audiences for Violent Imagery

It is difficult to think of a group of people that is not in some way an audience for violent imagery. Young children, Maria Tatar assures us, like grotesque, violent stories, even though these stories are written by adults to serve their needs and beliefs. Even so, "children find nearly all displays of excess exciting, though not necessarily attractive," she writes.

Every study of the subject finds that boys far more than girls are drawn to violent entertainment. This is true not only in the United States and Europe but elsewhere where it has been studied—India, Japan, the

Philippines. It is boys and young men who play with toy guns, fill soccer stadia every Saturday, watch *Faces of Death*, and embrace Beavis and Butt-head. Which young men? Based on research reviewed in several chapters of *Why We Watch*, those who find violent entertainment most attractive have a relatively high level of aggression and high need for physical arousal or excitement.

Not every boy and man finds images of violence enjoyable, and not every female finds them repugnant. Individuals differ in their need for excitement and tolerance for stimulation. Those with a greater need for sensation are apt to find portrayals of violence more enjoyable than those with a lesser need. According to unpublished research by Jo Groebel of the University of Utrecht (the Netherlands), this relationship is not linear. Individuals extremely high in sensation seeking tend to find passive activities, like watching films and television, insufficiently stimulating; they prefer active dangers like skydiving and bungee jumping.

Adolescent boys like violent entertainment more than any other group does, although this does not mean that they like only violent entertainment or that they are the only audience for it. Relative to other children, highly aggressive boys find war toys more appealing than other toys (Watson & Peng, 1992) and prefer violent sports, films, video games, and television programs (Brug, 1994; Cantor & Nathanson, 1997; Russell & Goldstein, 1995; Wiegmann et al., 1995). Even preschool children's choice of fairy tales is related to their degree of aggression. Collins-Standley, Gan, Yu, and Zillmann (1995) found a positive association between children's aggressiveness, as rated by their caretakers, and their preference for violent fairy tales.

When Violence Is Not Attractive

The premise that portrayals of violence are inherently appealing is simply untenable. Depending upon personal dispositions and social conditions, these portrayals are capable of evoking grief, disgust, or elation at extreme levels, say McCauley and Zillmann. From studies using bloody films that viewers found decidedly unappealing, Clark McCauley concludes that violent portrayals can be disturbing, disgusting, and depressing, but that these effects are insufficient to deter viewers.

Why We Watch

As nearly every chapter in this book has stressed, the attraction of violence is best explained by analyzing its portrayal and its audience. And we must examine it also on a "macro" level, by considering the context in which it is witnessed and the times in which it is experienced.

In discussions of violent entertainment there is much speculation about morbid curiosity and our baser instincts. But the research and analysis in *Why We Watch* suggest that violent entertainment may have less to do with our "violent nature" and more to do with old-fashioned virtues of morality and justice.

There have been attempts, mostly by film reviewers and literary critics, to explain our fascination with violent entertainment. Stephen King, the popular purveyor of fictional horror, has even written a book, *Danse Macabre* (1981), explaining why his fans like to be horrified. In examining these armchair analyses, researchers Joanne Cantor, Clark McCauley, and Dolf Zillmann could find no support for several popular (and a few truly bizarre) explanations. They have laid to rest many of the speculations regarding violent entertainment. For example, they could find no evidence to support the position that people experience a catharsis of deep-seated fears, such as fear of the dark, or fear of aging, death, AIDS, technology, or the unknown. Likewise, there is little evidence to support the claim that viewers identify with the aggressor. Violent entertainment does not purge us of aggression or the propensity for violence, nor does it provide relief from unpleasant emotions.

"We are told . . . that the atomic bomb created a new climate of fear, and that because people now are more death conscious than ever before, they seek exposure to displays of violence and death to work out their fears." This makes no more sense, Zillmann says, than "the claim that a fear of overpopulation is behind our interest in seeing as much slaughter of humanity as we can muster." Zillmann concludes that violent material "has not been found to provide relief from ill emotions and motivations." Indeed, the best evidence is that the audience is disturbed and disgusted by scenes of violence but continues to watch it anyway.

The forms and appeals of violent imagery are many. Below we consider attractions of violent images as proposed in *Why We Watch*.

Social Identity

Violent entertainment appeals primarily to males, and it appeals to them mostly in groups. People rarely attend horror films or boxing matches alone, and boys do not play war games by themselves. These are social occasions, particularly suitable for "male bonding" and establishing a masculine identity. Boys may be playing violent video games alone in their rooms, but they are certain to talk about them with their peers. They use video games to make friends and gain popularity. Violent entertainment may be experienced alone, but it has a social purpose. The documentary film *Faces of Death*, for example, was regarded by adolescent boys as a sort of rite of passage, where the acceptable reaction was to consider the gore "cool" rather than "gross" ("Echt dood, dat is pas spannend" [Real death, that's exciting], *de Volkskrant*, Amsterdam, Apr. 5, 1995). Even though it is disturbing, boys use violent entertainment to demonstrate to their peers that they are man enough to take it. Perhaps one reason the films used by McCauley in his studies were not attractive to viewers is that they were alone while viewing them. Thus the social value of the films was lost.

I once spent an evening with a group of teenage girls and boys watching horror films, which they themselves had selected. How would these middle-class American youngsters react to the horror of dismemberments and exploding bodies? It was gratifying to see that young people found it difficult to watch the bloody excesses, though boys and girls expressed their distress in different ways. When the music-enhanced story suggested impending bloodshed, the girls would look away from the screen and talk animatedly among themselves about an unrelated topic—school, friends, parties. The boys apparently did not feel free to look away; while still gazing determinedly at the screen, they distanced themselves emotionally from the action by commenting upon the special effects, how they were done, whether the gore looked convincingly real. For a moment they saw the film through the dispassionate eyes of a film critic. When the music gave the "all clear" signal, they resumed their interest in the story.

"Distancing" oneself from the mayhem makes it tolerable. These adolescent boys and girls were able to fine-tune their degree of involvement. I spoke with one young woman who watches horrific films. She makes them palatable by squeezing her leg until it hurts, distracting herself while gazing at the screen. She, too, wants to be "man enough" to take it.

Zillmann describes the process well: "Boys . . . must prove to their peers, and ultimately to themselves, that they are unperturbed, calm, and collected in the face of terror; and girls must similarly demonstrate their sensitivity by being appropriately disturbed, dismayed, and disgusted."

As Hoberman notes of reactions to *Bonnie and Clyde*, people defined themselves by their responses to screen excesses. The violence of the film became a subject of conversation and social posturing, the purposes served by our public responses to all forms of entertainment.

Mood Management

An undeniable characteristic of violent imagery is its emotional wallop. It gives most people a jolt. Not everyone finds this kind of stimulation pleasant, but some do. Furthermore, the occasion of violent imagery can be used to express emotions in ways generally prohibited.

Cantor's research confirms the importance of taking the type of violence into consideration when discussing the attractions of violent entertainment. "Typical violent television series might be characterized as anxiety-reducing, justice-restoring genres that attract anxious, more empathic children, who side emotionally with the 'good guy' over the 'bad guy' and use the programs to control their anxieties. Violence for violence's sake should be considered separately. Children who are attracted by something described only as 'very violent' are more likely to be children with a good deal of exposure to violence in their own lives" and who "enjoy the violence irrespective of moral considerations or outcomes to protagonists." But the basis for their attraction remains unclear: is it because, in contrast to what they witness on the screen, their own lives seem less wretched? Perhaps aggressive youngsters have a greater need for excitement, which underlies both their antisocial behavior and their entertainment preferences. It may be a test of their manliness, or a way to make or maintain friends.

Sensation Seeking and Excitement

Perhaps our attraction to violent imagery is an outcome of the "civilizing process" described by Norbert Elias and Eric Dunning (1986), a way to fill the void left by diminished opportunities to experience the real thing. Certainly the events described by Vicki Goldberg lend credence to this view: As the dying and dead became further removed from immediacy, interest in *images* of death and dying seems to have increased.

Regardless of whether we crave excitement because society is increasingly "civilized" and "unexciting," as Elias and Dunning contend, it is certainly so that some individuals crave excitement more than others. Zuckerman's (1979) concept of sensation seeking, described by McCauley, helps to explain individual differences in attraction to violence. Those who have a high need for sensation (as measured by Zuckerman's scale) find violent films and television programs more appealing than do other individuals.

McCauley reviews research on the role of sensation seeking in the appeal of horror films. "There is little doubt," he writes, "that high sensation seekers like horror movies more than low sensation seekers do. The relationship is not always strong, but it is consistent." Still, McCauley dismisses the importance of such individual differences by questioning whether they can explain the broad appeal of horror and other exceedingly violent films.

Emotional Expression

Guttmann notes that violent sports are occasions for "excitement openly expressed." In this regard, sports are similar to rock concerts and other public spectacles. They not only provide a physiological "kick" for the observer but also serve as social occasions for the expression of intense emotion.

Making airplane, automobile, and shooting sounds is one of the appeals of aggressive games, especially for boys. For men, such aggressive sports as football and boxing provide an opportunity to shout and yell. Perhaps males can overcome the social pressures on them not to be emotional or intimate with other males only in a hypermasculine context, like aggressive games and entertainment.

Commenting on expressive responses of horror audiences, Clover (1992) observes that extravagantly participatory audiences (shouting, throwing things) were the norm in all manner of performances (operatic, dramatic, symphonic) until toward the end of the nineteenth century, when they were silenced and "sacralized":

> Audiences express uproarious disgust ("Gross!") as often as they express fear, and it is clear that the makers of slasher films pursue the combination. More particularly: spectators tend to be silent during the stalking scenes (although they sometimes call out warnings to the stalked person), scream out at the first slash, and make loud noises of revulsion at the sight of the bloody stump. The rapid alternation between registers—between something like "real" horror on one hand and a camp, self-parodying horror on the other—is by now one of the most conspicuous characteristics of the tradition. (p. 41)

For the child, there are cognitive, emotional, and social reasons for engagement with taboo subjects. According to Maria Tatar, children's curiosity about the forbidden is satisfied. They learn to manage anxiety and defeat fear by distorting and exaggerating reality. And they bond with others, storytellers and peers, by sharing intense emotional experiences.

People say they like horror films because they are exciting and scary. Does enjoyment have something to do with arousal or fear? McCauley and Zillmann note that negative emotions can be mixed with positive ones. In research by de Wied, Zillmann, and Ordman (1994), those who most enjoyed the film *Steel Magnolias* were those who felt the most sadness during the film. The degree of enjoyment was directly related to the degree of sadness experienced during the film. People may be attracted to violent entertainment but they do not necessarily *enjoy* the gory details.

Why don't negative feelings, such as fear and sadness, make for an unpleasant viewing experience? Perhaps feelings of control mediate this process. Control is one of the factors that players enjoy about video games (Saxe, 1994). With the joystick or remote control in their hands, players can control not only what appears on the screen but, indirectly, what effects it will have on them. A remote control is ultimately a device for self-control, for producing satisfying emotional and physiological states in the user. In a study at the University of Utrecht, students who viewed a violent videotape while merely holding a remote control experienced less distress than those who viewed the same tape without a remote control. Presumably, the feeling of control made the gruesome scenes less unpleasant (Goldstein, Claassen, van Epen, de Leur, & van der Vloed, 1993; see chapter 3 in this volume).

Some see predictability as the most appealing feature of violent entertainment, from cowboy movies to horror films (Britton, 1986). We know that the bad guys will "buy it" in the end, or in the sequel. But this does not account for our interest in blood sports, where the outcome is not known in advance. Perhaps the unpredictability of events like a boxing match is attenuated by the knowledge that there will come another fight, another game. Maybe it isn't over when it's over. Perhaps a rematch is equivalent to a movie sequel. While the outcome of a specific game or match is unpredictable, a subsequent one may provide a sense of closure.

Fantasy

The potential of a book, a film, or a video game to engross one in an imaginary world is one of the most attractive features of entertainment media (Turkle, 1984). For a short time, one becomes totally immersed in an activity, a phenomenon referred to as "flow" by Csikszentmihalyi (1990). Violent entertainment may be enjoyed repeatedly because it lends itself to imaginative experiences and to a temporary loss of self-consciousness (flow). The willing suspension of disbelief, the leap into imaginary worlds, is emphasized in nearly every chapter of *Why We Watch*, whether considering literature, film, television, play, or sport. Although this potential inheres in all entertainment, it helps explain the tolerance for, if not the attraction of, violent imagery. Moreover, the richness of the fantasy may be enhanced by the emotional impact of violent images.

The Importance of Context

Both the context of violent images themselves and the circumstances in which they are experienced play crucial roles in their appeal. Violent images lose their appeal when the viewer does not feel relatively safe. When there are few cues to the unreality of the violence, as in the "disgusting" films studied by McCauley, violent images are not very appealing. If the violent imagery does not itself reveal its unreality, the physical environment may do so. We are aware of holding a book, of sitting in a movie theater or a sports stadium.

People go to horror films in order to experience in safety emotions that are usually associated with danger. Fairy tales that "end tragically in the punishment of likable wrongdoers still can be greatly enjoyed, as children find comfort in the arms of the tale-telling caretaker. The caretaker, by radiating security, constitutes a happy ending of sorts" (Zillmann).

Images of carnage on the nightly news are far more disturbing than exploding bodies in a war film or the worst images from Mortal Kombat. Without background music, awareness of the camera, exaggerated special effects, or film editing, images of violence are unattractive to both males and females, according to McCauley's experiments. In the Scandinavian study cited by Joanne Cantor, preschool children typically showed facial expressions of joy while watching cartoon violence but showed negative emotions while watching realistic physical violence (Lagerspetz, Wahlroos, & Wendelin, 1978).

The Justice Motive

The popularity of violent entertainment may reflect the wish to be reassured that good prevails over evil. Displays of violence result in distress, which is reduced when the bad guys get their comeuppance. Some might say there would be no wish to see justice restored if people did not watch the injustice on the screen in the first place. But people can bring a sense of generalized injustice in society with them to the theater.

According to Zillmann, negative attitudes about the victims "contribute greatly to the enjoyment of humiliation, disparagement, defeat, and destruction. . . . Observing the audience of any contemporary action film, especially the apparent euphoria of young men upon seeing the bad guys being riddled with bullets and collapsing in deadly convulsions, should convince the doubtful that Western audiences fully exercise their moral right of rejoicing in response to exhibitions of *righteous violence.* . . . There can be little doubt, then, that righteous violence, however brutal but justified by the ends, will prompt gloriously intense euphoric reactions the more it is preceded by patently unjust and similarly brutal violence."

Fictional characters toward whom an audience holds particular dispositions elicit affective responses and emotional involvement similar to real persons toward whom the same dispositions are held, writes Zillmann. These emotions are mediated by moral judgment. Viewers come to have strong feelings and fears regarding protagonists and antagonists, and decide in moral terms what fate they deserve. "[J]ustified hatred and the call for punishment allows us to uninhibitedly enjoy the punitive action when it materializes. *Negative affective dispositions, then, set us free to thoroughly enjoy punitive violence.* As we have morally condemned a villain for raping and maiming, for instance, we are free to hate such a person, can joyously anticipate his execution, and openly applaud it when we finally witness it" (Zillmann). Thus the typical story line of enjoyable entertainment involves the establishment of animosity toward wrongdoers, which makes later violence against them seem justified and hence enjoyable.

The Historical Context

Not only the viewing situation but also the larger social world influences the attractiveness of violence. Interest in violent imagery changes with the times. There are also historical shifts in what violent images are regarded as acceptable or excessive.

Real-life violence influences the desire for violent entertainment. War and war play are not independent of one another, nor are crime and crime entertainment. Real violence activates aggressive associations and images. These, in turn, may heighten the preference for further exposure to violent entertainment. If children first hear aggressive stories, they are more likely to choose toy guns for play (Jukes & Goldstein, 1993). The same relationship is evident in preferences for violent film entertainment (Cantor; Hoberman), war toys and video games (Goldstein, chapter 3), and enjoyment of blood sports (Guttmann). As noted in chapter 3, an increase in student patronage of violent films occurred at the University of Wisconsin following the murder of a coed on campus (Boyanowsky, Newtson, & Walster, 1974). Sales of replica missiles increased during the Persian Gulf War (Goldstein, 1994). Public support for military expenditures is correlated with an increase in the sale of war toys and in the prevalence of war movies (Regan, 1994).

Almost Real

An important issue not yet decided regarding the attractions of violent images is the degree to which realism enhances or diminishes their acceptance or appeal. In the discussions of ritual (Bloch), photographic images of death (Goldberg), and spectator sports (Guttmann), a close relationship is said to exist between the apparent realism of violent images and their appeal to their consumers. Zillmann writes that violence in sports is appealing not because of any "blood lust" among spectators but because it is a sign that the participants are willing to take risks for their sport, an indication of their passionate commitment. In other realms, such as film (McCauley), children's television (Cantor), and play (Goldstein), it appears that violent imagery must carry cues to its unreality or it will lose its appeal.

Based on his previous studies of disgusting films and research conducted for this project, McCauley concludes with two possibilities: (1) Emotions elicited by drama are weaker than everyday emotions. Thus, the arousal accompanying fear, disgust, and pity can be experienced as pleasurable. Within a dramatic or protective frame, violent imagery becomes exciting rather than anxiety provoking. (2) The emotions experienced in drama are qualitatively different from their real-life counterparts. "Indeed, this theory would assert that we err in calling dramatic emotions by the same names as everyday emotions; the dramatic emotions are a parallel but different reality." Perhaps when the violence is almost real, so too are the emotions it elicits. Both sides of the equation—the violent images as well as the emotions that result—are recognizably different from the genuine article. We are then able to tolerate both reasonably well, without the distress being too intense to spoil our enjoyment.

Violent Images as Social Control

Gerbner, Gross, Morgan, and Signorielli (1986) report that heavy viewers of violence in the media come to see the world as a frightening and dangerous place. As a result, they lend support to the forces of law and order. In Gerbner's "cultivation theory," media violence is seen to serve as a means of social control in a broad sense. Similarly, Maria Tatar considers children's stories as a form of moral instruction, produced by adults to frighten children into obedience. Do these scary tales with morals produce obedience? Yes, she says, if it is clear what must be done to reduce the jeopardy. Children who disobey their parents, lie, or steal in these tales meet horrific ends. The message is that obedience, truthfulness, and honesty will enable children to avoid these horrible consequences.

Summary

It is obvious that the attractions of violent imagery are many. The audiences for images of violence, death, and dying do not share a single motive—some viewers seek excitement, others companionship or social acceptance through shared experience, and still others wish to see justice enacted. For some, the immersion in a fantasy world is its primary appeal.

Table 10.1 lists the features that, according to the authors in *Why We Watch*, make violence attractive. These do not fit neatly into a single theory. They illustrate the range of phenomena that any theory would have to explain. An adequate theory must account for sex and personality differences, the social uses to which violent entertainment is put, and the broader cultural roles it plays.

Not all the elements in table 10.1 seem compatible. Some may even appear to be inherently incompatible. For example, it appears that violent imagery becomes more appealing when signs are present indicating that the violence is not real, yet historical analysis finds heightened interest in violent imagery when war and crime are salient to the audience. And while the real violence of war increases interest in violent entertainment, Vicki Goldberg finds increasing images of death and dying precisely when death and dying begin to disappear from sight.

TABLE 10.1 When Violence Is Attractive

Subject Characteristics

Those most attracted to violent imagery are
Males
More aggressive than average
Moderate to high in need for sensation or arousal
In search of a social identity, or a way to bond with friends
Curious about the forbidden, or interested because of their scarcity
Have a need to see justice portrayed or restored
Able to maintain emotional distance to prevent images from being too disturbing
Violent images are used
For mood management
To regulate excitement or arousal
As an opportunity to express emotion

Characteristics of Violent Images that Increase Their Appeal

They contain clues to their unreality (music, editing, setting)
They are exaggerated or distorted
Portray an engaging fantasy
Have a predictable outcome
Contain a just resolution

Context

Violent images are more attractive
In a safe, familiar environment
When war or crime are salient

One feature of violent entertainment that presumably enhances its appeal is a predictable outcome. Yet in sports, the outcome is not known in advance. Clearly, other appeals of aggressive sports—perhaps the opportunity they afford for the intense expression of emotions—outweighs their unpredictability.

Emotional expression and control and the ability to distance oneself emotionally from threatening images are not, strictly speaking, subject characteristics. But they are included in table 10.1 because violent imagery may enable its audience to seek and obtain a level of emotional or social engagement that is personally satisfying.

What We Don't Know

What we don't know about the attractions of violent entertainment could fill a book. Some of the issues remaining to be explored are considered below. Not only are the data currently available minute in quantity, but even where research on the subject does exist, it is often inadequate. It fails to consider the role of culture or of subcultural groups, fails to adequately define key terms, like "attraction," "entertainment," and "violence."

Do we need a "macro" or a "micro" theory to explain the attractions of violent entertainment? A macro-level explanation would focus on society's changing definitions and wavering opinions of violence and violent entertainment, as well as the relationship between violent imagery and social institutions, like religion, politics, business, and the military. The historical and anthropological chapters in *Why We Watch* (Bloch, Guttmann, Goldstein, Tatar, Hoberman) make just such connections. At the same time, we know from experimental, micro-level research a few features of violent images that make them appealing, and something about the individuals who find them most attractive.

Some explanations are very difficult to put to the test, but worth considering nonetheless. For example, violent imagery may be attractive to humans in general because we, alone among creatures, know that we will die but, except in rare cases, we do not know when or how. Hence, we may be motivated by morbid curiosity. Violent images may be compelling in part because we are tantalized by images of mortality.

Individual Differences

Aside from sex, sensation seeking, and individual differences in aggressiveness, we know little about characteristics of the audiences for different forms of violent entertainment. Who likes professional wrestling? Do they share traits or experiences with those who read detective fiction or watch slasher films? Why don't females find this material as appealing as men do? Is it because men have different needs than women (for arousal, for example), or because women have alternative means of satisfying the same needs (for example, expressing emotion more openly)?

Context

Except for Maurice Bloch's contribution to this volume, there has been virtually no cross-cultural or cross-national analysis of the extent, appeal, or functions of violent imagery. In Japan, extraordinarily violent images are the bases of countless comic books read by both men and women. Does such graphic violence appeal to the Japanese for the same reasons that Arnold Schwarzenegger films appeal to Westerners?

Can the future course of violent entertainment be predicted? The violence in some media, like fairy tales, has been toned down over time, while the violence in others, like Hollywood films, has increased. What is technologically feasible will almost inevitably be tried. Are the exploding bodies of Hollywood only a test of the limits of new technology?

If so, we can expect increasingly realistic shoot-'em-ups as virtual reality and other new technologies evolve.

Alternatives to Violent Entertainment

Violent entertainment did not suddenly arrive on the scene, and it is not likely any time soon to depart it. Zillmann's analysis suggests that people become acclimated to the arousal generated by violent images but that they have a continuing need for excitement. "Does this mean that we shall have to accept an ever increasing utilization of violence and terror for entertainment purposes?" he asks. "[I]t would appear to be so, indeed."

It is worth remembering that violent entertainment is the preferred form of entertainment only for a minority of the general audience. Most viewers appear to prefer comedies and sitcoms to violent entertainment. These attract large audiences of all ages and of both sexes. When violent entertainment is preferred, it is often not for the violence itself; for many males, it is a means toward an end—to achieve a desired level of stimulation, to help establish a masculine identity, or to be accepted by peers.

Is there something that meets the requirements and serves the purposes of violent entertainment without relying on the violence? Are there effective substitutes for violent entertainment? People use all forms of entertainment to achieve a desirable level of excitement or relaxation. Nonviolent but equally stimulating entertainment satisfies many of the same needs as violent entertainment. Arousal from visual media can be generated through editing and special effects. Hitchcock's famous shower scene in *Psycho*, while bloody, showed little direct violence.

Some essential features of attractive entertainment are an engaging fantasy, an unpredictable path toward a predictable end, the restoration of justice and the depiction of morality, and opportunities for arousal and its reduction. These attributes would seem to be present in most of the violent fare discussed in *Why We Watch*. Other features that may make violent images more attractive are the presence of humor, appealing graphics, and sound effects.

Can we do away with violent entertainment? Social and historical circumstances influence its popularity. During times of war, or when violence permeates our neighborhoods, it gains in popularity. Violent entertainment may be as inevitable as violence in society.

It is up to the image makers to put violence in perspective—to emphasize, as they still do, the unacceptability of random, arbitrary, anarchistic, and plain sadistic violence, and to applaud violence that ultimately serves justice and the good of humanity. The public can and does influence the determination of what are acceptable and what are unacceptable displays of violence. There is opposition to "ultimate fighting," and even the future of boxing is in doubt because of growing public discontent with its crippling injuries. Eventually it might suffer the fate of smoking. The portrayal of violent action is inevitable; nevertheless, the limits we place on it, the manner in which we consume it, and the ways we respond to it help to define a culture.

References

The Adventures of Master Headstrong, and Miss Patient in their journey towards the land of happiness. (1802). London: J. Harris.

Alle haben gekotzt, nur ich nicht. (1984). *Der Spiegel*, March 12, p. 42.

Alloway, L. (1972). Monster films. In R. Huss & T. J. Ross (Eds.), *Focus on the horror film.* Englewood Cliffs, N.J.: Prentice-Hall.

Almqvist, B. (1989). Age and gender differences in children's Christmas requests. *Play and Culture, 2,* 2–19.

American Psychiatric Association. (1994). *Diagnostic and statistical manual of mental disorders.* 4th ed. Washington, DC: American Psychiatric Association.

Anglo, S. (1968). *The great tournament roll of Westminster.* 2 vols. Oxford: Clarendon.

Ansen, D. (1995). The return of a bloody great classic: *The wild bunch* still pushes our buttons about violence. *Newsweek*, March 13, pp. 70–71.

Apter, M. J. (1992). *The dangerous edge.* New York: Free Press/Macmillan.

Ariès, P. (1960). *Centuries of childhood: A social history of family life.* R. Baldick, Trans. New York: Vintage.

Ariès, P. (1981). *The hour of our death.* H. Weaver, Trans. New York: Oxford University Press.

Ariès, P. (1985). *Images of man and death.* J. Lloyd, Trans. Cambridge, Mass.: Harvard University Press.

Armbruster, B., & Kuebler, H.-D. (1984). Die Klasse von 1984: Videobewaltigung in der Schule? Eine Tagung mit Lehrern. *Medien Praktisch, 2,* 4–9.

Arms, R. L., Russell, G. W., & Sandilands, M. L. (1977). Effects of observing athletic contests on hostility of spectators viewing aggressive sports. *Social Psychology Quarterly, 42,* 275–79.

Atkin, C., Greenberg, B., Korzenny, F., & McDermott, S. (1979). Selective exposure to televised violence. *Journal of Broadcasting, 23* (1), 5–13.

Auguet, R. (1972). *Cruelty and civilization.* London: Allen and Unwin.

Augustine. (1907). *Confessions.* E. B. Pusey, Trans. London: J. M. Dent.

Baldwin, B. (1984). The sports fans of Rome and Byzantium. *Liverpool Classical Monthly, 9* (2), 28–30.

Bandura, A. (1973). *Aggression: A social learning analysis.* Englewood Cliffs, N.J.: Prentice-Hall.

Barber, N. (1991). Play and energy regulation in mammals. *Quarterly Review of Biology, 66,* 129–47.

Barber, R. (1974). *The knight and chivalry.* Ipswich, U.K.: Boydell Press.

Baron, R. A. (1974). The aggression-inhibiting influence of heightened sexual arousal. *Journal of Personality and Social Psychology, 30,* 318–22.

Baron, R. A. (1977). *Human aggression.* New York: Plenum.

Baron, R. A., & Ball, R. L. (1974). The aggression-inhibiting influence of nonhostile humor. *Journal of Experimental Social Psychology, 10,* 23–33.

Baron, R. A., & Richardson, D. R. (1994). *Human aggression.* 2nd ed. New York: Plenum.

Barry, H., Bacon, M. K., & Child, I. L. (1957). A cross-cultural survey of some sex differences in socialization. *Journal of Abnormal and Social Psychology, 55,* 327–32.

Bartholomew, G. A., & Birdsell, J. B. (1953). Ecology and the protohominids. *American Anthropologist, 55,* 481–96.

Barton, C. A. (1993). *The sorrows of the ancient Romans.* Princeton, N.J.: Princeton University Press.

Bateson, G. (1955). A theory of play and fantasy. *Psychiatry Research Reports, 2,* 39–51.

Battaglio, S. (1991). A bigger dose of reality: Networks cut costs with more shows about police work, rescue missions. *Adweek, 12* (27), 18–19.

Beer, C. (1984). Fearful curiosity in animals. In J. A. Crook, J. B. Haskins, & P. G. Ashdown (Eds.), *Morbid curiosity and the mass media: Proceedings of a symposium.* Knoxville: University of Tennessee and the Gannett Foundation.

Belton, J. (1985). Technology and aesthetics of film sound. In E. Weis & J. Belton (Eds.), *Film sound: Theory and practice.* New York: Columbia University Press.

Bem, D. J. (1972). Self-perception theory. In L. Berkowitz (Ed.), *Advances in experimental social psychology.* Vol. 6. New York: Academic Press.

Bennett, W. J. (1993). *The book of virtues: A treasury of great moral stories.* New York: Simon and Schuster.

Benton, R., & Newman, D. (1971). Lightning in a bottle. In S. Wake & N. Hayden (Eds.), *The Bonnie and Clyde book.* New York: Simon and Schuster.

Bere, R. M. (1966). *The African elephant.* London: A. Barker.

Berenbaum, S. A., & Hines, M. (1992). Early androgens are related to childhood sex-typed toy preferences. *Psychological Science, 3,* 203–6.

Berenbaum, S. A., & Snyder, E. (1995). Early hormonal influences on childhood sex-typed activity and playmate preferences: Implications for the development of sexual orientation. *Developmental Psychology, 31,* 31–42.

Beresin, A. R. (1989). Toy war games and the illusion of two-sided rhetoric. *Play and Culture, 2,* 218–24.

Berger, S. M. (1962). Conditioning through vicarious instigation. *Psychological Review, 29,* 450–66.

Bergman, A. (1971). *We're in the money: Depression America and its films.* New York: Harper.

Berkowitz, L. (1964). Aggressive cues in aggressive behavior and hostility catharsis. *Psychological Review, 71,* 104–22.

Berkowitz, L. (1965). Some aspects of observed aggression. *Journal of Personality and Social Psychology, 2,* 259–369.

Berkowitz, L. (1984). Some effects of thought on anti-and prosocial influences of media events: A cognitive neo-associationist analysis. *Psychological Bulletin, 95,* 410–27.

Berkowitz, L. (1989). Frustration-aggression hypothesis: Examination and reformulation. *Psychological Bulletin, 106,* 59–73.

Berkowitz, L. (1993). *Aggression: Its causes, consequences, and control.* New York: McGraw-Hill.

Berkowitz, L., & Alioto, J. T. (1973). The meaning of an observed event as a determinant of its aggressive consequences. *Journal of Personality and Social Psychology, 28,* 206–17.

Berkowitz, L., & Geen, R. G. (1966). Film violence and the cue properties of available targets. *Journal of Personality and Social Psychology, 3,* 525–30.

Berkowitz, L., & Rawlings, E. (1963). Effects of film violence on inhibitions against subsequent aggression. *Journal of Abnormal and Social Psychology, 66,* 405–12.

Berkowitz, L., & Walster, E. (Eds.). (1976). *Advances in experimental social psychology: Vol. 9. Equity theory: Toward a general theory of social interaction.* New York: Academic Press.

Bettelheim, B. (1966). Violence: A neglected mode of behavior. In B. Bettelheim, *Surviving and other essays.* New York: Random House.

Bettelheim, B. (1976). *The uses of enchantment: The meaning and importance of fairy tales.* New York: Random House.

Biro, Y. (1982). *Profane mythology: The savage mind of the cinema.* I. Goldstein, Trans. Bloomington: Indiana University Press.

Bjorkqvist, K., Lagerspetz, K., & Kaukiainen, K. (1991). The development of direct and indirect strategies: Gender differences during ages 8, 11, 15, and 18. *Aggressive Behavior, 17,* 60.

Bjorkqvist, K., & Niemela, P. (Eds.). (1992). *Of mice and women: Aspects of female aggression.* San Diego, Calif.: Academic Press.

Black, J. (1991). *The aesthetics of murder.* Baltimore: Johns Hopkins University Press.

Bloch, M. (1985). From cognition to ideology. In R. Fardon (Ed.), *Power and knowledge: Anthropological and sociological approaches.* Edinburgh: Scottish University Press.

Bloch, M. (1986). *From blessing to violence: History and ideology in the circumcision ritual of Madagascar.* Cambridge: Cambridge University Press.

Bloch, M. (1992). *Prey into hunter: The politics of religious experience.* Cambridge: Cambridge University Press.

Blumenschine, R. J. (1987). Characteristics of an early hominid scavenging niche. *Current Anthropology, 28*, 383–407.

Bogeng, A. E. (Ed.). (1926). *Geschichte des Sports aller Volker und Zeiten.* 2 vols. Leipzig, Germany: Seemann.

Bollinger, T. (1969). *Theatralis licentia.* Winterthur, Switzerland: Hans Schellenberg.

Bonte, E. P., & Musgrove, M. (1943). Influences of war as evidenced in children's play. *Child Development, 14*, 179–200.

Boulton, M. J. (1991). Children's abilities to distinguish between playful and aggressive fighting: A developmental perspective. *British Journal of Developmental Psychology, 11*, 249–63.

Boyanowsky, E. O., Newtson, D., & Walster, E. (1974). Film preferences following a murder. *Communication Research, 1*, 32–43.

Bradburn, N. M. (1969). *The structure of psychological well-being.* Chicago: Aldine.

Branscombe, N. R., & Wann, D. L. (1990). Die-hard and fair-weather fans: Effects of identification on BIRGing and CORFing tendencies. *Journal of Sport and Social Issues, 14*, 103–17.

Branscombe, N. R., & Wann, D. L. (1992a). Physiological arousal and relations to outgroup members during competitions that implicate an important social identity. *Aggressive Behavior, 18*, 85–93.

Branscombe, N. R., & Wann, D. L. (1992b). Role of identification with a group, arousal, categorization processes, and self-esteem in sports spectator aggression. *Human Relations, 45*, 1013–33.

Branscombe, N. R., Wann, D. L., Noel, J. G., & Coleman, J. (1993). In-group or out-group extremity. *Personality and Social Psychology Bulletin, 19* (4), 381–88.

Brehm, J. (1972). *Responses to loss of freedom: A theory of psychological reactance.* Morristown, N.J.: General Learning Press.

Britton, A. (1986). Blissing out: The politics of Reaganite entertainment. *Movie, 31/32*, 1–7.

Brody, L. R. (1985). Gender differences in emotional development: A review of theories and research. *Journal of Personality, 53*, 102–49.

Brosius, H.-B., & Schmitt, I. (1990). Nervenkitzel oder Gruppendruck? Determinanten fur die Beliebtheit von Horrorvideos bei Jugendlichen. In H. Lukesch (Ed.), *Wenn Gewalt zur Unterhaltung wird . . . Beitrage zur Nutzung und Wirkung von Gewaltdarstellungen in audiovisuellen Medien.* Regensburg, Germany: Roderer.

Brosnan, J. (1976). *The horror people.* New York: New American Library.

Brown, K. D. (1990). Modeling for war: Toy soldiers in late Victorian and Edwardian Britain. *Journal of Social History, 24*, 237–54.

Bruce, L. (1995a). At the intersection of real-life and television violence: Emotional effects, cognitive effects, and interpretive activities of children. Unpublished doctoral dissertation, University of Wisconsin, Madison.

Bruce, L. (1995b). Interpretive activities of traumatized children in response to violent television fare. Convention of the International Communication Association, Albuquerque, N. Mex., May.

Brug, H. H. van der (1994). Football hooliganism in the Netherlands. In R.

Giulianotti, N. Bonney, & M. Hepworth (Eds.), *Football, violence, and social identity*. London: Routledge.

Bryant, J., Brown, D., Comisky, D. W., & Zillmann, D. (1982). Sports and spectators. *Journal of Communication, 32* (1), 109–19.

Bryant, J., Carveth, R. A., & Brown, D. (1981). Television viewing and anxiety: An experimental examination. *Journal of Communication, 31* (1), 106–19.

Bryant, J., Comisky, P. A., & Zillmann, D. (1981). The appeal of rough-and-tumble play in televised professional football. *Communication Quarterly, 29*, 256–62.

Bryant, J., & Zillmann, D. (1983). Sports violence and the media. In J. H. Goldstein (Ed.), *Sports violence*. New York: Springer-Verlag.

Bryant, J., & Zillmann, D. (1984). Using television to alleviate boredom and stress. *Journal of Broadcasting, 28*, 1–20.

Buhmann, H. (1975). *Der Sieg in Olympia und in den anderen panhellenischen Spielen*. Munich: UNI-Druck.

Burghardt, G. M. (1984). On the origins of play. In P. K. Smith (Ed.), *Play in animals and humans*. Oxford: Basil Blackwell.

Burns, S. B. (1990). *Sleeping beauty: Memorial photography in America*. Altadena, Calif.: Twelvetrees Press.

Buruma, I. (1984). *Behind the mask: On sexual demons, sacred mothers, transvestites, gangsters, and other Japanese heroes*. New York: Pantheon.

Calvert, S. L., & Tan, S.-L. (1994). Impact of virtual reality on young adults' physiological arousal and aggressive thoughts: Interaction versus observation. *Journal of Applied Developmental Psychology, 15*, 125–39.

Cameron, A. (1976). *Circus factions*. Oxford: Clarendon.

Cameron, E. (1972). McLuhan, youth, and literature. *Horn Book*, October, 433–40.

Cannon, W. B. (1929). *Bodily changes in pain, hunger, fear, and rage: An account of researches into the function of emotional excitement*. 2nd ed. New York: Appleton-Century-Crofts.

Cantor, J. R. (1994). Fright reactions to mass media. In J. Bryant & D. Zillmann (Eds.), *Media effects: Advances in theory and research*. Hillsdale, N.J.: Lawrence Erlbaum Associates.

Cantor, J., & Nathanson, A. I. (1997). Predictors of children's interest in violent television programs. *Journal of Broadcasting and Electronic Media, 41*, 155–67.

Carey, P. M. (1994). NY firms feed Asia's entertainment appetite. *Crain's New York Business*, May 9–15, International section, p. 19.

Carlsson-Paige, N., & Levin, D. E. (1987). *The war play dilemma*. New York: Teachers College Press.

Carroll, L. (1992). *Alice in wonderland*. D. J. Gray, Ed. New York: Norton.

Carroll, N. (1990). *The philosophy of horror, or paradoxes of the heart*. New York: Routledge.

Cavalcanti, A. (1985). Sound in films. In E. Weis & J. Belton (Eds.), *Film sound: Theory and practice*. New York: Columbia University Press.

Cawelti, J. (1973). *Focus on Bonnie and Clyde*. Englewood Cliffs, N.J.: Prentice-Hall.

Cialdini, R. B., Borden, R. J., Thorne, A., Walker, M. R., Freeman, S., & Sloan,

L. R. (1976). Basking in reflected glory. *Journal of Personality and Social Psychology, 34,* 366–75.

Clarens, C. (1980). *Crime movies: An illustrated history.* New York: Norton.

Clark, J. D. (1959). *The prehistory of southern Africa.* Baltimore: Penguin.

Clover, C. J. (1992). *Men, women, and chainsaws: Gender in the modern horror film.* Princeton, N.J.: Princeton University Press.

Cohen, A. J. (1990). Understanding musical soundtracks. *Empirical Studies of the Arts, 8* (2), 111–24.

Cole, J. (1995). *The UCLA television violence monitoring report.* Los Angeles: University of California, Center for Communication Policy.

Coleridge, S. T. (1951). Biographia literaria. In D. Stauffer (Ed.), *Selected poetry and prose of Coleridge.* New York: Random House.

Collins-Standley, T., Gan, S., Yu, H. J., & Zillmann, D. (1995). Choice of romantic, violent, and scary fairy-tale books by preschool girls and boys. Unpublished manuscript, University of Alabama, Tuscaloosa.

Comisky, P., Bryant, J., & Zillmann, D. (1977). Commentary as a substitute for action. *Journal of Communication, 27* (3), 150–53.

Comollie, J.-L., & Labarthe, A. (1973). *Bonnie and Clyde*: An interview with Arthur Penn. In J. Cawelti (Ed.), *Focus on Bonnie and Clyde.* Englewood Cliffs, N.J.: Prentice-Hall.

Connor, K. (1989). Aggression: Is it in the eye of the beholder? *Play and Culture,* 2, 213–17.

Cooper, J., Hall, J., & Huff, C. (1990). Situational stress as a consequence of sex-stereotyped software. *Personality and Social Psychology Bulletin, 16,* 419–29.

Cortez, V. L., & Bugental, D. B. (1995). Priming of perceived control in young children as a buffer against fear-inducing events. *Child Development, 66.*

Costabile, A., Genta, M. L., Zucchini, E., Smith, P. K., & Harker, R. (1992). Attitudes of parents to war play in young children. *Early Education and Development, 3,* 356–69.

Costabile, A., Smith, P. K., Matheson, L., Aston, J., Hunter, T., & Boulton, M. (1991). Cross-national comparison of how children distinguish serious and playful fighting. *Developmental Psychology, 27,* 881–87.

Covington, R. (1994). Lost in multimedia land. *International Herald Tribune,* January 19, p. 11.

Cripps-Day, F. H. (1918). *The history of the tournament in England and France.* London: B. Quaritch.

Csikszentmihalyi, M. (1990). *The flow experience.* San Francisco: Jossey-Bass.

Cumberbatch, G., Maguire, A. & Woods, S. (1993). *Children and video games: An exploratory study.* Birmingham U.K.: Aston University, Communications Research Group.

Dahl, R. (1964). *Charlie and the chocolate factory.* New York: Puffin.

Dart, R. A. (1953). The predatory transition from ape to man. *International Anthropological Linguistics Review,* 1, 201–19.

Darton, W. (1802). *Little truths, for the instruction of children.* London: Darton and Harvey.

de Grazia, E., & Newman, R. K. (1982). *Banned films: Movies, censors, and the First Amendment.* New York: R. R. Bowker.

Delgado, J. M. R. (1968). Electrical stimulation of the limbic system. *Proceed-*

ings of the 24th International Congress of Physiological Sciences, 6, 222–23.

Delgado, J. M. R. (1969). Offensive-defensive behavior in free monkeys and chimpanzees induced by radio stimulation of the brain. In S. Garattini & E. B. Sigg (Eds.), *Aggressive behavior*. New York: Harper and Row.

Denholm-Young, N. (1948). The tournament in the thirteenth century. In R. W. Hunt (Ed.), *Studies in medieval history*. Oxford: Clarendon.

Denne, J. D. (1972). Society and the monster. In R. Huss & T. J. Ross (Eds.), *Focus on the horror film*. Englewood Cliffs, N.J.: Prentice-Hall.

Denny, M. R. (Ed.). (1991). *Fear, avoidance, and phobias: A fundamental analysis*. Hillsdale, N.J.: Lawrence Erlbaum Associates.

Derry, C. (1987). More dark dreams: Some notes on the recent horror film. In G. A. Waller (Ed.), *American horrors: Essays on the modern American horror film*. Urbana: University of Illinois Press.

Deutsch, H. (1926). A contribution to the psychology of sport. *International Journal of Psychoanalysis, 7*, 223–27.

DeVore, I. (1965). *Primate behavior: Field studies of monkeys and apes*. New York: Holt, Rinehart and Winston.

de Waal, F. (1989). *Peacemaking among primates*. Cambridge, Mass.: Harvard University Press.

de Wied, M., Zillmann, D., & Ordman, V. (1994). The role of empathic distress in the enjoyment of cinematic tragedy. *Poetics, 23*, 91–106.

Dickstein, M. (1984). The aesthetics of fright. In B. K. Grant (Ed.), *Planks of reason: Essays on the horror film*. Metuchen, N.J.: Scarecrow Press.

Diener, E., & DeFour, D. (1978). Does television violence enhance program popularity? *Journal of Personality and Social Psychology, 36*, 333–41.

Diener, E., & Woody, L. W. (1981). TV violence and viewer liking. *Communication Research, 8*, 281–306.

Doane, M. A. (1985). Ideology and the practice of sound editing and mixing. In E. Weis & J. Belton (Eds.), *Film sound: Theory and practice*. New York: Columbia University Press.

Doherty, T. (1988). *Teenagers and teenpics: The juvenilization of American movies in the 1950s*. Boston: Unwin Hyman.

Donohue, T. R. (1975). Black children's perceptions of favorite TV characters as models of antisocial behavior. *Journal of Broadcasting, 19* (2), 153–67.

Douglas, D. (1966). *Horror!* New York: Macmillan.

Douglas-Hamilton, I., & Douglas-Hamilton, O. (1975). *Among the elephants*. New York: Viking.

Dunning, E., Murphy, P., & Williams, J. (1988). *The roots of football hooliganism*. London: Routledge and Kegan Paul.

Eaton, W. O., & Enns, L. R. (1986). Sex differences in human motor activity level. *Psychological Bulletin, 100*, 19–28.

Ebert, J. (1980). *Olympia*. Vienna: Tusch.

Eckerman, C., & Stein, M. R. (1990). How imitation begets imitation and toddlers' generation of games. *Developmental Psychology, 26*, 370–78.

Edwards, E. (1984). The relationship between sensation-seeking and horror movie interest and attendance. Unpublished doctoral dissertation, University of Tennessee, Knoxville.

Eisenberg, N., Tryon, K., & Cameron, E. (1984). The relation of preschoolers' peer interaction to their sex-typed toy choices. *Child Development, 55,* 1044–50.

Elias, N. (1982). *The civilizing process.* New York: Pantheon. (Orig. 1969)

Elias, N., & Dunning, E. (1970). The quest for excitement in unexciting societies. In G. Luschen (Ed.), *Cross-cultural analysis of sport and games.* Champaign, Ill.: Stipes.

Elias, N., & Dunning, E. (1986a). *Sport im Zivilisationsprozess.* Munster: LIT-Verlag.

Elias, N., & Dunning, E. (1986b). *Quest for excitement.* Oxford: Blackwell.

Epstein, S. (1967). Toward a unified theory of anxiety. In B. A. Maher (Ed.), *Progress in experimental personality research.* Vol. 4. New York: Academic Press.

Evans, W. (1984). Monster movies: A sexual theory. In B. K. Grant (Ed.), *Planks of reason: Essays on the horror film.* Metuchen, N.J.: Scarecrow Press.

Farber, J. (1987). Blood, sweat, and fears: Why are horror movies such a slashing success? *Seventeen,* July, 108–9, 140–41, 149.

Farrell, J. J. (1980). *Inventing the American way of death.* Philadelphia: Temple University Press.

Fenichel, O. (1954). *Collected papers: Second series.* New York: Norton.

Fenigstein, A. (1979). Does aggression cause a preference for viewing media violence? *Journal of Personality and Social Psychology, 37,* 2307–17.

Fenz, W. D., & Epstein, S. (1967). Gradients of physiological arousal in parachutists as a function of an approaching jump. *Psychosomatic Medicine, 24,* 33–51.

Feshbach, S., & Singer, R. D. (1971). *Television and aggression.* San Francisco: Jossey-Bass.

Festinger, L. (1954). A theory of social comparison processes. *Human Relations, 7,* 117–40.

Feuerbach, L. (1855). *The essence of Christianity.* M. Evans, Trans. New York: Calvin Blanchard. (Orig. 1843)

Fine, M. (1991). *Bloody Sam: The life and films of Sam Peckinpah.* New York: Donald I. Fine.

Finley, M. I., & Pleket, H. W. (1976). *The Olympic Games.* New York: Viking.

Fleckenstein, J. (Ed.). (1985). *Das ritterliche Turnier im Mittelalter.* Gottingen: Vandenhoek and Ruprecht.

Foley, D. J. (1962). *Toys through the ages.* Philadelphia: Chilton.

Forman, H. J. (1935). *Our movie made children.* New York: Macmillan.

Foucault, M. (1977). *Discipline and punish: The birth of the prison.* A. Sheridan, Trans. New York: Pantheon.

Fraser, A. (1966). *A history of toys.* London: Weidenfeld and Nicolson.

Freedman, J. L. (1984). Effects of television violence on aggressiveness. *Psychological Bulletin, 96,* 227–46.

Freeman, M. (1993). Reality TV. *Broadcasting and Cable, 123* (15), 30.

Freud, S. (1962). *Three essays on the theory of sexuality.* J. Strachey, Trans. New York: Avon. (Orig. 1905)

Freud, S. (1963). Das Unheimliche. In S. Freud, *Das Unheimliche: Aufsatze zur Literatur.* Hamburg: Fischer. (Orig. 1919)

Freud, S. (1964a). The ego and the id. In J. Strachey (Ed. and Trans.), *The standard edition of the complete psychological works of Sigmund Freud.* Vol. 19. London: Hogarth. (Orig. 1923)

Freud, S. (1964b). Group psychology and the analysis of the ego. In J. Strachey (Ed. and Trans.), *The standard edition of the complete psychological works of Sigmund Freud.* Vol. 19. London: Hogarth. (Orig. 1921)

Freud, S. (1968). *Die Traumdeutung.* Frankfurt am Main: Fischer-Verlag. (Orig. 1900)

Freud, S. (1987). Psychopathische Personen auf der Buhne. In A. Richards (Ed.), *Sigmund Freud: Gesammelte Werke.* Frankfurt am Main: Fischer-Verlag. (Orig. 1905–1906)

Friedberg, A. (1990). A denial of difference: Theories of cinematic identification. In E. A. Kaplan (Ed.), *Psychoanalysis and cinema.* New York: Routledge.

Friedländer, L. (1908–1913). *Roman life and manners under the early empire.* J. H. Freese & L. A. Magnus, Trans. 4 vols. London: Routledge.

Frodi, A., Macaulay, J., & Thome, P. (1977). Are women always less aggressive than men? A review of the experimental literature. *Psychological Bulletin, 84,* 634–60.

Froissart, J. (1814–1816). *Chronicles.* J. Bourchier, Trans. 4 vols. London: J. Davis.

Frost, R., & Stauffer, J. (1987). The effects of social class, gender, and personality on physiological responses to filmed violence. *Journal of Communication, 37* (2), 29–45.

Fry, D. P. (1990). Play aggression among Zapotec children: Implications for the practice hypothesis. *Aggressive Behavior, 16,* 321–40.

Fulton, R., & Owen, G. (1987–1988). Death and society in twentieth century America. *Omega, 18* (4), 379–95.

Gabbard, G. O. (1987). *Psychiatry and the cinema.* Chicago: University of Chicago Press.

Gardiner, E. N. (1930). *Athletics of the ancient world.* Oxford: Clarendon.

Garvey, C. (1991). *Play.* 2nd ed. Cambridge, Mass.: Harvard University Press.

Geen, R. G. (1975). The meaning of observed violence: Real vs. fictional violence and consequent effects on aggression and emotional arousal. *Journal of Research in Personality, 9,* 270–81.

Geen, R. G. (1994). Television and aggression: Recent developments in research and theory. In D. Zillmann, J. Bryant, & A. C. Huston (Eds.), *Media, children, and the family: Social scientific, psychodynamic, and clinical perspectives.* Hillsdale, N.J.: Lawrence Erlbaum Associates.

Geen, R. G., & Berkowitz, L. (1966a). Name-mediated aggressive cue properties. *Journal of Personality, 34,* 456–65.

Geen, R. G., & Berkowitz, L. (1966b). Some conditions facilitating the occurrence of aggression after the observation of violence. *Journal of Personality, 35,* 666–76.

Geen, R. G., & O'Neal, E. C. (1969). Activation of cue-elicited aggression by general arousal. *Journal of Personality and Social Psychology, 11,* 289–92.

Geen, R. G., & Quanty, M. B. (1977). The catharsis of aggression: An evaluation of a hypothesis. In L. Berkowitz (Ed.), *Advances in experimental social psychology.* Vol. 10. New York: Academic Press.

Geen, R. G., & Rakosky, J. J. (1973). Interpretations of observed violence and their effects on GSR. *Journal of Experimental Research in Personality, 6,* 289–92.

Gennep, A. van. (1960). *The rites of passage.* M. B. Vizedom & G. L. Caffee, Trans. Chicago: University of Chicago Press.

Gerbner, G. (1988). Violence and terror in the mass media. In *Reports and papers in mass communication.* No. 102. Paris: UNESCO.

Gerbner, G., & Gross, L. (1976). Living with television: The violence profile. *Journal of Communication, 26* (2), 173–99.

Gerbner, G., Gross, L., Morgan, M., & Signorielli, N. (1986). Living with television: The dynamics of the cultivation process. In J. Bryant & D. Zillmann (Eds.), *Perspectives on media effects.* Hillsdale, N.J.: Lawrence Erlbaum Associates.

Gerbner, G., Gross, L., Morgan, M., & Signorielli, N. (1994). Growing up with television: The cultivation perspective. In J. Bryant & D. Zillmann (Eds.), *Media effects: Advances in theory and research.* Hillsdale, N.J.: Lawrence Erlbaum Associates.

Gibson, J. W. (1994). *Warrior dreams.* New York: Hill and Wang.

Gibson, R., & Zillmann, D. (1994). Exaggerated versus representative exemplification in news reports: Perception of issues and personal consequences. *Communication Research, 21* (5), 603–24.

Gilmore, A. T. (1975). *Bad nigger! The national impact of Jack Johnson.* Port Washington, N.Y.: Kennikat.

Girard, R. (1972). *La violence et le sacré.* Paris: Galimard.

Girard, R. (1978). *Des choses cachées depuis la fondation du monde.* Paris: Grasset.

Gitlin, T. (1987). *The sixties: Years of hope, days of rage.* New York: Bantam.

Goldberg, V. (1988). *Photography in print.* Albuquerque: University of New Mexico Press.

Goldberg, V. (1991). *The power of photography: How photographs changed our lives.* New York: Abbeville Press.

Goldstein, J. H. (Ed.). (1983). *Sports violence.* New York: Springer-Verlag.

Goldstein, J. H. (1986). *Aggression and crimes of violence.* 2nd ed. New York: Oxford University Press.

Goldstein, J. H. (Ed.). (1989a). *Sports, games, and play.* 2nd ed. Hillsdale, N.J.: Lawrence Erlbaum Associates.

Goldstein, J. H. (1989b). Violence in sports. In J. H. Goldstein (Ed.), *Sports, games, and play.* 2nd ed. Hillsdale, N.J.: Lawrence Erlbaum Associates.

Goldstein, J. H. (1992). Sex differences in aggressive play and toy preference. In K. Bjorkqvist & P. Niemela (Eds.), *Of mice and women: Aspects of female aggression.* San Diego, Calif.: Academic Press.

Goldstein, J. H. (1994). Sex differences in toy play and use of video games. In J. H. Goldstein (Ed.), *Toys, play, and child development.* New York: Cambridge University Press.

Goldstein, J. H. (1995). Aggressive toy play. In A. D. Pellegrini (Ed.), *The future of play theory.* Albany: State University of New York Press.

Goldstein, J. H., & Arms, R. L. (1971). Effects of observing athletic contests on hostility. *Sociometry, 34,* 83–90.

Goldstein, J. H., Cajko, L., Oosterbroek, M., Michielsen, M., van Houten, O., & Salverda, F. (1997). Video games and the elderly, *Social Behavior and Personality, 25,* 345–352.

Goldstein, J. H., Claassen, C., van Epen, E., de Leur, W., & van der Vloed, G. (1993). Preference for violent films and the search for justice. Unpublished manuscript, University of Utrecht, the Netherlands.

Goode, E., & Hetter, K. (1994). The selling of reality: A hot tale and a good agent can buy fame and fortune. But at what cost? *U.S. News and World Report,* July 25, pp. 49–56.

Gorer, G. (1955). The pornography of death. *Encounter, 5* (4).

Grant, M. (1967). *The gladiators.* London: Weidenfeld and Nicolson.

Gray, J. A. (1971). *The psychology of fear and stress.* New York: McGraw-Hill.

Greenberg, B. S., & Gordon, T. F. (1972a). Children's perceptions of televised violence: A replication. In E. A. Rubinstein, G. A. Comstock, & J. P. Murray (Eds.), *Television and social behavior.* Vol. 2. Washington, D.C.: U.S. Government Printing Office.

Greenberg, B. S., & Gordon, T. F. (1972b). Social class and racial differences in children's perceptions of televised violence. In E. A. Rubinstein, G. A. Comstock, & J. P. Murray (Eds.), *Television and social behavior.* Vol. 2. Washington, D.C.: U.S. Government Printing Office.

Gretton, T. (1980). *Murders and moralities: English catchpenny prints, 1800–1860.* London: Colonnade Books.

Grings, W. W., & Dawson, M. E. (1978). *Emotions and bodily responses: A psychophysiological approach.* New York: Academic Press.

Groos, K. (1898). *The play of animals.* New York: Appleton.

Gudmundsen, J. (1959). *The great provider: The dramatic story of life insurance in America.* Norwalk, Conn.: Industrial Publications.

Guilland, R. (1948). The Hippodrome at Byzantium. *Speculum, 22,* 676–82.

Guttmann, A. (1978). *From ritual to record: The nature of modern sport.* New York: Columbia University Press.

Guttmann, A. (1984). *Sports spectators.* New York: Columbia University Press.

Guttmann, A. (1988). The modern Olympics: A sociopsychological interpretation. In J. O. Segrave & D. Chu (Eds.), *The Olympic Games in transition.* Champaign, Ill.: Human Kinetics Press.

Guttmann, A. (1991). *Women's sports: A history.* New York: Columbia University Press.

Haidt, J., McCauley, R. C., & Rozin, P. (1994). Individual differences in sensitivity to disgust: A scale sampling seven domains of disgust elicitors. *Personality and Individual Differences, 16,* 701–713.

Hamilton, J. T. (1994). Marketing violence: The impact of labeling violent television content. International Conference on Violence in the Media, St. John's University, New York, October.

Hanson, A. C. (1966). *Edouard Manet, 1832–1883.* Philadelphia: Philadelphia Museum of Art.

Hardy, S. (1974). The medieval tournament. *Journal of Sport History, 1* (2), 91–105.

Harrell, W. A. (1981). Verbal aggressiveness of spectators at professional hockey games. *Human Relations, 34,* 643–55.

Harrington, C. (1972). Ghoulies and ghosties. In R. Huss & T. J. Ross (Eds.), *Focus on the horror film*. Englewood Cliffs, N.J.: Prentice-Hall.

Harris, H. A. (1976). *Green athletics and the Jews*. Cardiff: University of Wales Press.

Hartmann, D. P. (1969). The influence of symbolically modeled instrumental aggression and pain cues on aggressive behavior. *Journal of Personality and Social Psychology, 11*, 280–88.

Hasegawa, T., Hiraiwa, M., Nishida, T., & Takasaki, H. (1983). New evidence on scavenging behavior in wild chimpanzees. *Current Anthropology, 24*, 231–32.

Haskins, C. H. (1927). The Latin literature of sport. *Speculum, 2*, 235–52.

Haskins, J. B. (1984). Morbid curiosity and the mass media: A synergistic relationship. In J. A. Crook, J. B. Haskins, & P. G. Ashdown (Eds.), *Morbid curiosity and the mass media: Proceedings of a symposium*. Knoxville: University of Tennessee and the Gannett Foundation.

Heller, T. (1987). *Delights of terror: An aesthetics of the tale of terror*. Urbana: University of Illinois Press.

Hemingway, E. (1932). *Death in the afternoon*. New York: Halcyon House.

Henderson, J. L. (1979). Ancient myths and modern man. In C. G. Jung (Ed.), *Man and his symbols*. Garden City, N.Y.: Doubleday.

Herman, G., & Leyens, J. P. (1977). Rating films on TV. *Journal of Communication, 27* (4), 48–53.

Herrmann, H. U. (1977). *Die Fussballfans*. Schorndorf, Germany: Karl Hofmann.

Hinde, R. A. (1970). *Animal behavior: A synthesis of ethology and comparative psychology*. 2nd ed. New York: McGraw-Hill.

Hirt, E. R., Zillmann, D., Erikson, G. A., & Kennedy, C. (1992). Costs and benefits of allegiance. *Journal of Personality and Social Psychology, 63*, 724–38.

Hitchcock, A. (1959). Interview by H. Brean. *Life*, July 13, p. 72.

Ho, R. K. K. (1994). How many children must we bury? *Chicago Tribune*, December 26, Perspective, p. 29.

Hoenle, A., & Henze, A. (1981). *Römische Amphitheater und Stadien*. Zurich: Atlantis.

Hoffman, A. (1968). *Revolution for the hell of it*. New York: Dial Press.

Hoffman, M. L. (1977). Empathy, its development and prosocial implications. In H. E. Howe Jr. (Ed.), *Nebraska symposium on motivation*. Vol. 25. Lincoln: University of Nebraska Press.

Hoffman, M. L. (1978). Toward a theory of empathic arousal and development. In M. Lewis & L. A. Rosenblum (Eds.), Lincoln: University of Nebraska Press.

Hofstadter, R., & Wallace, M. (1970). *American violence: A documentary history*. New York: Vintage.

Holmes, O. W. (1859). The stereotypes of the stereograph. *Atlantic Monthly*, June.

Holmes, O. W. (1863). Doings of the sunbeam. *Atlantic Monthly*, July.

Hopkins, K. (1983). *Death and renewal*. Cambridge: Cambridge University Press.

Horace. (1959). *The satires and epistles.* S. P. Bovie, Trans. Chicago: University of Chicago Press.

Hortleder, G., & Gunter, G. (1986). *Sport, Eros, Tod.* Frankfurt am Main: Suhrkamp.

Howell, F. C. (1968). *Early man.* New York: Time-Life Books.

Howell, S. (1989). *Societies at peace.* London: Routledge.

Huesmann, L. R., & Eron, L. E. (1986). *Television and the aggressive child: A cross-national comparison.* Hillsdale, N.J.: Lawrence Erlbaum Associates.

Humphreys, A. P., & Smith, P. K. (1984). Rough-and-tumble in preschool and playground. In P. K. Smith (Ed.), *Play in animals and humans.* Oxford: Basil Blackwell.

Huxley, A. (1971). *The devils of Loudon.* Harmondsworth, U.K.: Penguin.

Hyde, W. W. (1921). *Olympic victor monuments and Greek athletic art.* Washington, D.C.: Carnegie Institute.

Hygge, S. (1976). Information about the model's unconditioned stimulus and response in vicarious classical conditioning. *Journal of Personality and Social Psychology, 33,* 764–71.

Iaccino, J. F. (1994). *Psychological reflections on cinematic terror: Jungian archetypes in horror films.* Westport, Conn.: Praeger.

Jackson, C. O. (1980). Death shall have no dominion: The passing of the world of the dead in America. In R. A. Kalish (Ed.), *Death and dying: Views from many cultures.* Farmingdale, N.Y.: Baywood.

Jackson, M. V. (1989). *Engines of instruction, mischief, and magic: Children's literature from its beginnings to 1839.* Lincoln: University of Nebraska Press.

Janeway, J. (1977). *A token for children, being an exact account of the conversion, holy and exemplary lives and joyful deaths of several young children.* R. Miner, Ed. New York: Garland. (Orig. 1672)

Jennison, G. (1937). *Animals for show and pleasure in ancient Rome.* Manchester, U.K.: Manchester University Press.

Jenvey, V. B. (1993). Toys, play, and aggression. Unpublished doctoral dissertation, Faculty of Education, Monash University, Clayton, Victoria, Australia.

Johnson, D. M. (1972). *Western badmen.* New York: Ballantine Books.

Johnson, R. (1786). *Juvenile rambles through paths of nature.* London: E. Newbery.

Johnson, R. N. (1972). *Aggression in man and animals.* Philadelphia: W. B. Saunders.

Johnston, D. D. (1995). Adolescents' motivations for viewing graphic horror. *Human Communication Research, 21,* 522–52.

Jones, M., Jr. (1990). Bring back the monsters: Kids are inundated with preachy books, but a few good yarns stand out. *Newsweek,* December 3, pp. 64–66.

Jose, P. E., & Brewer, W. F. (1984). Development of story liking: Character identification, suspense, and outcome resolution. *Developmental Psychology, 20,* 911–24.

Jukes, J., & Goldstein, J. H. (1993). Preference for aggressive toys. *International Play Journal, 1,* 93–103.

Jung, C. G. (1959). Archetypes and the collective unconscious. R. F. C. Hull, Trans. In *Collected works of C. G. Jung*. Vol. 9, pt. 1. New York: Pantheon. (Orig. 1951)

Jung, C. G. (1970). Aion: Researches into the phenomenology of the self. R. F. C. Hull, Trans. In *Collected works of C. G. Jung*. Vol. 9, pt. 2. 2nd ed. New York: Pantheon. (Orig. 1951)

Jusserand, J. J. (1901). *Les sports et jeux d'exercise dans l'ancienne France.* Paris: Plon.

Juvenal. (1958). *Satires.* R. Humphries, Trans. Bloomington: Indiana University Press.

Kaplan, E. A. (Ed.). (1990). *Psychoanalysis and cinema.* New York: Routledge.

Karpoe, K. P., & Olney, R. L. (1983). The effect of boys' or girls' toys on sex-typed play in preadolescents. *Sex Roles, 9,* 507–18.

Keefer, R., Goldstein, J. H., & Kasiarz, D. (1983). Olympic Games participation and warfare. In J. H. Goldstein (Ed.), *Sports violence.* New York: Springer-Verlag.

Keen, M. (1984). *Chivalry.* New Haven, Conn.: Yale University Press.

Kendrick, W. (1991). *The thrill of fear.* New York: Grove Weidenfeld.

Kershaw, A. (1993). *A history of the guillotine.* New York: Barnes and Noble.

The killing screens: Media and the culture of violence [video]. (1994). Northampton, Mass.: Media Education Foundation.

Kincaid, J. (1992). *Child-loving: The erotic child and Victorian culture.* London: Routledge.

King, S. (1981). *Danse macabre.* New York: Berkley.

Kingsmore, J. M. (1968). The effect of a professional wrestling and a professional basketball contest upon the aggressive tendencies of male spectators. Unpublished doctoral dissertation, University of Maryland.

Klass, P. (1994). A "Bambi" for the 90's, via Shakespeare. *New York Times,* June 19, pp. 1, 20–21.

Klausner, S. Z. (1967). Sport parachuting. In R. Slovenko & J. A. Knight (Eds.), *Motivations in play, games, and sports.* Springfield, Ill.: Thomas.

Klausner, S. Z. (1968). *Why man takes chances: Studies in stress-seeking.* Garden City, N.Y.: Anchor.

Kline, S., & Pentecost, D. (1990). The characterization of play: Marketing children's toys. *Play and Culture, 3,* 235–55.

Knight, W. (1896). *The poetical works of William Wordsworth.* London: Macmillan.

Kohlberg, L. (1964). Development of moral character and moral ideology. In M. L. Hoffman & L. W. Hoffman (Eds.), *Review of child development research.* Vol. 1. New York: Russell Sage Foundation.

Kracauer, S. (1995). *The mass ornament.* Cambridge, Mass.: Harvard University Press.

Krause, J. H. (1972). *Olympia.* Hildesheim, Germany: Georg Olms.

Krüger, S. (1985). Das kirchliche Turnierverbot im Mittelalter. In J. Fleckenstein (Ed.), *Das ritterliche Turnier im Mittelalter.* Gottingen, Germany: Vandenhoek and Ruprecht.

Lagerspetz, K. M., Wahlroos, C., & Wendelin, C. (1978). Facial expressions of preschool children while watching televised violence. *Scandinavian Journal of Psychology, 19,* 213–22.

Lahey, M. P. (1996). Children in the midst of war: Paradoxes of play. *Society and Leisure, 19*, 363–73.

Langer, E. J., & Rodin, J. (1976). The effects of choice and enhanced personal responsibility for the aged: A field experiment in an institutional setting. *Journal of Personality and Social Psychology, 34*, 191–98.

Langley, T., O'Neal, E. C., Craig, K. M., & Yost, E. A. (1992). Aggression-consistent, -inconsistent, and -irrelevant priming effects on selective exposure to media violence. *Aggressive Behavior, 18*, 349–56.

Lawick-Goodall, J. van. (1968). The behavior of free-living chimpanzees in the Gombe Stream Reserve. *Animal Behaviour Monographs, 1* (3), 161–311.

Leff, L. J., & Simmons, J. L. (1990). *The dame in the kimono: Hollywood, censorship, and the production code from the 1920s to the 1960s.* New York: Doubleday.

Lefkowitz, M. M., Eron, K. D., Walder, L. O., & Huesmann, L. R. (1977). *Growing up to be violent: A longitudinal study of the development of aggression.* New York: Pergamon.

Leiris, M. (1981). *Miroir de la tauromachie.* Paris: Fata Morgana.

Lennon, J. X., & Hatfield, F. Q. (1980). The effect of crowding and observation of athletic events on spectator tendency toward aggressive behavior. *Journal of Sport Behavior, 3* (2), 61–80.

Lewin, R. (1984). Man the scavenger. *Science, 224*, 861–62.

Leyens, J., Herman, G., & Dunand, M. (1982). The influence of an audience upon the reactions to film violence. *European Journal of Social Psychology, 12*, 131–42.

Lienhardt, G. (1961). *Divinity and experience: The religion of the Dinka.* Oxford: Oxford University Press.

Lindsay, P. L. (1973). Attitudes toward physical exercise reflected in the literature of ancient Rome. In E. F. Zeigler (Ed.), *History of sport and physical education to 1900.* Champaign, Ill.: Stipes.

Linz, D. G., & Donnerstein, E. (1989). The effects of violent messages in the mass media. In J. Bradac (Ed.), *Message effects in communication science.* Newbury Park, Calif.: Sage.

Locke, J. (1693/1910). *Some thoughts concerning education.* N.Y. Collier.

Loomis, R. S. (1959). Arthurian influence and sport and spectacle. In R. S. Loomis (Ed.), *Arthurian literature in the Middle Ages.* Oxford: Clarendon.

Lovaas, O. I. (1961). Effect of exposure to symbolic aggression on aggressive behavior. *Child Development, 32*, 37–44.

Loy, J. W., & Hesketh, L. (1992). Competitive play on the Plains: An analysis of games and warfare among native American warrior societies, 1800–1850. International Council for Child's Play. Paris: May.

Loyette, H. (1994). History painting. In G. Tinterow & H. Loyette (Eds.), *Origins of Impressionism.* New York: Metropolitan Museum of Art.

Lyle, J., & Hoffman, H. R. (1972). Children's use of television and other media. In E. A. Rubinstein, G. A. Comstock, & J. P. Murray (Eds.), *Television and social behavior.* Vol. 4. Washington, D.C.: U.S. Government Printing Office.

Maccoby, E. E., & Jacklin, C. (1974). *The psychology of sex differences.* Stanford, Calif.: Stanford University Press.

Maccobby, E. E., & Wilson, W. C. (1957). Identification and observational learning from films. *Journal of Abnormal and Social Psychology, 55,* 76–87.

Maccobby, E. E., Wilson, W. C., & Burton, R. V. (1958). Differential movie-viewing behavior of male and female viewers. *Journal of Personality, 26,* 259–67.

MacLean, P. D. (1958). The limbic system with respect to self-preservation and the preservation of the species. *Journal of Nervous and Mental Disease, 127,* 1–11.

MacLean, P. D. (1964). Man and his animal brains. *Modern Medicine, 32,* 95–106.

MacLean, P. D. (1968). Contrasting functions of limbic and neocortical systems of the brain and their relevance to psychophysiological aspects of medicine. In E. Gellhorn (Ed.), *Biological foundations of emotion.* Glenview, Ill.: Scott, Foresman.

Malalas, J. (1940). *Chronicle.* M. Spinka & G. Downey, trans. Chicago: University of Chicago Press.

Malone, T. (1981). Toward a theory of intrinsically motivating instruction. *Cognitive Science, 4,* 333–69.

Maltby, R. (1983). *Harmless entertainment: Hollywood and the ideology of consensus.* Metuchen, N.J.: Scarecrow Press.

Mannix, D. P. (1960). *Those about to die.* London: Nicholls & Co.

Marin, R., & Katel, P. (1994). Miami's crime time live: News to "chill the flesh and warm the heart." *Newsweek,* June 20, pp. 71–72.

Marks, I. M. (1969). *Fears and phobias.* New York: Academic Press.

Marks, I. M. (1987). *Fears, phobias, and rituals: Panic, anxiety, and their disorders.* New York: Oxford University Press.

Marler, P., & Hamilton, W. J. (1968). *Mechanisms of animal behavior.* New York: Wiley.

Marsh, P., Rosser, E., & Harre, R. (1978). *Rules of disorder.* London: Routledge and Kegan Paul.

Marx, M. H., & Hillix, W. A. (1963). *Systems and theories in psychology.* New York: McGraw-Hill.

Masson, J. L., & Patwardhan, M. V. (1970). *Aesthetic rapture: The Rasadhyaya of the Natyasastra.* Poona, India: Deccan College.

McCauley, C., & Bremer, B. A. (1991). Subjective quality of life measures for evaluating medical intervention. *Evaluation and the Health Professions, 14* (4), 371–87.

McManners, J. (1985). *Death and enlightenment: Changing attitudes to death in eighteenth century France.* Oxford: Oxford University Press.

Medved, M. (1992). *Hollywood vs. America: Popular culture and the war on traditional values.* New York: Harper Collins.

Mendelsohn, H. (1966). *Mass entertainment.* New Haven, Conn.: College and University Press.

Mendner, S. (1956). *Das Ballspiel im Leben der Volker.* Munster: Aschendorff.

Mergen, B. (1982). *Play and playthings: A reference guide.* Westport, Conn.: Greenwood.

Meth, C. (1987). The horror beat goes on. *Video Software Dealer* (Los Angeles: VSD Publications), September, 61–65.

Meyer, P. (1891–1904). *L'histoire de Guillaume le Marechal*. 3 vols. Paris: Renouard.

Meyer-Bahlburg, H. F. L., Feldman, J. F., Cohen, P., & Ehrhardt, A. A. (1988). Perinatal factors in the development of gender-related play behavior: Sex hormones versus pregnancy complications. *Psychiatry, 51*, 260–71.

Miedzian, M. (1991). *Boys will be boys*. New York: Doubleday.

Mills, J. (1993). The appeal of tragedy: An attitude interpretation. *Basic and Applied Social Psychology, 14* (3), 255–71.

Mitchell, B. R. (1962). *Abstract of British historical statistics*. Cambridge: Cambridge University Press.

Moeran, B. (1986). The beauty of violence: Jidaigeki, yakuza, and "eroduction" films in Japanese cinema. In D. Riches (Ed.), *The anthropology of violence*. Oxford: Blackwell.

Moller, L. C., Hymel, S., & Rubin, K. H. (1992). Sex typing in play and popularity in middle childhood. *Sex Roles, 26*, 331–53.

Mönckeberg, V. (1972). *Das Marchen und unsere Welt: Erfahrungen und Einsichten*. Dusseldorf: Diederichs.

Morley, J. (1971). *Death, heaven, and the Victorians*. Philadelphia: University of Pennsylvania Press.

Murphy, P., Williams, J., & Dunning, E. (1990). *Football on trial*. London: Routledge.

National Television Violence Study Council. (1996). *National television violence study*. Studio City, Calif.: Mediascope.

Nevin, J. A. (1973). Conditioned reinforcement. In J. A. Nevin (Ed.), *The study of behavior: Learning, motivation, emotion, and instinct*. Glenview, Ill.: Scott, Foresman.

Nochlin, L. (1981). *Realism*. Harmondsworth, U.K.: Penguin.

Norfleet, B. P. (1993). *Looking at death*. Boston: David R. Godine.

Novatian. (1972). *De spectaculis*. Turnholt: Brepols.

O'Brien, M., & Huston, A. C. (1985). Development of sex-typed play behavior in toddlers. *Developmental Psychology, 21*, 866–71.

O'Connell, J. F., Hawkes, K., & Blurton Jones, N. (1988). Hadza scavenging: Implications for Plio/Pleistocene hominid subsistence. *Current Anthropology, 29*, 356–63.

Oliver, M. B. (1994). Portrayals of crime, race, and aggression in "reality-based" police shows: A content analysis. *Journal of Broadcasting and Electronic Media, 38*, 179–92.

Opie, I. (1993). *The people in the playground*. Oxford: Oxford University Press.

Orbach, I., Winkler, E., & Har-Even, D. (1993). The emotional impact of frightening stories on children. *Journal of Child Psychology and Psychiatry, 34*, 379–89.

Orwaldi, D. (1984). "Ich sehe sie mir gern an, obwohl mir dabei schlecht wird." Zum Gebrauch von Videofilmen durch Kinder und Jugendliche. *Medium: Zeitschrift für Horfunk, Fernsehen, Film, und Presse, 14*, 31–34.

Ovid. (1957). *The art of love*. R. Humphries, Trans. Bloomington: Indiana University Press.

Palaeogos, K. (1979). The organization of the Games. In N. Yalouris (Ed.), *The eternal Olympics*. New Rochelle, N.Y.: Caratzas Brothers.

Panksepp, J., Sacks, D. S., Crepeau, L. J., & Abbott, B. B. (1991). In M. R. Denny (Ed.), *Fear, avoidance, and phobias: A fundamental analysis*. Hillsdale, N.J.: Lawrence Erlbaum Associates.

Parker, S. T. (1984). Playing for keeps: An evolutionary perspective on human games. In P. K. Smith (Ed.), *Play in animals and humans*. Oxford: Basil Blackwell.

Parten, M. (1933). Social play among preschool children. *Journal of Abnormal & Social Psychology, 28*, 136–47.

Patrucco. R. (1972). *Lo sport nella Grecia antica*. Florence: Olschiki.

Paul, C. K. (1876). *William Godwin: His friends and contemporaries*. Boston: Roberts Brothers.

Pellegrini, A. D. (1988). Elementary-school children's rough-and-tumble play and social competence. *Developmental Psychology, 24*, 802–6.

Pellegrini, A. D. (1989). What about recess, really? *Play and Culture, 2*, 354–56.

Pelling, H. (1964). Religion and the nineteenth century British working class. *Past and Present*, April, 128–33.

Pellis, S. M. & Pellis, V. C. (1996). On knowing it's only play: The role of play signals in play fighting. *Aggression and Violent Behavior, 1*, 249–68.

Penn, A. (1967). *Bonnie and Clyde*: Private morality and public violence. *Take One, 1* (6).

Pennebaker, J. W., Hughes, C. F., & O'Heeron, R. C. (1987). The psychophysiology of confession: Linking inhibitory and psychosomatic processes. *Journal of Personality and Social Psychology, 52*, 781–93.

Pennebaker, J. W., & Susman, J. R. (1988). Disclosure of traumas and psychosomatic processes. *Social Science and Medicine, 26*, 327–32.

Petronius. (1959). *Satyricon*. W. Arrowsmith, Trans. Ann Arbor: University of Michigan Press.

Phillips, C. A., Rolls, S., Rouse, A., & Griffiths, M. D. (1995). Home video game playing in schoolchildren: A study of incidence and patterns of play. *Journal of Adolescence, 18*, 687–91.

Phillips, D. P. (1983). The impact of mass media on U.S. homicides. *American Sociological Review, 48*, 560–68.

Phillips, D. P., & Hensley, J. E. (1984). When violence is rewarded or punished. *Journal of Communication, 34* (3), 101–16.

Piaget, J. (1948). *The moral judgment of the child*. Glencoe, Ill.: Free Press.

Pickering, S. F. (1993). *Moral instruction and fiction for children: 1749–1820*. Athens: University of Georgia Press.

Pilz, G. A. (1982). *Wandlungen der Gewalt im Sport*. Ahrensburg, Germany: Czwalina.

Pilz, G. A., & Trebels, A. H. (1976). *Aggression und Konflikt im Sport*. Ahrensburg, Germany: Czwalina.

Plagens, P., Miller, M., Foote, D., & Yoffee, E. (1991). Violence in our culture: As America binges on make-believe gore, you have to ask: what are we doing to ourselves? *Newsweek*, April 1, pp. 46–49, 51–52.

Pleket, H. W. (1974). Zur soziologie des antiken sports. *Mededelingen Nederlands Instituut te Rome, 36*, 57–87.

Pleket, H. W. (1975). Games, prizes, athletes, and ideology. *Stadion, 1* (1), 49–89.

Polybius. (1922–1927). *Histories*. W. R. Paton, Trans. 6 vols. London: Hutchinson.

Posthumus, B., Kleynen, I., Royaards, S., Stok, E., & Goldstein, J. (1994). Kan controle emoties beinvloeden? Onderzoek naar de invloed van control op de sterkte van emoties [Can control influence emotions? Research on the influence of control on the strength of emotions]. Unpublished manuscript, University of Utrecht, the Netherlands.

Postman, N. (1982). *The disappearance of childhood*. New York: Vintage.

Potts, R., Huston, A., & Wright, J. C. (1986). The effects of television form and violent content on boys' attention and social behavior. *Journal of Experimental Child Psychology, 41*, 1–17.

Pudovkin, V. I. (1985). Asynchronism as a principle of sound film. In E. Weis & J. Belton (Eds.), *Film sound: Theory and practice*. New York: Columbia University Press.

Rachlin, H. (1995). Self control: Beyond commitment. *Behavioral and Brain Sciences, 18*, 109–35.

Rachman, S. J. (1990). *Fear and courage*. 2nd ed. New York: W. H. Freeman.

Ramirez, J., Bryant, J., & Zillmann, D. (1982). Effects of erotica on retaliatory behavior as a function of level of prior provocation. *Journal of Personality and Social Psychology, 43*, 971–78.

Ramsland, K. (1989). Hunger for the marvelous: The vampire craze in the computer age. *Psychology Today*, November, 31–35.

Rashid ad-Din. (1960). *Sbornik letopisei* [Collected chronicles]. Vol. 1/2. p. 265. O. I. Smirnova, Trans. Moscow: Izd-Vo Akademii Nauk SSSR.

Regan, P. M. (1994). War toys, war movies, and the militarization of the United States, 1900–1985. *Journal of Peace Research, 31*, 45–58.

Reid, S. (1993). Game play. In C. E. Schaefer (Ed.), *The therapeutic powers of play*. London: Jason Aronson.

Rheingold, H., & Cook, K. V. (1975). The contents of boys' and girls' rooms as an index of parents' behavior. *Child Development, 46*, 459–63.

Richardson, A. (1994). *Literature, education, and romanticism: Reading as social practice, 1780–1832*. Cambridge: Cambridge University Press.

Richters, J. E., & Martinez, P. (1990). *Checklist of child distress symptoms: Self-report version*. Bethesda, Md.: National Institute of Mental Health.

Richters, J. E., & Saltzman, W. (1990). *Survey of children's exposure to community violence: Self-report version*. Bethesda, Md.: National Institute of Mental Health.

Rickey, C. (1982). Hooked on horror: Why we like scary movies. *Mademoiselle*, November, 168–70.

Rimmon-Kenan, S. (1976). *Discourse in psychoanalysis and literature*. London: Methuen.

Rivett, G. (1986). *The development of the London hospital system, 1823–1982*. London: King Edward's Hospital Fund for London.

Robert, L. (1971). *Les gladiateurs dans l'orient grec*. Amsterdam: Hakkert.

Roberts, D. F., & Bachen, C. M. (1981). Mass communication effects. *Annual Review of Psychology, 32*, 307–56.

Roberts, J. M., & Sutton-Smith, B. (1962). Child training and game involvement. *Ethnology, 1*, 166–85.

Roberts, R. (1983). *Papa Jack*. New York: Free Press.

Rockett, W. H. (1988). *Devouring whirlwind: Terror and transcendence in the cinema of cruelty*. New York: Greenwood Press.

Rosaldo, R. (1986). Anthropological commentary. In R. Hamerton-Kelly (Ed.), *Violent origins*. Stanford, Calif.: Stanford University Press.

Rose, J. (1984). *The case of Peter Pan, or, the impossibility of children's fiction*. London: Macmillan.

Rose, T. (1969). *Violence in America: A historical and contemporary reader*. New York: Random House.

Rosenbaum, R. (1979). Gooseflesh. *Harpers*, September, 86–92.

Rossman, M. (1971). *The wedding within the war*. New York: Anchor.

Roth, J. J. (1980). *The cult of violence: Sorel and the Sorelians*. Berkeley: University of California Press.

Rousseau, J. J. (1979). *Emile: or on education*. A. Bloom, Trans. New York: Basic Books. (Orig. 1763)

Rozin, P., Haidt, J., & McCauley, R. C. (1988). Individual differences in disgust sensitivity: Comparisons and evaluations of paper-and-pencil versus behavioral measures. Unpublished manuscript. Department of Psychology. University of Pennsylvania, Philadelphia.

Ruble, D., Balaban, T., & Cooper, J. (1981). Gender constancy and the effects of sex-typed televised toy commercials. *Child Development, 52*, 667–73.

Russell, G. W. (1986). Does sports violence increase box office receipts? *International Journal of Sport Psychology, 17*, 173–83.

Russell, G. W., & Drewry, B. R. (1976). Crowd size and competitive aspects of aggression in ice hockey. *Human Relations, 29*, 723–35.

Russell, G. W., & Goldstein, J. H. (1995). Personality differences between Dutch football fans and non-fans. *Social Behavior and Personality, 23*, 199–204.

Saarni, C. (1989). Children's understanding of strategic control of emotional expression in social transactions. In C. Saarni & P. L. Harris (Eds.), *Children's understanding of emotion*. New York: Cambridge University Press.

Sagi, A., & Hoffman, M. L. (1976). Empathic distress in newborns. *Developmental Psychology, 12*, 175–76.

Sale, K. (1974). *SDS*. New York: Vintage.

Salvian. (1930). *On the government of God*. E. M. Sanford, Trans. New York: Columbia University Press.

Sanson, A., & DiMuccio, C. (1993). The influence of aggressive and neutral cartoons and toys on the behaviour of preschool children. *Australian Psychologist, 28*, 93–99.

Sapolsky, B. S., & Molitor, F. (1995). Content trends in contemporary horror films. In J. Weaver & R. Tamborini (Eds.), *Horror films: Current research on audience preferences and reactions*. Hillsdale, N.J.: Lawrence Erlbaum Associates.

Saxe, J. (1994). Violence in videogames: What are the pleasures? International Conference on Violence in the Media, St. John's University, New York, October.

Schaller, M. (1993). Feeling bad to feel good: Comments and observations. *Basic and Applied Social Psychology, 14* (3), 285–94.

Schaufelberger, W. (1972). *Der Wettkampf in der alten Eidgenossenschaft*. Bern: Paul Haput.

Schickel, R. (1970). Mastery of the "dirty western." In J. Morgenstern & S. Kantor (Eds.), *Film 69/70: An anthology by the National Society of Film Critics*. New York: Simon and Schuster.

Schlesinger, A., Jr. (1968). *Violence: America in the sixties*. New York: New American Library.

Schumach, M. (1964). *The face on the cutting room floor: The story of movie and television censorship*. New York: Morrow.

Schwartz, L. A., & Markham, W. T. (1985). Sex stereotyping in children's toy advertisements. *Sex Roles, 12,* 157–70.

Seneca. (1917–1925). *Ad Lucilium epistulae morales*. R. M. Gummere, Trans. 3 vols. London: Heinemann.

Shell, R., & Eisenberg, N. (1990). The role of peers' gender in children's naturally occurring interest in toys. *International Journal of Behavioral Development, 13,* 373–88.

Shennum, W. A., & Bugental, D. B. (1982). The development of control over affective expression in nonverbal behavior. In R. Feldman (Ed.), *Development of nonverbal behavior in children*. New York: Springer-Verlag.

Shepard, L. (1962). *The broadside ballad: A study in origins and meanings*. London: Herbert Jenkins.

Sherwood, M. B. (1828). *The history of the Fairchild family*. In *The works of Mrs. Sherwood*. New York: Harper.

Shipman, P. (1986). Scavenging or hunting in early hominids: Theoretical framework and tests. *American Anthropologist, 88,* 27–43.

Shorter, E. (1987). *The health century*. New York: Doubleday.

Silvern, S. B., Lang, M. K., & Williamson, P. A. (1987). Social impact of video-game play. In G. A. Fine (Ed.), *Meaningful play, playful meaning*. Champaign, Ill.: Human Kinetics Press.

Simner, M. L. (1971). Newborn's response to the cry of another infant. *Developmental Psychology, 5,* 136–50.

Simonds, P. E. (1974). *The social primates*. New York: Harper and Row.

Sinclair, C. (1985). *Holiday house*. In R. L. Wolff (Ed.), *Masterworks of children's literature*. New York: Chelsea House. (Orig. 1864)

Singer, J. L. (1994). Imaginative play and adaptive development. In J. H. Goldstein (Ed.), *Toys, play, and child development*. New York: Cambridge University Press.

Singer, J. L., & Singer, D. G. (1990). *The house of make-believe*. Cambridge, Mass.: Harvard University Press.

Singer, R. N., et al. (1993). *Handbook of research on sport psychology*. New York: Macmillan.

Sipes, R. G. (1973). War, sports, and aggression: An empirical test of two rival theories. *American Anthropologist, 75,* 64–86.

Skal, D. J. (1993). *The monster show: A cultural history of horror*. New York: Penguin.

Skinner, B. F. (1969). *Contingencies of reinforcement*. New York: Appleton-Century-Crofts.

Skura, M. A. (1981). *The literary use of the psychoanalytic process*. New Haven, Conn.: Yale University Press.

Sloan, L. R. (1979). The function and impact of sports for fans. In J. H. Goldstein (Ed.), *Sports, games, and play.* Hillsdale, N.J.: Lawrence Erlbaum Associates.

Smith, P. K. (1994). The war play debate. In J. H. Goldstein (Ed.), *Toys, play, and child development.* New York: Cambridge University Press.

Smith, P. K., & Boulton, M. (1990). Rough-and-tumble play, aggression, and dominance: Perception and behaviour in children's encounters. *Human Development, 33,* 271–82.

Sneed, C., & Runco, M. A. (1992). The beliefs adults and children hold about television and video games. *Journal of Psychology, 126,* 273–84.

Sparks, G. G. (1984). Development of a scale to assess cognitive responses to frightening mass media. Convention of the International Communication Association, San Francisco, May.

Sparks, G. G. (1991). The relationship between distress and delight in males' and females' reactions to frightening films. *Human Communication Research, 17,* 625–37.

Spencer, H. (1891). Essays scientific, political, and speculative. New York: Appleton.

Sperber, D. (1974). *Le symbolisme en général.* Paris: Hermann.

Starobinski, J. (1971). *Jean-Jacques Rousseau: La transparence et l'obstacle.* Paris: Gallimard.

Stein, G. L., Kimiecik, J. C., Daniels, J., & Jackson, S. A. (1995). Psychological antecedents of flow in recreational sport. *Personality and Social Psychology Bulletin, 21,* 125–35.

Stipp, H. (1995). Children's viewing of news, reality-shows, and other programming. Convention of the International Communication Association, Albuquerque, N. Mex., May.

Stone, G., & Grusin, E. (1984). Network television as the bad news bearer. *Journalism Quarterly, 61,* 517–23.

Stone, G., Hartung, B., & Jensen, D. (1987). Local TV news and the good-bad dyad. *Journalism Quarterly, 64,* 37–44.

Stotland, E. (1969). Exploratory investigations of empathy. In L. Berkowitz (Ed.), *Advances in experimental social psychology.* Vol. 4. New York: Academic Press.

Strong, R. (1973). *Splendor at court.* Boston: Houghton Mifflin.

Strum, S. C. (1983). Baboon cues for eating meat. *Journal of Human Evolution, 12,* 327–36.

Suetonius. (1957). *The twelve Caesars.* R. Graves, Trans. Harmondsworth, U.K.: Penguin.

Sutton-Smith, B. (1988). War toys and childhood aggression. *Play and Culture, 1,* 57–69.

Sutton-Smith, B., Gerstmyer, J., & Meckley, A. (1988). Play-fighting as folkplay amongst preschool children. *Western Folklore, 47,* 161–76.

Tacitus. (1959). *Annals of imperial Rome.* M. Grant, Trans. Harmondsworth, U.K.: Penguin.

Tamborini, R., & Stiff, J. (1987). Predictors of horror film attendance and appeal: An analysis of the audience for frightening films. *Communication Research, 14* (4), 415–36.

Tamborini, R., Stiff, J., & Heidel, C. (1990). Reacting to graphic horror: A model of empathy and emotional behavior. *Communication Research, 17,* 616–640.

Tamborini, R., Stiff, J., & Zillmann, D. (1987). Preference for graphic horror featuring male versus female victimization: Personality and past film viewing experiences. *Human Communication Research, 13* (4), 529–52.

Tamborini, R., Zillmann, D., & Bryant, J. (1984). Fear and victimization: Exposure to television and perceptions of crime and fear. In R. N. Bostrom (Ed.), *Communication Yearbook 8.* Beverly Hills, Calif.: Sage.

Tan, E. S.-H. (1994). Film-induced affect as a witness emotion. *Poetics, 23,* 7–32.

Tatar, M. (1992). *Off with their heads! Fairy tales and the culture of childhood.* Princeton, N.J.: Princeton University Press.

Taylor, A., & Taylor, J. (1984). *Rhymes for the nursery.* In R. Bator (Ed.), *Masterworks of children's literature.* New York: Chelsea House. (Orig. 1835)

Tertullian. (1931). *De spectaculis.* T. R. Glover, Trans. London: Heinemann.

Thomas, J. (1972). Gobble, gobble . . . one of us! In R. Huss & T. J. Ross (Eds.), *Focus on the horror film.* Englewood Cliffs, N.J.: Prentice-Hall.

Timponi, A. (1994). Interview by J. Hoberman. September.

Toy Manufacturers of America. (1996). *Toy industry fact book, 1995–1996.* New York: Toy Manufacturers of America.

Tudor, A. (1989). *Monsters and mad scientists: A cultural history of the horror movie.* Oxford: Blackwell.

Turkle, S. (1984). *The second self.* New York: Simon and Schuster.

Turner, E. T. (1968). The effects of viewing college football, basketball, and wrestling on the elicited aggressive responses of male spectators. Unpublished doctoral dissertation, University of Maryland.

Twitchell, J. (1989). *Preposterous violence.* Oxford: Oxford University Press.

Vaughan, K. B., & Lanzetta, J. T. (1980). Vicarious instigation and conditioning of facial expressive and autonomic responses to a model's expressive display of pain. *Journal of Personality and Social Psychology, 38,* 909–23.

Velikovsky, I. (1956). *Worlds in collision.* Garden City, N.Y.: Doubleday.

Verdon, J. (1980). *Les loisirs au moyen age.* Paris: Tallandier.

Ville, G. (1960). Les jeux des gladiateurs dans l'empire chrétien. *Mélanges d'Archeologie et d'Histoire de l'Ecole Française de Rome, 72,* 273–335.

Ville, G. (1981). *La gladiature en occident.* Rome: Ecole Francaise de Rome.

Violence and the media: A staff report to the National Commission on the Causes and Prevention of Violence. (1969). Vol. 9A. Washington, D.C.: U.S. Government Printing Office.

Vogt, M. (1926). Der Sport im Altertum. In A. E. Bogeng (Ed.), *Geschichte des Sports aller Volker und Zeiten.* 2 vols. Leipzig: Seemann.

Wakshlag, J., Vial, V., & Tamborini, R. (1983). Selecting crime drama apprehension about crime. *Human Communication Research, 10,* 227–42.

Wann, D. L., & Branscombe, N. R. (1990). Person perception when aggressive or nonaggressive sports are primed. *Aggressive Behavior, 16,* 27–32.

Wann, D. L., & Branscombe, N. R. (1993). Sports fans: Measuring degrees of identification with their team. *International Journal of Sport Psychology, 24,* 1–17.

Wann, D. L., & Dolen, T. J. (1994a). Influence of spectators' identification on evaluation of the past, present, and future performance of a sports team. *Perceptual and Motor Skills, 78,* 547–52.

Wann, D. L., & Dolen, T. J. (1994b). Spectators' evaluations of rival and fellow fans. *Psychological Record, 44,* 351–58.

Wardetzky, K. (1990). The structure and interpretation of fairy tales composed by children. *Journal of American Folklore, 103,* 157–76.

Warr, P., Barter, J., & Brownbridge, G. (1983). On the independence of positive and negative affect. *Journal of Personality and Social Psychology, 44,* 644–51.

Warren, A. (1994). *Roald Dahl: From the gremlins to the chocolate factory.* San Bernardino, Calif.: Borgo Press.

Watson, M. W., & Peng, Y. (1992). The relation between toy gun play and children's aggressive behavior. *Early Education and Development, 3,* 370–89.

Weddle, D. (1994). *"If they move . . . kill 'em": The life and times of Sam Peckinpah.* New York: Grove.

Wegener-Spöhring, G. (1989). War toys and aggressive games. *Play and Culture, 2,* 35–47.

Wegener-Spöhring, G. (1994). War toys and aggressive play scenes. In J. H. Goldstein (Ed.), *Toys, play, and child development.* New York: Cambridge University Press.

Weiler, I. (1974). *Der Agon im Mythos.* Darmstadt, Germany: Wissenschaftliche Buchgesellschaft.

Weinraub, B. (1993). Despite Clinton, Hollywood is still trading in violence. *New York Times,* December 28, p. A1.

Wells, H. G. (1913). *Little wars: A game for boys from twelve years of age to one hundred and fifty and for that more intelligent sort of girls who like boys' games and books.* London: Frank Palmer.

White, C. (1970). An analysis of hostile outbursts in spectator sports. Unpublished doctoral dissertation, University of Illinois, Champaign.

Wiegmann, O., van Schie, E., Kuttschreuter, M., Boer, H., Breedijk, A., & Wiedijk, C. (1995). *Kind en computer-spelletjes* [Children and computer games]. University of Twente, Enschede, the Netherlands: Center for Communication Research.

Wildt, K. C. (1957). *Leibesübungen im deutschen Mittelalter.* Frankfurt am Main: Wilhelm Limpert.

Williams, J. (1989). When horror hits home: The biggest fans of violence are kids who live with it every day. *Washington Post,* November 26, pp. G1, G8–9.

Williams, J., Dunning, E., & Murphy, P. (1984). *Hooligans abroad.* London: Routledge and Kegan Paul.

Willis, R., & Howell, S. (1989). *Societies at peace.* Oxford: Routledge.

Willner, A. H. (1991). Behavioral deficiencies of aggressive 8–9-year-old boys: An observational study. *Aggressive Behavior, 17,* 135–54.

Wilson, B. J., & Cantor, J. R. (1987). Reducing children's fear reactions to mass media: Effects of visual exposure and verbal explanation. In M. McLaughlin (Ed.), *Communication Yearbook 10.* Beverly Hills, Calif.: Sage.

Wilson, B. J., Cantor, J. R., Gordon, L., & Zillmann, D. (1986). Affective response of nonretarded and retarded children to the emotions of a protagonist. *Child Study Journal, 16* (2), 77–93.

Winerip, M. (1995). Making peace with the Power Rangers. *Parenting*, February, 77–82.

Wolfe, T. (1977). *Mauve gloves and madmen, clutter and vine*. New York: Bantam.

Wood, R. (1984). An introduction to the American horror film. In B. K. Grant (Ed.), *Planks of reason: Essays on the horror film*. Metuchen, N.J.: Scarecrow Press.

Yalouris, N. (Ed.). (1979). *The eternal Olympics*. New Rochelle, N.Y.: Caratzas Brothers.

Young, D. C. (1984). *The Olympic myth of Greek amateur athletics*. Chicago: Ares.

Zahavi, A. (1975). Mate selection: A selection for a handicap. *Journal of Theoretical Biology, 53*, 205–14.

Zammuner, V. L. (1987). Children's sex-role stereotypes: A cross-cultural analysis. In P. Shaver & C. Hendrick (Eds.), *Review of personality and social psychology*. Vol. 7. Newbury Park, Calif.: Sage.

Zillmann, D. (1971). Excitation transfer in communication mediated aggressive behavior. *Journal of Experimental Social Psychology, 7*, 419–34.

Zillmann, D. (1978). Attribution and misattribution of excitatory reactions. In J. H. Harvey, W. J. Ickes, & R. F. Kidd (Eds.), *New directions in attribution research*. Vol. 2. Hillsdale, N.J.: Lawrence Erlbaum Associates.

Zillmann, D. (1979). *Hostility and aggression*. Hillsdale, N.J.: Lawrence Erlbaum Associates.

Zillmann, D. (1980). Anatomy of suspense. In P. H. Tannenbaum (Ed.), *The entertainment functions of television*. Hillsdale, N.J.: Lawrence Erlbaum Associates.

Zillmann, D. (1983a). Disparagement humor. In P. E. McGhee & J. H. Goldstein (Eds.), *Handbook of humor research: Vol. 1: Basic issues*. New York: Springer-Verlag.

Zillmann, D. (1983b). Transfer of excitation in emotional behavior. In J. T. Cacioppo & R. E. Petty (Eds.), *Social psychophysiology: A sourcebook*. New York: Guilford.

Zillmann, D. (1984). *Connections between sex and aggression*. Hillsdale, N.J.: Lawrence Erlbaum Associates.

Zillmann, D. (1987). Mood management: Using entertainment to full advantage. In L. Donohew, H. Sypher, & T. Higgins (Eds.), *Communication, social cognition, and affect*. Hillsdale, N.J.: Lawrence Erlbaum Associates.

Zillmann, D. (1988). Mood management through communication choices. *American Behavioral Scientist, 31* (3), 327–40.

Zillmann, D. (1991a). Empathy: Affect from bearing witness to the emotions of others. In J. Bryant & D. Zillmann (Eds.), *Responding to the screen: Reception and reaction processes*. Hillsdale, N.J.: Lawrence Erlbaum Associates.

Zillmann, D. (1991b). The logic of suspense and mystery. In J. Bryant & D. Zillmann (Eds.), *Responding to the screen: Reception and reaction processes*. Hillsdale, N.J.: Lawrence Erlbaum Associates.

Zillmann, D. (1991c). Television viewing and physiological arousal. In J. Bryant

& D. Zillmann (Eds.), *Responding to the screen: Reception and reaction processes.* Hillsdale, N.J.: Lawrence Erlbaum Associates.

Zillmann, D. (1994). Mechanisms of emotional involvement with drama. *Poetics, 23,* 33–51.

Zillmann, D. (1995a). Sequential dependencies in emotional experience and behavior. In R. D. Kavanaugh, B. Zimmerberg-Glick, & S. Fein (Eds.), *Emotion: Interdisciplinary perspectives.* Hillsdale, N.J.: Lawrence Erlbaum Associates.

Zillmann, D. (1995b). The psychology of suspense in dramatic exposition. In P. Vorderer, H. J. Wulff, & M. Friedrichsen (Eds.), *Suspense: Conceptualizations, theoretical analyses, and empirical explorations.* Hillsdale, N.J.: Lawrence Erlbaum Associates.

Zillmann, D., (1996a). Sequential dependencies in emotional experience and behavior. In R. D. Kavanaugh, B. Zimmberberg-Glick, & S. Fein (Eds.), *Emotion: Interdisciplinary perspectives.* Hillsdale, N.J.: Erlbaum.

Zillmann, D., (1996b). The psychology of suspense in dramatic exposition. In P. Vorderer, H. J. Wulff, & M. Friedrichsen (Eds.), *Suspense: Conceptualizations, theoretical analyses, and empirical explorations,* Hillsdale, N.J.: Erlbaum.

Zillmann, D., & Bryant, J. (1975). Viewer's moral sanction of retribution in the appreciation of dramatic presentations. *Journal of Experimental Social Psychology, 11,* 572–82.

Zillmann, D., & Bryant, J. (1986). Exploring the entertainment experience. In J. Bryant & D. Zillmann (Eds.), *Perspectives on media effects.* Hillsdale, N.J.: Lawrence Erlbaum Associates.

Zillmann, D., & Bryant, J. (1994). Entertainment as media effect. In J. Bryant & D. Zillmann (Eds.), *Media effects: Advances in theory and research.* Hillsdale, N.J.: Lawrence Erlbaum Associates.

Zillmann, D., Bryant, J., & Sapolsky, B. S. (1989). Enjoyment from sports spectatorship. In J. H. Goldstein (Ed.), *Sports, games, and play.* 2nd ed. Hillsdale, N.J.: Lawrence Erlbaum Associates.

Zillmann, D., & Cantor, J. R. (1976). A disposition theory of humor and mirth. In A. J. Chapman & H. C. Foot (Eds.), *Humour and laughter: Theory, research, and applications.* London: Wiley.

Zillmann, D., & Cantor, J. R. (1977). Affective responses to the emotions of a protagonist. *Journal of Experimental Social Psychology, 13,* 155–65.

Zillmann, D., & Gibson, R. (1995). Evolution of the horror genre. In J. Weaver & R. Tamborini (Eds.), *Horror films: Current research in audience preferences and reactions.* Hillsdale, N.J.: Lawrence Erlbaum Associates.

Zillmann, D., Hay, T. A., & Bryant, J. (1975). The effect of suspense and its resolution on the appreciation of dramatic presentations. *Journal of Research in Personality, 9,* 307–23.

Zillmann, D., & Paulus, P. B. (1993). Spectators: Reactions to sports events and effects on athletic performance. In R. N. Singer, et al. (Eds.), *Handbook of research on sport psychology.* New York: Macmillan.

Zillman, D., Rockwell, S., Schweitzer, K., & Sundar, S. S. (1993). Does humor facilitate coping with physical discomfort? *Motivation and Emotion, 17,* 1–21.

Zillmann, D., & Wakshlag, J. (1985). Fear of victimization and the appeal of crime drama. In D. Zillmann & J. Bryant (Eds.), *Selective exposure to communication.* Hillsdale, N.J.: Erlbaum.

Zillmann, D., & Weaver, J. B. (1995). Gender-socialization theory of horror. In J. Weaver & R. Tamborini (Eds.), *Horror films: Current research in audience preferences and reactions.* Hillsdale, N.J.: Lawrence Erlbaum Associates.

Zillmann, D., & Weaver, J. B. (1997). Psychoticism in the effect of prolonged exposure to gratuitous media violence on the acceptance of violence as a preferred means of conflict resolution. *Personality and Individual Differences, 22,* 613–627.

Zillmann, D., Weaver, J. B., Mundorf, N., & Aust, C. F. (1986). Effects of an opposite-gender companion's affect to horror on distress, delight, and attraction. *Journal of Personality and Social Psychology, 51,* 586–94.

Zillmann, D., & Zillmann, M. (1996). Psychoneuroendocrinology of social behavior. In E. T. Higgins & A. W. Kruglanski (Eds.), *Social psychology: Handbook of basic principles.* New York: Guilford Press.

Zipes, J. (1993). *The trials and tribulations of Little Red Riding Hood.* 2nd ed. New York: Routledge.

Zots, T. (1985). Adel, Bürgertum, und Turnier in deutschen Stadten vom 13. bis 15. Jahrhundert. In J. Fleckenstein (Ed.), *Das ritterliche Turnier im Mittelalter.* Gottingen, Germany: Vandenhoek and Ruprecht.

Zuckerman, M. (1979). *Sensation seeking: Beyond the optimal level of arousal.* New York: Wiley.

Zuckerman, M., & Litle, P. (1986). Personality and curiosity about morbid sexual events. *Personality and Individual Differences, 2,* 49–65.

Subject Index

Name Index